THEOLOGY
AND
PASTORAL
COUNSELING

Theology and Pastoral Counseling

A NEW INTERDISCIPLINARY APPROACH

Deborah van Deusen Hunsinger

WILLIAM B. EERDMANS PUBLISHING COMPANY
GRAND RAPIDS, MICHIGAN

© 1995 Wm. B. Eerdmans Publishing Co.
255 Jefferson Ave. S.E., Grand Rapids, Michigan 49503

Printed in the United States of America

00 99 98 97 96 95   7 6 5 4 3 2 1

Library of Congress Cataloging-in-Publication Data

Hunsinger, Deborah van Deusen.
    Theology and pastoral counseling: a new interdisciplinary approach /
Deborah van Deusen Hunsinger.
        p.   cm.
    Includes bibliographical references.
    ISBN 0-8028-0842-5 (pbk.: alk. paper)
    1. Pastoral counseling. 2. Barth, Karl, 1886-1968. 3. Psychology and religion.   I. Title.
BV4012.2.H833   1995
253.5 — dc2095-12857
CIP

Contents

Preface

PASTORAL COUNSELORS have not usually been interested in the theology of Karl Barth, and Barth himself paid little attention to the discipline of pastoral counseling. As a practicing pastoral counselor for nearly fifteen years, however, I have always found in Barth's theology an incomparable wealth of insight and wisdom. This book addresses some of the theoretical and practical questions that arise when a pastoral counselor actually operates from a Barthian theological perspective. Here I would simply like to say something about how this combination of interests became so important in my own life.

As an undergraduate in an interdisciplinary humanities program, I became captivated by the thought of C. G. Jung. Art history, comparative literature, religion, cultural anthropology, even modern dance — it seemed that everything of interest to me could be illuminated by Jung's psychology. Jung was the first thinker I had ever striven to understand in any depth. I loved his passion, his insistence on the rich lived experience of the psyche, and his unswerving commitment to discovering and living out what he described as his personal myth. Immersed in his writings and not least in their capacity to help me understand my own inner life, I readily granted him his basic assumptions. This was also true of his religious ideas, which suggested to me a new way of understanding religious symbols. In good Jungian fashion I learned to make connections between traditional Christian beliefs and unconscious motifs that appeared in dreams and myths. After college I pursued my enthusiasm for Jung through a year abroad in Zurich, where I enrolled in courses at the Jung Institute. At that time I began recording my dreams and entered Jungian analysis myself.

Through a series of "synchronistic events" — that is, "meaningful coincidences," according to Jung, and as I also understood them at the time, having as yet no real concept of God's providence — I found myself considering divinity school. I was interested in the life of the soul. Psychology as taught in most American universities seemed more concerned with rats in mazes than with human souls in need. I ended up at Yale Divinity School in the early 1970s, where, through a number of outstanding professors, I encountered the theology of Karl Barth. Before long Barth's thought had become as compelling to me as Jung's, but it led in such different directions! Whereas Jung approached the world through the hidden recesses of the psyche, Barth approached it by confessing the radical otherness of God.

Encountering Barth with my Jungian background, I was astounded by his apparent audacity. "How," I would exclaim in exasperation, "does he think he can speak of God as he is in himself?" Following Jung I had come to suppose that any such move since Kant was impossible. On what basis could Barth conceivably speak as he did of God? Such questions vexed and engaged me. I wanted to know how to relate Jung's thought more directly to Barth's. Although each writer seemed so convincing as I read him one by one, how could they come to such completely different conclusions — for example, about the Book of Job? Did their interpretive frameworks ever allow for any elements of compatibility, despite the disparity in their views? I began to sense that I was not yet ready to compare the thought of Jung, which I knew fairly well, with that of Barth, the likes of which I had never seen before. I first had to understand what Barth was saying. Theology, at least as he represented it, was a very different enterprise than I, with my Jungian assumptions, had ever imagined it could be.

Jesus Christ, according to Barth, was the living Lord — the incarnate presence of God in his unsubstitutable identity — and not merely the symbolic expression of a universal archetype that could be presented just as well in another form (for example, in various myths of dying and rising gods). Barth could speak of divine reality as it is in itself (and therefore in truth, independently of our symbols and conceptions) because he took Jesus seriously — not as the receiver of a collective process of unconscious projection but as God's actual self-revelation to the world. Scripture, according to Barth, was not to be read as a register of ancient religious experience but as one form of the Word of God, through which God continues to speak to us today. Here the views of Jung and Barth could not be more widely divergent. What is more, Barth took a rather dim view of what Jung valued so highly as "immediate religious experience." No way exists from our religious experiences to God, be they ever so sublime, Barth maintained, but only from God to us — in any of our life experiences, be they ever so ordinary or mundane. Regardless of what form it takes in experience (and the possibilities are ever new), our knowledge of God is always somehow mediated through Jesus Christ as attested by Scripture. When I studied the Barmen Declaration, that theological manifesto through which the Confessing Church in Germany denied revelatory status to Hitler and confessed Jesus Christ alone as Lord, I began to understand something of Barth's suspicion toward religious experiences and their supposed "revelations." Hitler, it was clear, was no contemporary word of God, yet so much of contemporary theology, based as it was on "religious experience," contained no viable criteria by which to prevent such a claim. Barth's voice in the Barmen Declaration, which allowed for no other norm than Jesus Christ himself, sounded a clear note in a cacophony of theological confusion.

While sorting through these questions, I was also engaged in the practice of ministry, primarily through summer programs in Clinical Pastoral Education. There I learned to rely ever more deeply on Scripture and prayer as I ministered to the sick and the dying. At the same time, however, my study of Jung was also bearing fruit. Jung had taught me the value of listening carefully to the actual lived experience of each particular individual, to attend to the seemingly obscure significance of fantasies and dreams, to uncover the threads of meaning that run through a person's life. Jung helped me to see that a person's image of God could contain unconscious representations formed from early childhood experiences. Newly appreciating what I had gleaned from Jung, I was all the more perplexed by how it should fit with my increasing esteem for Barth. Was there a *conjunctio oppositorum* between the two that would eventually unfold itself to me? Or was I destined always to be split between two opposed universes of discourse? Feeling this disjunction acutely, I remember telling my Jungian analyst that no matter how hard I tried I could not bring Barth and Jung together. His reply was strangely comforting. "They are already together," he observed. "They are both *in you*."

These questions seemed important enough to pursue further. I enrolled as a doctoral student at Union Theological Seminary in New York, where I had the opportunity to study in the Psychiatry and Religion program under Professor Ann Belford Ulanov. Ulanov, a trained Jungian analyst and pastoral counselor, impressed me especially by her gift for enlivening the ideas of a wide range of depth psychologists. Through her courses, always interspersed by rich clinical examples from her own practice, I was exposed to many psychological approaches to religious phenomena (most notably Freud, the neo-Freudians, and the so-called "object relations" school), which enabled me to see Jung in a broader context. However, although all this enriched the psychological side of my knowledge, it did little to resolve my interdisciplinary question of how to bring such material into relationship with a theology like Barth's. It became increasingly clear that there was little to build upon, since so few pastoral theologians or psychologists were interested in Barth and the kind of theology he stood for. They were more attracted to someone like Tillich, whose thought seemed more obviously compatible.

With so little being done in my own field, I turned to writers who were interested in Barth and other disciplines. Perhaps through them I could at least clarify what the formal issues might be. How did Barth approach dialogue between theology and philosophy, for example, or between theology and culture in general? At one point a remark by Hans W. Frei especially struck me. Commenting on how matters of theology and culture are related from a Barthian perspective, Frei wrote that they are "logically diverse even when they are existentially connected, that is to say, even when they reside in the same breast. In that case, one could not systematically correlate the two." Here was an insight that began to make sense of my dilemma. Somehow these matters could be "existentially connected" ("both *in you*") even though they remained "logically diverse" so that their subject matters could not be "systematically correlated." They could be integrated in oneself as a person without needing to be integrated in a unified theoretical scheme. But what did it mean to say that they were "logically diverse?"

My search for an answer to this question eventually led to the

distinctive conception of "asymmetry" as set forth in this book. Two
further factors in my own life played a significant role in pointing me
in this direction. First, in the course of my practice as a pastoral
counselor (which I had meanwhile begun as I worked on my dissertation for Union), I was continually confronted by counselees for
whom theological questions of faith were variously intermingled with
psychological questions of disorder and health. Nevertheless, my
counselees clearly presupposed in one way, as did my various inter-
ventions in another, that these sorts of questions were indeed "logically diverse." Insofar as my counselees expected me to take their faith
seriously and not to reduce it to some kind of psychological disorder,
for example, they assumed that I would honor certain differences
between psychological and theological interpretation. In terms of actual practice, I strove to address psychological problems psychologically and questions of faith theologically. Thus psychological evaluation (for example, of current relationships, family of origin, dreams,
fantasies) proceeded alongside a ministry of spiritual care (for example,
through reading Scripture together and prayer). Working intuitively,
I was without the benefit of a developed rationale for these two diverse
sets of practices. My clinical work thus reinforced all the more my
desire to find a conceptual resolution that might keep the two different
kinds of discourse both closely related and yet distinct.

Second, conversations over the years with my husband, George
Hunsinger, which had helped in sustaining the theological side of my
interests, led me to see parallels between his way of relating theology
and radical politics from a Barthian perspective and the way I was
seeking to relate theology and psychology as a practicing pastoral
counselor. In particular I found that much depended in either case on
respecting the ontological otherness of God. God's otherness is not
taken seriously, Barth urged, if treated as though it could be correlated
with phenomena of creaturely existence (whether political, psychological, or whatever) by means of a unified system or conceptual
scheme. But if theology and disciplines like psychology cannot be so
unified, then how can they be related at all?

As already suggested, much came to depend for me on the possibility of distinguishing symmetrical from asymmetrical relationships.
A "symmetrical" relationship between psychology and theology
would be one in which concepts from each discipline were somehow

logically reversible. In other words, it would be possible to restate a psychological concept in theological terms, or a theological concept in psychological terms, without any significant loss in content or meaning. An "asymmetrical" relationship, however, would be one in which this sort of mutual restatement across the disciplines is not possible. Theological and psychological concepts would thus be what Frei called "logically diverse." Respecting God's ontological otherness, as understood by Barth, would seem to require this kind of logical irreversibility.

At the same time, it would also seem to require "asymmetry" in another, more substantive sense. From a Barthian perspective, as I eventually came to see, the alternative to systematic correlation involved the construction of ad hoc analogies. The turn to analogy seemed to bring a number of advantages. It respected the basic competence of each discipline within its own distinctive field and, therefore, allowed each to have its own realm of significance. It also seemed to make reciprocal influence possible without resulting in a loss of identity for either discipline. Above all, it allowed psychological concepts to take on analogical significance in relation to concepts from theology. Although, from a Barthian viewpoint, there was no way from psychology to theology, there was a way from theology to psychology — the way of analogy within a frame of reference supplied by theology itself. Here was another asymmetrical pattern that seemed to follow from the otherness of God. Analogical relations were possible between the two fields as long as they respected God's fundamental uniqueness and preeminence.

This new interdisciplinary approach is what finally resolved the tension I felt between the two fields, even as it allowed me to understand the rationale behind my various intuitive strategies in pastoral counseling practice. It is now the point of view that I seek to explain and elaborate in this book.

Acknowledgments

MANY FRIENDS, colleagues, teachers, and family members have encouraged and sustained me during the writing of this work. Among them all I must single out Marilyn Chandler McEntyre for special mention because she gave so generously of her time in order to improve the felicity of my presentation. I am also indebted to those counselees who have kindly consented to my use of their personal material. Without such consent, major portions of the book could not have been written and the work as a whole would have been greatly impoverished.

I would like most especially to thank Professor Ann Belford Ulanov of Union Theological Seminary in New York, who supervised this work in its previous form as a doctoral dissertation and who, by her patient guidance and wisdom and her unfailing encouragement, helped me develop my own point of view.

Finally, no words could adequately convey my gratitude to my husband, George Hunsinger, for the support he has gladly offered in every area of our common life so that I could complete this work. The book is dedicated to him with love and joy.

Abbreviations

I/1   *Church Dogmatics,* vol. I, part 1 (Edinburgh: T. & T. Clark, 1936).

I/2   *Church Dogmatics,* vol. I, part 2 (Edinburgh: T. & T. Clark, 1956).

II/1   *Church Dogmatics,* vol. II, part 1 (Edinburgh: T. & T. Clark, 1957).

III/2   *Church Dogmatics,* vol. III, part 2 (Edinburgh: T. & T. Clark, 1960).

III/3   *Church Dogmatics,* vol. III, part 3 (Edinburgh: T. & T. Clark, 1961).

III/4   *Church Dogmatics,* vol. III, part 4 (Edinburgh: T. & T. Clark, 1961).

IV/1   *Church Dogmatics,* vol. IV, part 1 (Edinburgh: T. & T. Clark, 1956).

IV/2   *Church Dogmatics,* vol. IV, part 2 (Edinburgh: T. & T. Clark, 1958).

IV/3   *Church Dogmatics,* vol. IV, part 3, first half (Edinburgh: T. & T. Clark, 1961); second half (Edinburgh: T. & T. Clark, 1962).

rev.   revised translation

CHAPTER ONE

Pastoral Counseling as a Ministry of the Church: The Promise of Karl Barth

PASTORAL COUNSELING, as a ministry of the church, is essentially interdisciplinary. Becoming equipped for this ministry requires both psychological and theological training. Like psychotherapists, pastoral counselors must have studied a variety of psychological theories, received extensive training in clinical practice, and undergone a sufficient investigation of their own intrapsychic conflicts to be able to protect others from their personal areas of difficulty. At the same time, pastoral counselors are not simply trained clinicians. As ministers of the church (whether ordained or lay), pastoral counselors are members of the believing community who have been called to a particular vocation. Normally, they have been trained in such disciplines as biblical studies, church history, and theology; have learned to preach and conduct worship; and have received instruction in the art of pastoral care. In the course of this training it is expected that pastoral counselors will develop both a psychological and a theological perspective that will benefit people with a variety of emotional and spiritual problems.

The Constitution of the American Association of Pastoral Counselors (AAPC) describes pastoral counseling as the "exploration, clarification and guidance of human life, both individual and corporate, at the experiential and behavioral levels *through a theological perspective.*"[1]

---

1. "The Constitution of the American Association of Pastoral Counselors," in *AAPC Handbook,* 1986 revised edition (privately printed by the AAPC, Fairfax, Va.), p. I-1; emphasis added.

1

While pastoral counselors will necessarily possess psychological expertise, the distinctiveness of the profession depends upon its ability to combine such expertise with a theological perspective. Certain questions thus arise. What does it mean to bring a theological perspective to the task of interpretation? How should pastoral counselors relate their theological training to their training in psychology? Should they somehow strive to integrate the disciplines of theology and psychology into a unified system of thought? Or should they view them as two distinct universes of discourse, each making its own special hermeneutical contribution? Moreover, how do each of these disciplines apply to the actual clinical situations faced by pastoral counselors in their practice? How can pastoral counselors conceptualize the task of concrete application so that both theological and psychological integrity are retained? One contemporary commentator, Charles Gerkin, poses the question in this way: "How can pastoral counseling be at the same time an authentically theological and a scientifically psychological discipline?" This, he contends, is the "root question" facing the pastoral counseling movement at the present time.[2]

While there has always been concern to emphasize the pastoral counselor's expertise, both theoretical and practical, in the disciplines of psychology and theology, most of its emphasis over the years has been psychotherapeutic and clinical. Gerkin says, for example, "Through the first four decades of the modern period in pastoral care and counseling, psychological and psychotherapeutic concerns have unquestionably been dominant."[3] Theological competency has been more or less taken for granted while the primary focus has been on developing the theoretical (i.e., psychological) and clinical competence of the practitioner. Charles Van Wagner, for example, in writing a recent history of the AAPC says:

> In my own experience with the AAPC's demanding process of accreditation, the focus has been primarily upon clinical competence. The membership committee in my own region seems generally to have accepted paper statements regarding previous pastoral experi-

2. Charles V. Gerkin, *The Living Human Document: Re-Visioning Pastoral Counseling in a Hermeneutical Mode* (Nashville: Abingdon, 1984), p. 11.

3. Gerkin, p. 11.

ence, pastoral identity and ecclesiastical endorsement without much question, and then has moved on . . . to deal intensively with applicants' personhood and therapeutic competency with their clients.[4]

But while membership committees focus on clinical and therapeutic competency, others in the field worry about the loss of theological competency among pastoral counselors. Even more, they are concerned that ministers and pastoral counselors are losing their distinctive professional identity by embracing new psychological perspectives and abandoning their own discipline of theology. Prominent among such critics is Paul Pruyser, a clinical psychologist with interests in the psychology of religion and strong ties to the pastoral counseling movement. Although not a pastoral counselor himself, Pruyser has an astute understanding of the needs that a theological perspective might meet, and he encourages ministers and pastoral counselors to continue to develop their expertise in its use. He writes:

> I have the growing conviction that people turn to pastors — correctly — because they want to have the opportunity *to look at themselves and their problems in the light of their faith and their religious tradition,* with the help of an expert in just this perspective.[5]

Pruyser is concerned that as ministers seek to help their parishioners by psychological means, they lose confidence in their own theological perspective, substituting, as it were, "psychological-mindedness for theological-mindedness, sometimes to the point of doubting the relevance to their pastoral work of the theological disciplines, the Church tradition and the religious language conventions."[6] While Pruyser applauds an openness to learning from other disciplines, especially his own, he does not want pastoral counselors to do so at the cost of losing their distinctive professional identity. Pruyser's remarks show, by implication, that certain attitudes and skills

---

4. Charles A. Van Wagner, *AAPC in Historical Perspective: 1963–1991,* edited and abridged by Allison Stokes (privately published by the AAPC, Fairfax, Va., 1992), pp. 81-82.

5. Paul W. Pruyser, "The Diagnostic Process in Pastoral Care," in *Psychiatry, Ministry, and Pastoral Counseling,* ed. A. W. Richard Sipe and Clarence J. Rowe (Collegeville, Minn.: Liturgical Press, 1984), p. 109.

6. Pruyser, p. 104.

associated with a theological perspective can no longer be taken for granted.

> Professional identity, then, consists in being identified with a chosen perspective and acquiring skill in systematically "looking at all things" from within this perspective. It entails reliance on one's basic sciences; respect for the perspective's relevance, potency and explanatory power; skill in using the discipline's transformational propositions and procedures; and versatility in using the discipline's particular language game.[7]

Thomas Oden, a theologian who writes on interdisciplinary questions, worries about similar trends but focuses his concern somewhat differently. Oden feels that pastoral counselors tend to adopt various psychological perspectives without first evaluating them critically from a theological standpoint. Pastors need psychology, but their psychology needs to be compatible with their theological convictions. Such compatibility could be tested only through critical conversation between the disciplines. After 1920, Oden says, the pastoral counseling movement "began to swing headlong toward modern psychological accommodation. . . . During these decades we have witnessed wave after wave of various hegemonies of emergent psychologies being accommodated, often cheaply, into pastoral care, without much conscious identity formation from the tradition."[8] Oden urges the recovery of the pastoral counselor's distinctive identity through relearning and reacquiring the classical traditions of care in the church.

Perhaps contemporary pastoral counseling needs not so much a return to "classical traditions of care," as Oden proposes, but rather methodological clarity about the relationship of the disciplines of psychology and theology to the overall task of the pastoral counselor. How might pastoral counseling as a ministry of the church be conceived so that a theological perspective would not only give genuine shape and substance to the therapeutic work but also interact critically and fruitfully with the pastoral counselor's psychological perspective?

Learning to work from a theological perspective means becoming

---

7. Pruyser, p. 108.

8. Thomas C. Oden, *Care of Souls in the Classic Tradition* (Philadelphia: Fortress, 1984), p. 32.

skilled in a particular way. If a pastoral counselor's theological perspective were as refined as her psychological perspective, it would equip her to perceive both problems and their solutions; it would equip her to frame her questions and to develop hypotheses about what directions to pursue. Acquiring such skills is, as George Lindbeck has noted, similar to acquiring a language. In commenting on what it means to "become religious," Lindbeck captures something essential about "looking at all things" from a theological perspective.

> Unless we acquire language of some kind we cannot actualize our specifically human capacities for thought, action and feeling. . . . To become religious involves becoming skilled in the language, in the symbol system of a given religion. To become a Christian involves learning the story of Israel and of Jesus well enough to interpret and experience oneself and one's world in its terms. A religion is above all an external word, a *verbum externum,* that molds and shapes the self and its world. . . . To become religious — no less than to become culturally or linguistically competent — is to interiorize a set of skills by practice and training. One learns how to feel, act and think in conformity with a religious tradition.[9]

If pastoral counseling is essentially interdisciplinary, then in Lindbeck's sense pastoral counselors must learn to become "bilingual." They must learn to be as skilled in the language or symbol system of theology as they are in that of psychology. They must be equipped to interpret and experience themselves and their world in theological as well as in psychological terms. They must become as linguistically competent in the one discipline as in the other, interiorizing by practice and training two very different sets of skills. They must learn how to feel, act, and think in conformity with two different modes of thought.

Becoming bilingual in this sense would have definite methodological implications for how pastoral counselors understand their task. Just as a linguist would not choose to integrate French and German into a single tongue, so also the pastoral counselor would not need to integrate theology and psychology into some single, unified

---

9. George A. Lindbeck, *The Nature of Doctrine: Religion and Theology in a Postliberal Age* (Philadelphia: Westminster, 1984), pp. 34-35.

whole. Each language would maintain its own integrity, and each would require the learning of its own grammatical rules. The pastoral counselor would not need to find an overarching systematic theory that would conceptually integrate these two diverse language worlds any more than a linguist needs Esperanto. "The 'sad little joke' about universal languages," Mary Midgley once said, "is that almost nobody speaks them."[10]

In ways that will become clear as my argument unfolds, theology and psychology represent material that cannot be integrated into a unified whole. They are logically diverse; they have different aims, subject matters, methods, and linguistic conventions. They do not exist on the same level. Both perspectives are fully a part of the pastoral counselor, that is, they are integrated into the *person,* but as language and thought worlds, they are not to be integrated *with one another* in any systematic way. What Hans Frei once observed about how theology and culture are related from a Barthian perspective would apply also to theology and psychology. They are, suggests Frei, "logically diverse even when they are existentially connected, that is to say, even when they reside within the same breast. In that case one could not systematically correlate the two."[11]

To practice pastoral counseling with bilingual fluency, therefore, would mean that one interprets the counselee's material by employing two logically diverse perspectives, the psychological and the theological. Each language would have its own integrity and make its own unique contribution. Neither would need casting into terms of the other in order to be made meaningful. Thus theology would not need to be psychologized, nor psychology theologized. Nor would it be necessary to unify them conceptually or to integrate them systematically. Although from time to time certain analogies might be drawn between them, this would be done primarily as a way to test critically whether one's psychological and theological goals converge or diverge in any given case.

Each perspective — the psychological and the theological — is

10. Mary Midgley, *Beast and Man* (New York: Meridian, 1980), p. 306; cited in Jeffrey Stout, *Ethics after Babel* (Boston: Beacon, 1988), p. 166.

11. Hans W. Frei, "An Afterword to Eberhard Busch's Biography of Barth," *Karl Barth in Re-View,* ed. H. Martin Rumscheidt (Pittsburgh: Pickwick, 1981), p. 103.

understood to offer categories of perception and discernment in the counseling situation. Each has a vocabulary that pertains to "diagnosis" and to "treatment," even though the two vocabularies may be quite different. It is one thing, for instance, to think of oneself as beset with a terrible "negative mother complex" and as needing to learn to trust one's "feminine side." It is quite another to think of oneself as mistrusting God's providential goodness and needing to confess the sin of unbelief. Yet both ways of conceiving oneself and one's predicament might be apt in a particular case. Although very different from each other, they might each illumine aspects of the self and its situation. One would not integrate them with each other, for they are not really talking about the same thing. Yet, analogies might be drawn between them. One might work simultaneously for two different goals: to trust in one's "feminine side" and to trust in God's providential goodness. The goals are clearly not the same, yet they might be related. One could not say without first examining what each of the terms mean within its own language world.

The more fluent the pastoral counselor is in using both languages, the more differentiated her perceptions will be, the more apt her questions, and, at least theoretically, the more helpful her interpretations. For the two perspectives she brings to the interpretive task give her a set of maps that will be useful in traversing through unknown territory. As counselor and counselee set out together, each begins to learn something about the other's language world. For the counselee obviously also has a set of categories of perception based on the languages he or she has already learned. Gerkin aptly describes the process as a mutual undertaking.

> If one is to hear truly what the other person has to say in its own integrity, there must be a breaking through of the barrier that stands between the language world of the hearer and that of the speaker. . . . Hermeneutically speaking, this is possible only because of and to the extent that we are able to enter the other's language world, the world of the other's meanings. In the same way, if we are to be known by the other person, the other must in some degree enter our world, the language of meaning which we bring to the encounter.[12]

12. Gerkin, p. 43.

The shared language that grows up between counselor and counselee is in some sense a unique creation between them. Shared meanings develop over time as the person's life story unfolds. The language that the pastoral counselor uses to interpret that story will inevitably shape the story itself. The story is understood differently depending on its overall context. Gerkin observes:

> If [the counselor's language world] is inhabited by the images of theology and faith, the counselee will be invited into a world shaped by those images. If that be, on the other hand, a language world shaped by the images of secularity, it is into that world that the counselor invites the one seeking help.[13]

The kind of methodological clarity that this book seeks, therefore, is a way of thinking about the pastoral counselor's distinctive task. It conceives of pastoral counseling as an interpretive enterprise where the counselor needs to become fluent in two distinctively different languages: the language of faith and the language of depth psychology. The pastoral counselor uses vocabularies from both language worlds to interpret the counselee's personal story, but the vocabularies are strictly distinguished from each other and are neither confused with nor integrated with one another. At the same time the pastoral counselor is required to reflect critically on the aptness of her psychological perspective from a theological standpoint and vice versa. With each new case, a kind of ad hoc internal conversation begins where one's psychological and theological perspectives enter into dialogue. Loose analogies may be drawn between them as one seeks to determine the aptness of one's psychological goals in the light of one's theological convictions.

This book seeks to shed light, from a particular theological point of view, on the twofold task of interpretation in pastoral counseling. Its specific focus may be stated as follows: How would the relationship between theology and psychology be understood by a pastoral counselor who works from a Barthian perspective? Having been such a pastoral counselor for nearly fifteen years, the question was one of more than academic interest. How did I understand psychological theory in relation to theological claims and both in relation to the

13. Gerkin, p. 43.

human beings who came to me for help? How would understanding the relationship between these two kinds of theoretical material help those who came, not only with psychological problems, but also with important questions of faith? It seemed to me that the goals of psychotherapy did not always easily mesh with the aims of Christian faith. Pastoral counseling, so it seemed, was the child of two very different parents. What kind of household rules might be created in that new family whose parents came from such different backgrounds and traditions?

Barth's theology, I found, could illumine some of these basic methodological issues. In particular, it could shed light on the question of how to conceive the relationship of the two disciplines. This book aims to develop an approach for relating psychotherapeutic and theological interpretation from a Barthian perspective. This proposal will be explored for both its theoretical and its practical implications.

After identifying a formal pattern of thought in Barth's theology, this book then goes on to use this pattern to bring theology and psychology into relationship. This formal conceptual device, which is referred to as the "Chalcedonian pattern" and which involves elements of "differentiation," "unity," and "order," actually underlies a variety of different discussions in Barth's theology. In this book, however, the use of the pattern is extended beyond anything quite found in Barth in order to illumine theoretical and practical issues in pastoral counseling.

The metaphor of "becoming bilingual," which governs the entire argument, suggests that pastoral counselors need to reflect more carefully on what it would mean to be proficient in two different languages, one the language of depth psychology, the other the language of faith. Particularly with those counselees who seek not just psychotherapeutic help but psychotherapeutic help in the context of their Christian faith, pastoral counselors need to be clear about the nature of the interpretive task they are undertaking. Cases that require explicitly theological as well as psychotherapeutic interpretation will be regarded as "paradigmatic" for pastoral counseling, for such cases draw directly upon the dual range of competencies that the pastoral counselor has acquired. Just such cases call most clearly for a "bilingual" approach. Such a paradigmatic case (one explicitly requiring both forms of interpretation) will be considered at length in order to demonstrate what the theoretical proposals of my argument look like when applied to pastoral counseling practice.[14]

The thesis of this book is, therefore, twofold. At the theoretical level it argues that from a Barthian theological perspective, theology and psychology are to be related according to the Chalcedonian pattern, that is, without separation or division, without confusion or change, and with the conceptual priority of theology over psychology. At the practical level, on the other hand, it argues that the bilingual competencies of the pastoral counselor are also to be used according to the stipulations of the Chalcedonian pattern. At both levels, therefore, the Chalcedonian pattern provides methodological clarity for the pastoral counselor in interpreting theological and psychological material.

The Promise of Barth

At first glance Barth might seem to be an unlikely choice for interdisciplinary dialogue. After all he himself seldom engaged in extensive conversation with the psychologists of his day. Unlike some of his theological contemporaries, notably Paul Tillich, Barth seemed to have scant interest in depth psychology. Nevertheless, there are at least three reasons for choosing Barth: first, his acknowledged stature as a theologian; second, his relative neglect by professionals in the field of pastoral care and counseling; and third, the promise his theology offers to pastoral counseling when conceived as a ministry of the church.

Barth's stature as a theologian has been widely acknowledged. Pope Pius XII, for example, once described him as the greatest theo-

---

14. Cases that explicitly require both forms of interpretation also provide a benchmark for reflecting upon cases that somehow fall outside the paradigm. Typically, not all counselees desire the full range of what the pastoral counselor potentially has to offer. Some counselees who seek only psychotherapeutic help will feel they have no need of a spiritual or theological perspective. On the other hand, occasionally a counselee will seek spiritual guidance without any expressed need for psychological assistance. Or a person may be agnostic, atheistic, or of another religious tradition. These sorts of cases will be briefly considered with respect to the paradigm in the last chapter. The overall focus, however, is on the paradigmatic situation where a pastoral counselor's bilingual expertise is explicitly sought by the counselee.

logian since Thomas Aquinas.[15] From a more academic perspective, furthermore, what James Gustafson has written about Barth's ethics could also be said of his theology as a whole:

> Why read Barth's ethics? They are not to be read, but studied and heard. They are not to be heard in order to be accepted at face value, but in order to be intellectually and spiritually wrestled with. One does this because of their richness. . . . They provide in their way the most systematic theological and practical ethics written in our time, and have a consistency which requires appreciation in order to penetrate and respond. . . . I would not consider myself a Barthian to any great extent, and on fundamental questions of ethics quite anti-Barthian. But to be what I think we need to be as independent ethical thinkers, we need to think in response to the richness of Karl Barth.[16]

Second, despite his stature, Barth has been relatively neglected in the field of pastoral care and counseling. Having first become fascinated with Barth as a divinity student, I was astonished to see how little-known he seemed to be among pastoral counselors. Why was this? Was it perhaps merely prejudice? Was it the unfortunate anti-psychological tone that has crept into the writings of some of his followers? Were Barth's own polemics somehow responsible for alienating those with interests in depth psychology and other human sciences? Or was it perhaps true, as so many had surmised, that pastoral counselors were in fact far more interested in psychology than in basic questions of faith? If they were interested in Christian theology at all, it seemed evident to me that there was a wealth of material in Barth for pastoral counselors, though they have done so little to draw upon it. Of the three full-length studies known to me whose main interest is in relating Barth's theology to psychological questions, none of them focuses specifically on pastoral counseling.[17] A handful

15. J. B. Torrance, "Karl Barth," in *The Encyclopedia of Religion,* ed. Mircea Eliade, vol. 2 (New York: Macmillan, 1987), p. 68.

16. James M. Gustafson, "Why Read Barth's Ethics?" *Reflection* 66, no. 4 (1969): 12.

17. These studies, which will be discussed fully in the next chapter, are: Dorothy W. Martyn, *The Man in the Yellow Hat: Theology and Psychoanalysis in Child Therapy* (Atlanta: Scholars Press, 1992); Thomas C. Oden, *Kerygma and Counseling*

of books and articles by pastoral counselors and others draw from time to time on Barth's theology, but for the most part little sustained attention has been devoted to Barth's possible contribution to this field.[18]

Finally, when pastoral counseling is understood as a ministry of the church, Barth is promising for interdisciplinary dialogue, largely because the theology he offers is intended as a theology of the church.[19] As perhaps the most distinguished modern theologian to work critically yet sympathetically within the framework set forth by the Councils of Nicea and Chalcedon, Barth uniquely represents the historic tradition of the ecumenical church. Especially since he sees theology as grounded solely in God's self-revelation in Jesus Christ, Barth offers pastoral counselors a perspective that is significantly distinguished from psychological modes of thought and that can, therefore, help them to gain what Thomas Oden has called a "sharper kerygmatic identity."[20] The need for a more distinct theological profile in interdisciplinary dialogue is often recognized in the field. As T. W. Jennings has written:

> The range of dialogue between theology and the human sciences is inordinately restricted when it is limited to representatives of the human sciences who appear to have a positive regard for the religious life and its vocabulary (so Jung vs. Freud) or to theologians who have appropriated some of the conceptuality of the human sciences (e.g. Tillich vs. Barth). But this overlap of vocabulary and conceptuality is by no means a prerequisite to dialogue and *may even prevent dialogue by the reduction of both sides of the discussion* to areas of explicit agreement.

(Philadelphia: Westminster, 1966); and Daniel J. Price, "Karl Barth's Anthropology in Light of Modern Thought: The Dynamic Concept of the Person in Trinitarian Theology and Object Relations Psychology" (unpublished dissertation, University of Aberdeen, Scotland, 1990).

18. One notable exception, also to be discussed in the next chapter, is Shirley C. Guthrie, Jr., "Pastoral Counseling, Trinitarian Theology, and Christian Anthropology," *Interpretation* 33 (April 1979): 130-43.

19. In his book on pastoral counseling as a ministry of the church, John Patton interestingly draws upon Barth's fourfold description of basic humanity as a "normative" concept. See John Patton, *Pastoral Counseling: A Ministry of the Church* (Nashville: Abingdon, 1983), p. 30.

20. Oden, *Kerygma and Counseling,* p. 127.

Thus one side is but the echo (or translation) of the other. . . . The reduction of different discourses to a table of equivalences (neurosis = sin, wholeness = salvation, acceptance = justification, etc.) is certainly *not* an enrichment but the reduction of one discourse to another or of both to a lowest common denominator.[21]

Barth's theology by its very nature resists this kind of reductionism. Because of his methodological point of departure, it is virtually impossible to undertake any such translation of his theology into psychological modes of thought. His consistent concern to delimit the boundaries of theology, differentiating it from fields not based on God's self-revelation, makes Barth a promising conversation partner not only for dialogue that is truly interdisciplinary but also for pastoral counseling as a bilingual form of ministry.

Chapter Two, as previously mentioned, offers a survey of writers who have brought Barth's theology into dialogue with depth psychology and counseling. Two lines of inquiry in particular are pursued. First, what sort of question is each writer asking, and how is Barth's theology drawn into the discussion? Second, what might be learned from each approach by a pastoral counselor seeking both bilingual fluency and methodological clarity?

In Chapter Three the "Chalcedonian pattern" is set forth and applied to some perennial questions about how to relate theological concepts like "sin" and "salvation" to psychological concepts like "neurosis" and "healing." The pattern is then used to analyze the work of three writers whose proposals for interdisciplinary dialogue are essentially theoretical. At the theoretical level, the pattern is shown to offer categories of discernment that may be used to assess and criticize these proposals from a Barthian standpoint. Finally, in a more practical application of the pattern, two hypothetical clinical examples are introduced in which the pattern assists in sorting through the psychological and theological issues at stake.

In Chapter Four the proposed procedure for relating theology and psychology through the Chalcedonian pattern is extended to examine the psychological process of forming a God representation. Psycho-

---

21. T. W. Jennings, "Pastoral Theological Methodology," in *Dictionary of Pastoral Care and Counseling,* ed. Rodney Hunter (Nashville: Abingdon, 1990), p. 864; emphasis added.

analytic understanding of how one internalizes and develops a God representation is investigated along with a Barthian understanding of how one acquires a knowledge of God. Psychoanalytic method and Barth's theological method are differentiated from each other, showing how each is appropriate to its intended object of study. A normative understanding of the God representation from the perspective of the two different disciplines — broadly conceived as "psychological functionality" and "theological adequacy" — is also presented. These respective norms are then brought into relationship with each other, exploring the logically possible ways in which they might be related. The close interweaving of psychological and theological issues is discussed with reference to a number of hypothetical pastoral counseling situations.

An extended case study is presented in Chapter Five in order to set forth the "paradigmatic situation" in which a counselee seeks both psychological healing and theological guidance in the Christian faith. The discussion shows how the pastoral counselor's "bilingual" competencies can be informed in practice by the Chalcedonian pattern. The case is analyzed from two different perspectives, one drawing upon depth psychology, the other drawing upon Barth. Theological and psychoanalytic materials are thus differentiated from each other and considered as conceptually distinct. At the same time, however, these materials are also seen not only as actually commingled in the life of the counselee but also as capable of coexisting in an analogical unity disclosed through the theological material. Finally, through this procedure of conceptual distinction and analogical relation, psychoanalytical interpretation is thereby placed in a larger context of theological interpretation and meaning. The chapter thus presents a concrete example of how the proposed method of relating the two disciplines may guide a pastoral counselor in formulating the kinds of complex judgments needed when theological and psychoanalytical materials are explicitly entwined in a particular case. The chapter also illustrates what it means to bring a Barthian theological perspective to the ministry of pastoral counseling.

With Chapter Six the book concludes by summarizing the proposed method for relating the two disciplines in the theory and practice of pastoral counseling. The analysis is briefly extended to touch upon how the pastoral counselor might use bilingual competencies in various cases where the counselee does not explicitly bring both theological and psychological questions to the work. The Chalcedonian pattern again demonstrates its fruitfulness for distinguishing and relating the complex materials confronting the pastoral counselor.

CHAPTER TWO

Barth and Counseling: A Survey

THIS CHAPTER surveys selected discussions that examine Barth's theology in relation to central issues in the theory and practice of counseling. Four authors will be considered, three theologians and one practicing psychotherapist, each bringing a particular set of questions to the interdisciplinary dialogue. Some of the authors have interests that are more theoretical, others that are more practical. In each case it will be important to notice what sort of question each author is raising and how Barth's theology is being employed. After the author's argument is presented in its own terms, its potential relevance for the "bilingual" pastoral counselor will be considered. What might be helpful to the pastoral counselor who seeks both methodological clarity and bilingual fluency?

Shirley Guthrie: Barthian Insights for Pastoral Counseling

Among the various discussions being reviewed in this chapter, the only one whose focus is explicitly on pastoral counseling is Shirley Guthrie's.[1] Yet Guthrie himself is not a pastoral counselor but, rather, a systematic theologian. His reflections are not, strictly speaking, interdisciplinary, in that he does not engage with contemporary psychological theory. He does, however, raise a number of substantive theo-

---

1. Shirley C. Guthrie, Jr., "Pastoral Counseling, Trinitarian Theology, and Christian Anthropology," *Interpretation* 33 (April 1979): 130-43. Subsequent references will be given parenthetically in the text.

logical questions that have important implications for the contemporary theory and practice of pastoral counseling. Guthrie's article is perhaps best characterized as an exercise in theological application. Drawing on central insights from Barth's theological anthropology, Guthrie asks how a (Reformed) Christian doctrine of the human person might inform the pastoral counselor's work. Guthrie is thus not interested in interpreting Barth so much as in using Barth's anthropology to make his own constructive contribution. Guthrie's essay sheds considerable light on our question of what it means to bring a theological perspective to the therapeutic task. Pastoral counseling's distinctiveness as a profession, he argues, comes precisely from its theological self-understanding.

> What makes Christian pastoral counseling unique is that fact that without arrogance but also without apology the work of counselors is based on the attempt to understand both themselves and their counselees in light of the God who is Creator, Redeemer and Life-Giver and thus the answer to questions about the ultimate origin, meaning and goal of life which lie behind all other problems and questions. (Guthrie, p. 132)

From the above quotation it is already evident that Guthrie has adopted Barth's methodological procedure of basing his theological anthropology on the doctrine of the Trinity. Following this method, Guthrie outlines a Christian doctrine of the human person on the basis of a doctrine of the triune God. Human beings are thus understood from a threefold perspective: first, as created in the image of God (derived from knowledge of God the Creator); second, as sinners who fail to live out God's purposes and who stand in need of redemption (derived from knowledge of Christ, the Redeemer); and third, as people who are promised a new humanity in Christ (derived from knowledge of the Holy Spirit). Guthrie emphasizes the importance of the pastoral counselor's keeping all three aspects of human reality in a kind of creative tension, so that the created goodness, the sinful fallenness, and the promised new life of human beings are all clearly seen and affirmed as being simultaneously true. He spells out the implications of this complex affirmation later in the essay when he raises questions about the freedom and bondage of the human will.

Because pastoral counselors understand both their counselees and themselves on this basis, Guthrie goes on to say, they understand themselves to be on the same plane with their counselees. Counselors are ministers who may indeed have specialized skills but who, like their counselees, are themselves "limited, fallible, sinful human beings who themselves are judged, need reconciliation and salvation, and can only receive the wisdom and power they cannot produce from themselves to help others" (Guthrie, p. 132).

In applying this trinitarian anthropology to current questions in pastoral counseling, Guthrie deftly wends his way through a complex set of issues about the counselor's attitude toward the physical body and the human emotions. He sees the contemporary emphasis on the importance of the body and the emotions to be a justified reaction to a kind of false spirituality in the church that has overemphasized the rational and volitional aspects of humanity. Here as elsewhere, Guthrie employs Barth's method in moving characteristically from theological affirmation to anthropological implication. God himself is not a disembodied idea, he argues, but an incarnate Lord, one who in Jesus Christ shared our bodily existence and felt human emotions. Moreover, God himself "has a 'heart' and he created human beings in his own image with a heart" (Guthrie, p. 134). Because God has affirmed humanity's bodily and emotional needs, he argues, human beings are also free to do so. At the same time, however, human beings were created as "rational, purposive beings. . . . Body without spirit is as inhuman as spirit without body."[2] Guthrie sees the Christian pastoral counselor working toward a goal in which "body, heart, mind and will are understood in their integrated relationship to each other" (Guthrie, p. 134).

Guthrie then takes up the question of the proper relationship between the individual and the community. He again addresses what he sees as a legitimate concern of contemporary counseling: the need for human self-affirmation and self-determination. While he affirms the validity of these goals for counseling, he places them into a larger theological context that critically appraises them and effectually rela-

---

2. Guthrie, p. 134. Here one can perceive an echo of Barth's rich discussion of the differentiated unity of the soul and the body in *Church Dogmatics* III/2.

tivizes them. He argues that a Christian pastoral counselor can work for such goals only if they are put into a context of Christian love. "Human individuality is realized in human community," he writes (Guthrie, p. 135). Again arguing from theological to anthropological affirmation, Guthrie emphasizes God's decision to enter into partnership with his creatures. God's "deity is not transcendent loneliness and self-sufficiency," he states, "but his desire and ability to be God-in-relationship" (Guthrie, p. 135). So also human beings are not meant to be isolated but rather in relationship. God created human beings to relate to other people in "faithful, mutually giving and helping love" (Guthrie, p. 135), and in a concern for the poor and the weak. The claims put on us by our relationships, both interpersonal and societal, he argues, are precisely the means by and through which we are able to affirm ourselves.

Guthrie thus maintains that we are truly fulfilled as individuals only as we love and serve others. Ably drawing out the implications of such a position, he argues that larger political, economic, and cultural issues are not peripheral but integral to the pastoral counseling task, for fulfillment in interpersonal relationships cannot be divorced from the larger social context. At the same time, Christian pastoral counseling, he says, needs to be practiced "in the context of the Christian community and invite people to find wholeness in that community" (Guthrie, p. 136). Guthrie thus suggests a vision of the place of pastoral counseling in the overall life and work of the church. "Pastoral counselors who ignore the promises and requirements of the preaching, sacraments, fellowship and mission of the church deprive themselves and their counselees of the source and goal of the healing counselors seek to offer and counselees want to receive" (Guthrie, p. 136).

Returning to the core Christian affirmations about the goodness, fallenness, and redemption of human beings in light of the gospel, Guthrie applies them to the pastoral counseling setting. Once again Barth's distinctive theological anthropology is evident when Guthrie says that human beings are not sinful "by nature." Although fallen, human beings were created good, in the image of God, the Creator. Our real humanity is also affirmed in the "real man," Jesus (Barth's characteristic term) who lived in thankful obedience to God. Sin is thus "unreality," self-contradiction, the contradiction of what God created us to be. While our "radical sinfulness" is exposed by the gospel, the gospel also shows us that sin is not the last word. Christian pastoral counselors can thus encourage their counselees to become their authentically human selves when they understand that to mean the humanity created, redeemed, and promised by God and thus the "contradiction of the self-contradiction in which all human beings live" (Guthrie, p. 138). In this way the Christian pastoral counselor is able to affirm human creatureliness and the essential goodness of being human, on the one hand, without underestimating or denying the power of sin, on the other.

Guthrie next tackles a complex set of problems addressed by a theological understanding of the freedom and determination of human life by virtue of God's grace and human sin. Guthrie clearly differentiates between the psychological and the theological dimensions of the kinds of problems pastoral counselors face. He says quite explicitly that "the question of human freedom poses both a theological and a psychological problem for pastoral counselors." While he closely associates the "enslaving power of sin" with the various "hereditary, environmental and historical forces" (Guthrie, p. 138) that contribute to the inhibition of human freedom, he does not collapse the two languages into one but keeps them clearly distinct. Skillfully wending his way through extremely complex issues, Guthrie shows how it is possible for the Christian pastoral counselor to encourage human responsibility and freedom while understanding what realistic limits to that freedom (both theological and psychological) may entail.

Thus, for example, he affirms the theological proposition that "we are not able to be and to do the one thing that makes people really free: We cannot be people who decide to, and actually do, love God with our whole being and our neighbor as ourselves" (Guthrie, p. 139). Awareness of this bondage is a sobering reality to anyone who perceives the awful dimensions of human sin. Human beings really are not able to do what is needed. On the other hand, Guthrie speaks concretely about the relative but real freedom people do in fact have. Trusting that God genuinely "wills and gives human freedom," the pastoral counselor will encourage steps that lead toward freedom:

> It is true, for instance, that sinful human beings cannot simply "decide" to love God with their whole being, but they can at least go to church, or talk to people (including the counselor), or read a book (including the Bible) in order to find out who the God is who promises and gives freedom. It is true that they cannot "decide" to be loving and just, but they can risk the personal encounters and social contexts in which love and justice can happen. . . . None of these small steps are a guarantee that freedom will come. . . . But Christian pastoral counselors will encourage these small steps nevertheless. They are steps toward the freedom God intends and promises to give to all people. (Guthrie, pp. 140-41)

With these kinds of examples, which not only are rich in suggestive detail but also are differentiated psychologically and theologically, Guthrie exemplifies the kind of clarity and depth of understanding that the pastoral counselor needs.

This same kind of exemplary clarity is apparent in the last section of Guthrie's essay where he speaks of the freedom to be human as gift, task, and promise. He alludes to the analogy between the basic acceptance shown by counselors toward their counselees and God's love and acceptance for all people. While not affirming its trivialization (as for instance in "I'm OK, you're OK"), Guthrie indicates that in this arena counseling lives out in its own sphere the truth of God's justifying and forgiving love. As he proceeds to wrestle with core theological issues about the relationship between freedom and responsibility, Guthrie takes a fairly Barthian position of "Gospel preceding Law":

> To the extent that counselors neglect law and order and morality and responsibility, it is not because they take *too* seriously but because they do not take seriously *enough* the meaning of God's grace and the human freedom it brings. What is needed is not less but more complete emphasis on these doctrines. Then God's law and human responsibility will fall into their proper place as an *expression* of (rather than as an alternative to or qualification of) the Christian Gospel of a gracious God that sets people free. (Guthrie, p. 141)

Thus God's sovereign grace is understood to be the basis and foundation of the free self-determination of people. Because God *loves* sinners, Guthrie maintains, people do not have to grasp after justification or basic acceptance. But because God loves *sinners,* people will not become complacently satisfied with themselves but will strive to be gratefully obedient to this gracious and loving God. When pastoral counselors are clear about these important theological distinctions, they can better help their counselees to avoid both the Scylla of self-hatred and the Charybdis of moral laxity.

Pastoral counselors, as ministers of the gospel, thus stand for something distinctive. Guthrie asserts that they "will give up all neutrality about the *goal* of change, growth or becoming." Because they understand themselves to be serving a God who promises, invites, and commands a new humanity, they are open about the goals toward which they are working. Guthrie says, "Without manipulating people to attitudes and actions they do not freely choose for themselves, the counselor will openly stand for the Christian understanding of what fulfilled humanity looks like." Guthrie's own formulation of that goal is the "integration of bodily, rational, emotional and volitional selfhood in thankful and obedient relationship to God and a loving and just relationship with other people" (Guthrie, p. 143).

As we have indicated throughout this section, the strength of Guthrie's essay is its clarity about how actually to bring a theological perspective to pastoral counseling. Rather than talking *about* method, he *uses* a distinctively Barthian method of developing anthropological affirmations on the basis of theological convictions about the nature of God. He then applies his insights directly to a number of central issues in the practice of pastoral counseling, such as the nature of the relationship among mind, body, heart, and spirit, between individual and community, and between the bondage and the freedom of the human will. Although he himself does not use case material (being not a pastoral counselor but a theologian), he discusses the kind of theological issues that need addressing before looking at actual cases. Any pastoral counselor with case material at hand could readily make a number of applications based on Guthrie's remarks.

Guthrie clearly differentiates between psychological and theological perspectives and respects the domain and importance of each. While not focusing on method but, rather, on the content of Christian claims, he brings a great deal of methodological clarity to his work. Thus he does not look for any overarching theoretical framework to yoke together any theological and psychological concerns. Rather, he raises a number of issues in an ad hoc way, looking for ways that his theological perspective might illuminate some central issues in the practice of pastoral counseling. In my estimation he succeeds admirably in what he set out to do. He thus provides for us a kind of model of what it means to bring a theological perspective to pastoral counseling. Although he himself does not directly attempt to become bilingual and speaks only a theological tongue, he does so fluently and with integrity.

Dorothy Martyn: Barth in Clinical Practice Other than Pastoral Counseling

Dorothy Martyn, a psychotherapist with theological interests, uses Barth in a manner quite different from that of Guthrie. The primary focus of Martyn's work is not on pastoral counseling but, rather, on understanding some important theoretical issues in her practice as a psychotherapist. In her book she pursues two basic questions: First, how do children's use of symbols facilitate their emotional growth and change? And second, what is the significance of their relationship with the psychotherapist in bringing about this therapeutic change? Martyn combines these two questions into one focused theoretical issue: "How are the child's use of symbol and the contextual relationship related to . . . therapeutic change?"[3] She pursues this question by examining a number of psychological theoreticians (such as Freud, Jung, Winnicott, Sullivan, and Klein) and only then does she ask how her conclusions might be seen from a theological perspective (by way of Barth).

Because Martyn is a psychotherapist and not a pastoral counselor, she does not directly require the kind of bilingual fluency that this book proposes as a model for pastoral counseling. In a certain sense, one might say that her theological interests are more nearly reflective than practical. By this I mean to say only that as a rule she makes no

---

3. Dorothy Martyn, *The Man in the Yellow Hat: Theology and Psychoanalysis in Child Therapy* (Atlanta: Scholars Press, 1992), p. 33. Subsequent references will be given parenthetically in the text.

direct or explicit use of a theological perspective within the clinical setting. As is fitting in her role as a psychotherapist, in the actual course of her practice, theological language is not explicitly used to interpret her clients' material. One might acknowledge that her theological reflection would add a dimension of depth and richness to her interpretations or that it might provide her with insights not acquirable by other means, but there is no apparent way that such a perspective would find direct expression in her clinical work.

In a compelling first chapter, Martyn presents three case studies, rich in concrete detail, drawing the reader into a vivid encounter with the children. Her theoretical questions thus seem to evolve naturally out of the clinical setting. What *does* make it possible for these children to change? How does their play make such emotional growth occur? And what is the significance of the therapist's being present to interact with the child and interpret what she sees?

Martyn explores a number of depth psychological theories in an effort to answer these questions, beginning with Freud and Jung. She shows how they both conclude (though with very different formulations) that "symbolic creativity cannot be separated from a context of human relationship" (Martyn, p. 55). For Freud the libido that is bound up in symptoms is freed through the transference of a portion of that energy onto the therapist. Summarizing Freud, Martyn states, "The sublimation of the instinctual drives happens in connection with a new object relationship" (Martyn, p. 43). According to Jung's conception, the process of individuation unfolds as psychic energy is reworked through symbolic activity. Drawing on the work of Jungian writer Erich Neumann, Martyn traces how the ego is differentiated and developed out of the unconscious matrix, which, like a Great Mother, sustains and nourishes the ego, on the one hand, and threatens to overwhelm or swallow it up, on the other. The process of separating oneself from one's human mother while still relating to her is thus analogous to developing the ego out of the unconscious matrix. In fact, according to Neumann, the two processes are not significantly distinguishable. One develops as an individual only in the complex, ongoing process of psychic identification and differentiation with one's human parents and the archetypal realities they mediate. Thus for both Freud and Jung, symbolic activity and interpersonal relationship are inextricably tied together.

It is through the psychic mechanisms of introjection, the child's symbolic "eating" of the parents, which enable him or her to sublimate early instinctual drives. Martyn outlines the theories of a number of depth psychologists (such as Sullivan, Winnicott, and Klein) as she traces how they each conceptualize the complex interplay between inner and outer world in the process of symbol formation as one develops. She gives particular attention to the phenomenon of ambivalence and the kind of therapeutic attitudes required to help children to come to terms with their ambivalent feelings. For repressing one's aggressive or destructive impulses is seen to give them greater power, while allowing them to become externalized through play is understood to give the ego a greater sense of mastery over them. Martyn shows how each of the three children she presents had to come to terms with their "badness," anger, and hate and did so by creating such characters as wicked mothers, soldiers, and highway robbers in the playroom. Within the "holding environment" provided by the therapist, they were enabled to work through their inner conflicts by means of their creative play. Martyn concludes these theoretical reflections with a succinct statement of her own thesis:

> My own way of conceptualizing how the children's symbolic play and the relationship are connected . . . is that the children through their play were, in the simplest terms, "eating" the therapist. That is to say, they were appropriating, *through participating via the symbol* in a vital force present in the containing relationship. . . . I am convinced that there are certain qualities in the therapeutic relationship that make possible the arousing of the creative urge in the child, the mobilizing of that individual's own vital force in bringing forth what had lain dormant. There is some power at work. (Martyn, pp. 142-43)

It is at this point that Martyn begins to reflect theologically on what she has discovered. She asks about the nature of this power in the chapter entitled "A Theological Perspective." What qualities of relationship promote emotional growth? Martyn has already reflected on a number of these qualities from within a psychological frame of reference. But now she shifts that frame of reference by drawing on Barth. Significantly, Martyn does not turn, as Guthrie does, to Barth's theological *anthropology* but, rather, to his *doctrine of God* (in II/1). In her own way, then, she employs Barth's method of basing one's anthropology on a doctrine of the triune God. While she does not engage in any sustained methodological reflection regarding the possible interrelations between theology and psychology, she does draw explicit attention to the importance of Barth's methodological point of departure as a theologian:

> If I were to state what I understand to be the most significant, lasting contribution of Karl Barth, it would be his point of departure in the attempt to enlighten the human condition. Barth was convinced that no anthropological perspective is useful as a starting point for understanding who we are. The human subject, in Barth's view, can be understood only by the light of God's own revealing of Himself. In effect, Barth reverses the usual procedure for thinking about God and humanity, which is to begin with human experience, to identify something that seems good, to project this idea of goodness to an ultimate dimension and call it "God." (Martyn, p. 147)

Martyn closely follows the logic of Barth's argument by pointing out that the usual procedure of beginning with human considerations and projecting them in turn upon God puts us in the predicament of "divinizing . . . the human being's own image" (Martyn, p. 148). Martyn understands Barth to be saying that we learn nothing about God nor even about ourselves in such an undertaking but simply deify our inner experience or perhaps some cultural pattern (Martyn, p. 147).

Unlike Oden and Price (writers whose work will be examined next), Martyn does not enter technical discussions about the relative merits of the *analogia fidei* (analogy of faith) over the *analogia entis* (analogy of being), but she clearly builds on Barth's conclusions. So she adopts a stance based on the *analogia fidei* when she writes, "I am aware also that I have taken a stance that involves an attitude of faith as well as an attitude of investigation. . . . One always begins and ends an intellectual endeavor with an implicit, if not an explicit, premise of faith in what one believes to be ultimate" (Martyn, p. 166).

In this case, Martyn makes the premise explicit by adopting Barth's theological premise as her own. Thus she begins by reflecting on God's action in Jesus Christ and moves into the human sphere where she can ask about the interpersonal qualities of relationship that engender emotional growth and change. Martyn focuses her reflection on the divine qualities of relationship that Barth discusses under the heading of "The Perfections of the Divine Loving" (II/1, 351-439). She discusses the three dialectical pairs developed there by Barth: God's grace and holiness, God's mercy and righteousness, and God's patience and wisdom. She shows how each of these qualities might be embodied in a derivative way in human relationships. Because the ultimate ground of these qualities is understood to be divine, human beings are understood to embody them only when they have first received them from another person who has nurtured them. Quoting St. Paul, Martyn asks, "What have ye that ye did not receive?" (1 Cor. 4:7; Martyn, p. 146).

What follows is a creative but highly distilled exercise in theological application. Martyn does not directly enter Barth's argument but, rather, uses his thinking to construct her own applications of the evolving relationship between therapist and child. Thus she finds pithy and apt quotations from Barth for focusing her own remarks on the quality of the relationship she is investigating. The bulk of her discussion focuses on the possible applications of Barth's understanding of God's grace. First she quotes Barth: "Grace is the distinctive mode of God's being in so far as it seeks and creates fellowship by its own free inclination and favor, unconditioned by any merit or claim in the beloved, but also unhindered by any unworthiness or opposition in the latter — able on the contrary to overcome all unworthiness and opposition" (II/1, 353; Martyn, p. 150). Martyn focuses on four points she believes are particularly applicable to her work with children. She skillfully draws out the implications for her work as a child psychotherapist, drawing theory and practice into close conversation.

1. "The cannot-earn quality of grace."[4]

Since grace is an unmerited gift from God, there is obviously nothing human beings can do to earn it. Martyn observes that this idea is

4. Martyn, p. 151.

emotionally "assaultive" because it completely contradicts our normal belief that we reap what we sow. She explicates Barth's view that our innate resistance to this idea is directly commensurate with our preference for our own moral activity to God's gift of grace. The idea of a prior, uncontingent, prevenient God moving toward us, independent of our deserving, grates on our sense of justice, Martyn maintains. We are more comfortable thinking in terms of just desserts, of reward and punishment, consequences, or quid pro quo (Martyn, p. 151).

A parent or therapist approaching a child with a grace-filled attitude is not interested in the kind of moral bribery that achieves a child's compliance through offers of reward or threats of punishment. Rather than trying to manipulate the child, the adult seeks to support the child, bringing the child genuine help against the child's own destructive impulses. Two basic attitudes are thus contrasted: one that relies on power *over* the child and one that sustains the child by standing alongside the child. The first "uses the position of power to control — however disguised the tyranny — rather than to sustain and support the child's emerging being" (Martyn, p. 153). Martyn maintains that such an attitude is essentially powerless to bring about any deep motivational change and merely perpetuates a power struggle between the child and adult. The second attitude gives the child the message that the therapist is on his side. The child's destructive impulse *"is then revealed to the child also as alien and undesirable"* (Martyn, p. 133). The child's gratitude and motivation to change is thus evoked toward the supportive adult.

2. *"Grace is unhindered by unworthiness or opposition."*[5]

Just as God's purposes are not deterred by human sin, so the good parent or therapist moves forward with benevolent attitudes despite the child's destructive aggression. In a vivid example, Martyn shows how it was the therapist's steady offer of support to a young boy that "communicated the message that there was something bigger and more powerful than his own bad feelings. Each time he discovered — in joyous relief — that this bigger reality survived his aggression,

5. Martyn, p. 154.

he learned to lean more heavily on the good feelings instead of the bad feelings inside himself" (Martyn, pp. 154-55).

3. "Grace precedes law, not vice-versa."[6]

Grace itself creates the capacity for obedience to the law. If God were to insist upon the fulfillment of the law as a requirement for his gracious activity, human beings would remain mired in their sin. Christ died for us "while we were yet sinners" (Rom. 5:8), that is, precisely when we were disobedient to the law. Obedience thus is seen to arise out of gratitude for love and acceptance, not out of fear. Martyn basically presupposes Barth's discussion and proceeds directly to the implications for the therapist-child relationship. She writes:

> Rules and regulations, or the order of the law, have little meaning for youngsters like William — except as a source of fear of punishment or loss of reward — until they have experienced a relationship characterized by acceptance and respect. . . . One begins with the free gift of acceptance. It is the response of gratitude, not forced compliance, that engenders true obedience. (Martyn, p. 155)

4. "Grace is inherently powerful and overcomes enmity against it without violating the self-determination of those in the grip of the enmity."[7]

Martyn uses Barth's conclusion as a springboard for her own reflections and applications. Just as God respects our otherness and sustains us with divine grace even in the midst of our disobedient choices, so the wise parent or therapist seeks to respect the child as a separate being who cannot, indeed must not, be forced into compliance.

> A relationship informed by the nature of grace would mean that the parent takes up the position toward the child in a way analogous to the way God loves us into loving without compelling or forcing our

6. Martyn, p. 155.
7. Martyn, p. 155.

self-determination. The informed parent, or teacher, understands
that the true power does not lie in the violation of the child's own
being by open or hidden tyranny. (Martyn, p. 156)

The therapist's no-strings-attached acceptance of the child is seen
as the source of true power for maturational growth. Martyn's discussion of God's grace and its applications to the clinical setting is
then enriched by her drawing on Barth's discussion of its dialectical
opposite, God's holiness. She again finds a remark from Barth that
aptly captures the essence of the quality she seeks to understand.

> [God] neither compromises with [human] resistance, nor ignores it,
> still less calls it good. But as the gracious God he affirms himself over
> against the one to whom he is gracious by opposing and breaking
> down his resistance, and in some way causing his own good will to
> exert its effect upon him. Therefore the one to whom he is gracious
> comes to experience God's opposition to him. (II/1, 361; Martyn,
> p. 157)

Analogously, the child who is acting out destructive impulses will
experience the opposition of the therapist, for the therapist will actively
oppose those impulses. Yet, at the same time the therapist will continue to support the child. Just as a holy God opposes human sin, so
a good parent is firm in opposing anything that will hurt the child or
others. "The aggressive behavior that is destructive," states Martyn,
"is actively opposed; the child is not abandoned to it, nor is it sanctioned" (Martyn, p. 157).

In a similar fashion, Martyn draws on Barth's discussions of God's
mercy and righteousness and God's patience and wisdom to illustrate
their possible applications in the therapist–child relationship. Thus she
speaks of the therapist's compassion for her children as the "mediated
mercy of God" and her advocacy of helpless children as an analogy
to God's righteous concern for the oppressed poor.[8] Human patience

---

8. Martyn, p. 159. Martyn does not comment on the ambiguity of the idea of
"mediation" from a Barthian standpoint. Insofar as the idea carries connotations that
a human act of compassion can reflect or attest divine compassion by way of an
analogy and that the efficacy of this attestation or reflection remains entirely in God's
hands, Barth would have no objections. Insofar as the idea of "mediation" might
carry stronger connotations, however (i.e., that the human compassion automatically

is understood as a derivative of God's patience, which allows God's creatures space and time to develop in freedom. Similarly, the wise therapist will wait patiently for the child to grow and develop in her own way at her own pace. In so doing she aligns herself with God's wisdom, learning to trust the unfolding pattern that will emerge over time.

Martyn concludes the chapter by recalling the christocentric nature of Barth's theology. She writes, "God . . . seeks to regrasp his creatures by invading their sphere of bondage through a person, his own Son. His way is to draw human beings into a community characterized by participation in his Son, Jesus Christ" (Martyn, p. 171). She draws together the major strands of her thesis — on the use of the symbol and the healing relationship in which the transforming symbol emerges — by reflecting on the symbolic meal of the Eucharist. Just as we participate in God's love by incorporating God into our being via the symbolic elements of bread and wine, so also the children were able through their play to "eat" their therapist, that is, to incorporate those powerful qualities of relationship that mysteriously brought about human growth and maturation.

Thus the qualities of relationship that foster growth are understood to be, finally, of divine origin. By "mediating" these divine qualities of relationship in human form, therapists make possible liberation from all kinds of compulsive and destructive behavior. While this liberation can be explained psychoanalytically, Martyn maintains that to understand it at its deepest level, a theological perspective is also needed. Martyn provides us with just such a perspective through her creative use of Barth's doctrine of God.

Throughout her book, Martyn clearly differentiates between her use of psychoanalytic and of theological language. She does not attempt to synthesize them into a single, compound language or even to correlate them in anything other than an ad hoc way. She uses no overarching conceptual scheme by which to integrate or correlate them systematically. Instead, she simply suggests a kind of loosely ordered relationship between them when she envisions these qualities

---

effects or transmits or communicates divine compassion at the same time), Barth would demur. Despite this ambiguity, it seems clear that Martyn intends the former, not the latter connotation.

of relationship as divine qualities reflected, attested, or mediated in a secondary way by humans. The qualities that can be described psychologically are thus placed within a larger theological framework, whose own peculiar language operates essentially on another or different level. In doing this, Martyn carefully follows Barth's logic and does not attempt to understand the divine qualities as human projections of imagined goodness. The ground of knowledge is inverted so that certain psychological phenomena are interpreted as images or reflections of a prior divine reality — a reality known not directly by means of those phenomena but only on the peculiar basis of its own unique self-disclosure.

A more precise indication of how Martyn conceives of the relationship between the two disciplines is described in her article "A Child and Adam: A Parable of the Two Ages."[9] There she describes her conception of psychotherapy as a kind of "parable of the truth." She apparently first encountered the concept in C. K. Barrett, though Barth, too, developed it at some length (IV/3, 85-135). Psychotherapy, when it is truly healing, is conceived by Martyn as a kind of eschatological sign, where one may witness the kind of liberation and new life indicative of Christ's lordship and coming reign.

In her essay, Martyn develops three analogies between Christian theology and depth psychology. First she finds an analogy between the internalization of Christ as new family head for the Christian and the internalization of a caring therapist who represents a different kind of parent to the counselee. In the process of faith, there is a kind of double internalization that occurs, the believer is said to be incorporated into Christ and Christ is said to dwell within the believer. In the therapeutic process, the therapist is psychologically internalized through the process of introjection. In both cases, new life comes through the internalization of a loving and gracious other. The second analogy develops a parallel between the free gift of grace offered by God and the therapist's gracious acceptance of the child, an idea developed at much greater length in the book.

Finally, Martyn develops an analogy between God's recapitulative work in Christ and the recapitulative work of psychotherapy. Drawing

9. Martyn, "A Child and Adam: A Parable of the Two Ages," *Journal of Religion and Health* 16 (1977): 275-87.

on Irenaeus, "for whom the doctrine of recapitulation underlay all theology,"[10] Martyn calls to mind the divine work of creation in Adam and of redemption in the "second Adam," or Christ. Analogously, children who receive inadequate nurturing are understood to be in a kind of bondage to forces of evil and death. As they take part in the psychotherapeutic journey, which symbolically recapitulates their own family history, they are in a sense grafted onto a new family. The therapist symbolically becomes a loving parent who can help heal the childhood wounds of neglect or abuse by being internalized into the deepest strata of the child's psychic life. Just as Christians find themselves living in the tension of the "already" and the "not yet," so similarly for psychotherapeutic clients: something has fundamentally changed; they are freer, but they are not yet completely delivered. They, too, stand with the rest of creation, longing for the consummation of God's gracious plan.

In conclusion, the significance of Martyn's work for the pastoral counselor who seeks to become both psychologically and theologically fluent, may be seen as essentially twofold. First, her descriptions of actual cases are vivid and compelling. One is drawn into the material both intellectually and emotionally, for the author has the gift of bringing her readers along, helping them to think her thoughts after her, so to speak. Thus the theoretical questions that evolve out of the case studies become gripping for the reader as well. Pastoral counselors who regularly reflect theoretically on their cases cannot help but be interested in Martyn's way of formulating her questions, for it seeks to combine the two central elements — symbolic creativity and interpersonal relationship — that are repeatedly identified as being the key to the healing process.

Second, when she submits her conclusions to theological scrutiny, she does so with genuine clarity about the nature of the task she is undertaking. She is clear, for instance, about the need to indicate that she is shifting from an attitude of investigation to an attitude of faith when she uses Barth's reflections on the reality of God and brings them into relationship with the qualities of relationship that make for emotional growth. Although she characteristically seems to focus on the element of similarity rather than of dissimilarity in the analogies

10. Martyn, "A Child and Adam," p. 285.

that she constructs, leaving the latter element mostly implicit, she is also clear about the conceptual and linguistic boundaries that exist between the two fields, and she is clear about how to develop analogies between them. Although she does not explicitly specify the pattern that governs the relationship between theology and psychology, nor undertake any second-order reflection on the methodological issues at stake, she implicitly constructs her analogies according to the pattern described in our next chapter. Although she does not use the language of theological interpretation in the clinical setting as a pastoral counselor might, the clarity and creativity that she brings to her reflections would be helpful to any pastoral counselor pondering these and similar questions.

Thomas Oden: Dialogue at the Theoretical Level Between Barth and Secular Counseling

Thomas Oden is concerned neither with bringing a theological perspective to pastoral counseling, nor with theological reflection on the basis of a clinical investigation, but rather with developing correspondences between theology and psychology at the theoretical level.[11] While his book does not focus on interpreting Barth's own thought (as does Price's book, to be reviewed next), he does use Barth's theology to draw out the correspondences he sees. While Oden wants to generalize about the relationship between psychotherapy and Christian proclamation, as we will see, he actually defines his task somewhat more narrowly by focusing on the theoretical formulations of Carl Rogers and bringing them into relation with what he sees as the central affirmations of the gospel. The core of Oden's argument is conveyed by his own succinct statement: "The central thesis of this inquiry is that there is an implicit assumption hidden in all effective psychotherapy which is made explicit in the Christian proclamation" (Oden, *Kerygma,* p. 9).

Drawing on Rogers's conclusions regarding the therapeutic skills and attitudes needed by effective psychotherapists, Oden draws a

11. Thomas C. Oden, *Kerygma and Counseling* (Philadelphia: Westminster, 1966). Subsequent references will be given parenthetically in the text.

series of analogies between these and his understanding of the "Christ event." Thus he argues that all effective psychotherapy operates on an implicit assumption of the basic ontological acceptability of human beings. Rogers's formulation of therapeutic acceptance, permissiveness, and unconditional positive regard are understood to be analogous to the central message of the gospel, which Oden sums up in the phrase *Deus pro nobis,* God is for us. Oden maintains that the counselor's unconditional acceptance of the counselee is grounded in the nature of reality itself. The counselor is obviously not the source of this acceptance but is, rather, one who "mediates" it. Therapy, according to Oden, will be interpreted by faith "as *mediating* the love of God hiddenly present through interpersonal relationships."[12]

Although Oden speaks frequently of his debt to Barth and understands himself to be operating within a framework of a theology of revelation, he curiously draws on theologians such as Tillich or Bultmann at important junctures, a procedure that tends to efface the very distinctions he himself is attempting to make. Thus when Oden clarifies what he means by the gospel's claim of *Deus pro nobis,* he translates it into terms that Barth himself would probably disavow. Oden speaks of the gospel's message as "the final reality that we confront in life is for us," and that "the client is acceptable as a human being by the ground of being itself" (Oden, *Kerygma,* p. 21). Such Tillichian-sounding formulations lose the distinctiveness of Barth's voice and tend to obscure the boundaries between theology and psychology that Barth was keen to preserve.

Preaching the gospel is seen by Oden to be the explicit proclamation of an acceptance that is enacted behaviorally by the effective psychotherapist. By this Oden does not mean to suggest that a counselor must become a preacher to do good counseling. On the contrary, Oden wants to make a sharp distinction between the two roles. He

---

12. Oden, p. 30; emphasis added. The questions already raised about the term "mediation" need to be made even stronger here (see pp. 31-32 above). From a Barthian standpoint, it would be better not to say that human beings "mediate" divine love. Human beings may be capable of giving and receiving human love, which in turn might be seen as a witness to or attestation of divine love, but they would not thereby be "mediators" of divine love. Strictly speaking, there is only one Mediator of divine love, Jesus Christ himself, in relation to whom all others would function primarily as witnesses, not as little mediators in their own right.

sees the counselor's role as essentially a Socratic one of listening and clarifying from within the client's own frame of reference. Proclamation, by contrast, is understood to come from outside that frame of reference and is thus considered to be an "intrusion" into the counseling process. Oden apparently does not see how the language of faith might be used legitimately within the counseling setting (admittedly he is speaking of secular and not pastoral counseling) because he feels that by such use of the gospel, counselors can all too easily fall into the temptation to "become moralizers, judgers, and answer-givers, introjecting their viewpoint and imposing it upon troubled persons" (Oden, *Kerygma*, p. 30). He sounds another warning against such proclamation when he claims that "the intent of the kerygma is so easily distorted by the neurotic mind" (Oden, *Kerygma*, p. 28).

While Oden has raised an important issue here — certainly one does not want to use the therapeutic setting as a forum for moralizing or preaching — by drawing such a stark contrast between counseling and proclamation, he seems to leave no room for the more modest goal of bringing a theological perspective to the work of interpretation. Naturally it would be inappropriate to use the therapeutic relationship as a vehicle for imposing one's ideas — theological or any other — on the counselee. On the other hand, the old maxim would seem to apply here that "abuse does not bar use." While Oden rightly worries about the possibility of abuse (e.g., of imposing ready-made moralistic answers on the counselee), he is apparently unable to conceive of a legitimate way to speak the language of faith in the counseling setting. One could argue, however, that all things, and not just the intent of the kerygma, are easily distorted by the neurotic mind, for that is precisely one indication of what it means to be neurotic.[13]

13. Nearly twenty years later, Oden himself came to express some interesting misgivings on this point. In *Care of Souls in the Classic Tradition* (Philadelphia: Fortress, 1984), he writes: "As I now return to the early Christian pastoral tradition, however, I do not wish to negate the learning of this early journey of psychological discovery, nor do I want to disown my own work except for a few brief excessive passages in which I harshly inveighed against a deliberately religious orientation in counseling" (p. 24). Later he asks, "What can the classical tradition usefully contribute to modern pastoral counseling?" He answers, "The new synthesis would interweave evangelical witness more deliberately into the process of pastoral conversation rather than disavowing witness or dissociating proclamation from therapeutic dialogue" (pp. 38-39).

Unlike Martyn, Oden reflects at length on what he considers to be the crucial distinction between the *analogia entis* and the *analogia fidei* as Barth developed these ideas. One chapter of Oden's book focuses explicitly on the implications of the *analogia fidei* for developing analogies between disciplines. Drawing on Barth's distinctions, Oden states that he wants to reverse the normal procedure of moving from therapeutic experience to possible theological analogies by asking instead about "what we can learn about therapy from the self-disclosure of God" (Oden, *Kerygma,* p. 48). While his substantive question can thus be seen as quite similar to Martyn's, the difference lies in the sort of second-order reflection Oden brings to the discussion.

Oden tries to convey the significance of Barth's work by contrasting theology understood as projection and theology understood as revelation. The *analogia entis,* he suggests, presupposes that we can learn about God by observing human beings. Analogies between divine and human being may be developed because both are understood to share in "being," God perfectly and humanity imperfectly. We can thus learn about God by our observations of humanity. "If God loves us as the good father loves his child," Oden writes, "then we can learn something about the fatherhood of God by observing the character of good human fatherhood. So goes the process of natural theology — reading to the divine from the human on the basis of what is known about finite being" (Oden, *Kerygma,* pp. 47-48).

This is the kind of reasoning that Oden correctly sees Barth as repudiating, but nowhere in Oden's argument does he delineate the substantive reasons for this repudiation. Oden does seem to understand the important methodological implications of Barth's basing his theology on the divine self-disclosure of revelation, but he doesn't seem to have a clear grasp of the material reasons Barth has for rejecting the *analogia entis.* For Barth, the stark facts of sin and death are understood to be so radical as essentially to negate any continuity that might otherwise exist between divine and human being. Rather than continuity, Barth sees an ontological divide, a radical discontinuity between God's being and human being, which only God can overcome.[14]

14. For an assessment of the significance of Barth's distinction between the *analogia fidei* and the *analogia entis,* see Chapter Four, pp. 118-19.

Oden goes on to give some concrete illustrations of the *analogia fidei*. One example, which perhaps has more relevance today than when Oden wrote (1966), has to do with the fatherhood of God.[15] Rather than beginning with our perceptions of a good father and projecting that idea onto God, we are told to begin instead with God's self-disclosure as the "Father of our Lord, Jesus Christ." We thus learn of true fatherly goodness in the gospel's account of it. On that basis, we can construct analogies between God's fatherhood and human fatherhood. A true human father is thus understood to be one whose love in some way mirrors the divine self-giving love of God the Father. Such a perception is obviously possible only from a standpoint of faith, hence the *analogia fidei*.

The discussion of the analogy of faith is intended to pave the way for Oden's own constructive contribution. By asking about what we might learn about therapy from the self-disclosure of God, Oden proceeds to develop a series of analogies, culminating in an inventive chart that summarizes his remarks. The scope of these analogies can be seen from Oden's chart on page 40 (Oden, *Kerygma*, p. 80).

To give an example of the kind of argument undertaken, Oden's discussion of the analogy he sees between therapeutic empathy and the humanity of God will be summarized. The therapist's empathy for the client (as formulated by Rogers) is developed as an extended analogy to God's incarnation, where in the most radical way imaginable, "God assumes our frame of reference, entering into our human situation of finitude and estrangement, sharing our human condition even unto death" (Oden, *Kerygma*, p. 50). Just as God takes on our human form and suffers with us every kind of anguish known to human beings, so the empathetic therapist enters fully into the counselee's personal hell, descending with compassion into the most alienated aspects of the counselee's life.[16] As a result of this empathetic

15. In my exposition I will follow the ordinary practice of Scripture and tradition in which masculine pronouns are used to refer to God. Although this practice has recently become controversial, a defense of the practice and a critical discussion of the wider theological issues may be found in *Speaking the Christian God: The Holy Trinity and the Challenge of Feminism*, ed. Alvin F. Kimel, Jr. (Grand Rapids: Eerdmans, 1992).

16. If the counselor cannot achieve empathy with a particular counselee, it would seem to follow that the therapeutic relationship should be discontinued. At least by

	Therapist's Activity	Healing Process	Christ Event	Believer's Response
Understanding (cognitive)	Empathetic Understanding	Self-understanding	Humanity of God	Being Known
Existing (ontic)	Congruence	Self-identity	Deity of God	Being Oneself
Feeling (emotive)	Acceptance	Self-acceptance	Forgiveness of God	Being Forgiven
Willing (volitional)	Permissiveness	Self-direction	Grace of God	Being Liberated
Acting (relational)	Unconditional Positive Regard	Freedom for Others	Love of God	Loving Others

descent on the part of the counselor, the counselee feels known, understood, and accepted. Oden maintains that just this experience of being known and accepted for the whole of who one is is analogous to the explicit proclamation of the gospel: "*God is with us.* God himself has taken up our cause! We are able to affirm our humanity, because God himself has affirmed it."[17]

Oden's example moves from divine revelation to forms of human understanding. The loving human action finds its theological significance through an analogy with the prior action of God in Christ, known to us in revelation. Oden states: "Thus the kerygma makes a

---

Rogers's definition, which Oden is following here, only an empathic counselor would be able to bring about any therapeutic result.

17. Oden, *Kerygma,* p. 51. Given Oden's thesis — that Christian proclamation merely makes explicit something already implicit in all effective therapy — it would seem to follow that any effective counselor, not just one who is theologically conscious or trained, would have the capacity to know, accept, and understand a counselee in this way. The analogy drawn between the fruitful therapeutic experience and the material content of the gospel would be germane in a particular way, of course, for the counselee who was a believer.

radical cosmic affirmation of the very same sort of empathetic condescension or entry into another man's estrangement, which we find fragmentarily in psychotherapy" (Oden, *Kerygma,* p. 52). Thus Oden seeks to put the psychotherapeutic experience into a larger theological context and to differentiate between the two modes of discourse. At this point at least, Oden is careful to discuss not only the similarities between divine and human action but also the dissimilarities. For analogy does not mean identity, he reminds us, but rather *"a similarity in spite of a greater dissimilarity"* (I/1, 274).[18] Human empathy is analogous or similar to divine empathy but is clearly not identical to it. The dissimilarity between the two is not merely a matter of degree but also of kind. It is not just that human empathy by its very nature is limited but also that there is a substantive difference between human compassion and God's atoning sacrifice. In the gospel account, God in Jesus takes human sin and brokenness upon himself, into his own body and inner trinitarian life so that human beings might be made righteous and whole. There is thus an action of substitutionary atonement, where Christ suffers not only *with* us but *for* us, in our place. The effective counselor, by contrast, may suffer *with* us by entering imaginatively into our personal anguish but is unable (even if willing) to suffer *for* us.

In a similar vein, Oden fills out the rest of his chart by discussing in turn each of the therapeutic qualities identified by Rogers as necessary for effective counseling: congruence, acceptance, permissiveness, and unconditional positive regard. In each instance, Oden differentiates between the divine activity in the Christ event and the therapist's activity in the counseling relationship by stating what he understands to be the dissimilarities as well as the similarities between them. The chart and Oden's discussion of it represent the creative substance of the book.

Unfortunately, however, after making such careful distinctions, and after delineating the dissimilarities between theological and psychological discourse, Oden proceeds to ignore them in a chapter entitled "The Theology of Carl Rogers." Rather than drawing out possible analogies between a Christian understanding of the Fall and redemption and the therapeutic process of neurosis and healing, for

18. Quoted in Oden, *Kerygma,* p. 122; emphasis added by Oden.

instance, Oden seeks to show how Rogers's psychological views are a kind of "dekerygmatized" theology (Oden, *Kerygma,* p. 83). He translates Rogers's explicitly psychological categories into theological categories (in a way that I imagine Rogers himself would disavow) and then seems to criticize Rogers for not being more explicitly theological. In effect he doesn't allow Rogers to remain a psychologist but makes him sound like a crypto-theologian.

For instance, Oden writes, "If we mean by theology a deliberate and systematic attempt to speak self-consistently of man's predicament, redemption and authenticity, then the therapeutic work of Carl Rogers has deep theological concerns, even though he has little to say formally about God" (Oden, *Kerygma,* p. 83). Or again, drawing on Bultmann's formulation of sin, he writes, "If sin means missing the mark of one's authentic self, then surely Rogers' analysis of the dynamics of incongruence constitutes a rich explication and fresh restatement of the doctrine of sin" (Oden, *Kerygma,* p. 94). Rogers, however, is clearly *not* concerned with developing a "doctrine of sin" but, rather, with describing the psychological dynamics within and between people that push them toward incongruence. Oden is the one who speaks of "redemption" and of "a saving event," where Rogers's own formulations are much more modest and appropriate to the object of his investigation, that is, the therapist-client relationship and the therapeutic process. Although Oden readily acknowledges that Rogers himself does not speak in this way, he continues to force a kind of theological translation of Rogers's manifestly psychological constructs. Oden's disclaimer that the "saving event in client-centered therapy is not to be uncritically equated with the saving action of God in Jesus Christ" is unconvincing, because he himself seems to equate them throughout his discussion (Oden, *Kerygma,* p. 100).

One might trace the problem with Oden's logic at this point to his "if" clauses, which conceal a kind of reduction of theological language into anthropological language. Of course, theology in one sense might be understood to speak self-consistently of the human predicament, authenticity, and redemption, but it does so only on the basis of God's revelation, as Oden himself has already argued. One may make theological statements about humanity, at least if one wants to argue on the basis of the *analogia fidei,* only in the light of who God has revealed himself to be. Clearly such is not Rogers's self-defined task. Similarly, sin might possibly be defined as "missing the mark of one's authentic self," but it is also much more than that, from a strictly theological perspective. One misses the mark presumably because of disobedience and rebellion toward God. Oden's formulations seem only to confuse the matter at hand.

The lack of clarity at this point is puzzling, for here Oden blurs the very distinctions he himself is so pained to make. He collapses theological concepts into anthropological and psychological ones. As a result he loses the distinctiveness of both psychology and theology. Contrary to Oden, I would argue that Rogers does *not* offer us a "humanistic soteriology" (Oden, *Kerygma,* p. 111); indeed, he does not offer a soteriology at all but rather a description, based on empirical observation, of what factors help bring about emotional healing in a therapeutic relationship. It is curious how Oden translates Rogers's appropriately modest psychological terms into soteriological categories and then criticizes him for not having an explicitly Christian soteri- ology. He writes: "Consequently Rogers develops a soteriology without a Christology. . . . It is a humanistic soteriology without any acknowledged celebration of God's act, God's acceptance, God's un- conditional positive regard" (Oden, *Kerygma,* p. 111).

One might also notice that Oden has now confused the two catego- ries of thought in yet another regard. For not only does he speak of Rogers's "theology" and "soteriology," but he also speaks of God's "acceptance" and "unconditional positive regard," rather than, for in- stance, God's love, forgiveness, and grace. This is precisely the kind of reduction and confusion of theological and psychological categories that an understanding of Barth's theology should help one to avoid. Oden would have perhaps been helped at this point had he pondered Barth's idea of "secular parables of the truth," which Martyn developed as a way to conceive of the pattern of relationship between the two disciplines. Thus Oden might have said that the work of therapy, when it is effectively done, could be seen as a secular parable of the saving action of God.

Near the end of his book, Oden draws some analogies between the concepts of therapist and minister by examining the meaning of their Greek roots. He enriches one's understanding of psychotherapy by suggesting that in its deepest meaning it is a kind of careful, skilled, and meticulous service of one person to the "soul" of another. As such, Oden sees it as a "persistent and urgent theme of the New Testament" (Oden,

Kerygma, p. 150), with Christ himself portrayed as the prototypical *therapon,* healing the sick and restoring the broken to wholeness. Kerygma and therapeia, the foci of Oden's two concerns, are thus conceived as being intimately conjoined in the life of Jesus Christ. Oden writes, "The Servant-Messiah was remembered as one who uniquely blended the dual ministries of kerygma and therapeia in genuine involvement with the world" (Oden, *Kerygma,* p. 153). Jesus not only preached the kingdom of God and taught in the synagogues, he also cast out demons and healed the sick. Preaching, teaching, and healing as the threefold ministry of the church, Oden states, "remains today as a concise summary of the mission of the church" (Oden, *Kerygma,* p. 154).

Oden ends the book with some reflections on the comfort of God, making allusions to a wide range of New Testament passages. In so doing, he puts the emotional suffering of the person in therapy into a larger theological framework. By linking one's personal pain with Christ's redemptive suffering love, "personal afflictions thus take their place within the broader context of God's redeeming action, and suffering loses its power to subvert human health when seen within the framework of God's *paraklêsis* (understanding, encouragement, comfort) so that for those who love the Lord, everything works for the good (Rom. 8:28)" (Oden, *Kerygma,* p. 161). One is not delivered from suffering but rather is comforted in its midst. As one is comforted by God, one is able in turn to comfort others with the comfort given by God (2 Cor. 1:3-4). For Oden, this message of divine comfort is best mediated, at least in the counseling relationship, not directly in the words of proclamation but indirectly through the loving attitudes and active encouragement of the therapist toward the client.

Oden may thus be seen as having mixed success in his attempts to clarify and use Barth's theology. Sometimes his use of Barth is apt and to the point. At other times he seems to blur what he himself had previously been so careful to distinguish. For the pastoral counselor seeking methodological clarity about the relationship between the two linguistic worlds, Oden is both helpful and unhelpful. His understanding of the possible use of theological language or perceptions in the counseling setting is, in my opinion, too narrowly focused on proclamation. Perhaps because of the way he conceives of such proclamation (as "preaching" in the most pejorative sense of the term), he quite understandably gives it no role (or only a very minor role hedged about with all kinds of special considerations) in the counseling setting. Related to this same conception, perhaps, is his conclusion that the counselor's acceptance of the counselee is to be behaviorally enacted, not verbally relayed. But such restrictions are perhaps too narrow and do not take into account the peculiarities of each relationship. All this notwithstanding, Oden's creativity and inventiveness are clearly evident in the analogies he draws between Rogers's marks of therapeutic effectiveness and classical loci in Christian doctrine. When he keeps them as analogies and resists the temptation to turn them into identities, he gives the pastoral counselor food for thought for critically evaluating a psychological perspective from the standpoint of Christian faith.

Daniel Price: Dialogue at the Theoretical Level Between Barth's Theological Anthropology and Object Relations Psychology

Among the authors reviewed in this chapter, Daniel Price is the only one whose primary focus is on interpreting Barth. Unlike the others who are interested primarily in the application of Barth's ideas, in one way or another, to the theory or practice of counseling, Price is concerned with Barth himself, that is with understanding his work in its own context. Only after giving careful attention to placing Barth in his proper historical context does Price go on to compare certain of Barth's ideas with those of object relations psychology. His principal purpose is to clear up various misunderstandings, as he interprets them, that have arisen over the years about Barth's theology and especially about the possible use of Barth for interdisciplinary dialogue. He states explicitly, "My purpose in making such a comparison [between Barth's theological anthropology and object relations psychology] is primarily to see Barth's relation to the sciences properly understood."[19] Price has a secondary interest as well, for he goes on to say, "But such a comparison may also hold some practical value;

19. Daniel Price, "Karl Barth's Anthropology in Light of Modern Thought: The Dynamic Concept of the Person in Trinitarian Theology and Object Relations Psychology" (unpublished dissertation, University of Aberdeen, Scotland, 1990), p. 40. Subsequent references will be given parenthetically in the text.

providing a more adequate anthropology for the church can surely provide an important step toward improving the ancient art of the cure of souls in a modern world" (Price, p. 40). Price's focus may, therefore, be seen as twofold: first, to understand Barth accurately, especially in relation to what Price calls the "social sciences," and second, to provide a more adequate anthropology for the church in the hope that it will aid in the practice of pastoral care.

Price does not seek to apply Barth's ideas to the practice of counseling (as Guthrie does), nor does he present any case studies (as Martyn does). He writes neither as a psychologist nor as a practicing pastoral counselor, but as a "student of theology" (Price, p. 46). Unlike Oden, who begins with an exposition of his understanding of effective psychotherapy, Price begins with Barth's particular historical situation, giving extended attention to the broad philosophical and theological contexts of Barth's thought. Perhaps for this reason Price is more consistently clear than Oden about the implications of Barth's theology for interdisciplinary dialogue. He does not, as we saw Oden doing from time to time, confuse the two worlds of discourse, but keeps them clearly differentiated from each other, with each retaining its own integrity. Price's interest is also, one might say, more strictly theoretical than Oden's. That is, he is not asking directly about counseling at all, but rather about the relation of Barth's anthropology to the anthropology developed by certain object relations theorists, in particular, that of Ronald Fairbairn. He seeks to construct a methodologically careful dialogue between theory and theory so to speak, and does not raise direct questions about practice. Though he is aware that his study has broad implications for practice, indicating such from time to time, he himself does not explore them in a sustained way.

Price is especially helpful, it seems to me, because he does not attempt a systematic or conceptual synthesis between the two disciplines he is studying, nor is he interested in reducing or translating the terms of one discipline into those of the other. He seeks, rather, to find *analogies* between particular ways of conceiving human relationships from the perspective of each discipline. He is concerned, therefore, not only with the similarities but also with the differences between them, and he clearly spells out both. He has an especially good grasp, based on his close study of Barth's theology, of the proper boundaries between the disciplines:

> When it comes to carefully delineating the respective roles of theology and the natural sciences, Barth is particularly helpful. This is because of his insistence that theology must stand its own ground, remaining faithful to its own particular object of inquiry, which is the self-disclosure of the triune God. At the same time, Barth also realized that theology could not be done in isolation from modern thought. Barth believed theology could best serve the other sciences by engaging in dialogue — a dialogue which respected, and sometimes *defended* the establishment of clear boundaries between the disciplines. (Price, pp. 7-8)

The particular analogy or "material parallel" between Barth's theological anthropology and object relations psychology that Price explores is their common conviction that human beings cannot be understood apart from the complex web of interpersonal relationships in which they find themselves (Price, p. 14). Neither Barth nor object relations psychology is interested in studying the "isolated thinking individual." Instead, from their respective points of departure, they each examine the interpersonal relationships that they claim to be constitutive of essential humanity.

> In Barth's theology, the field of relations which define our essential humanity begins with the being of the triune God: God's being is dynamic because He is antecedently in relation within himself as Father, Son and Holy Spirit. The dynamic of God's relation to himself within the Trinity is reflected in our relations to self and others. In object relations the field of relations begins with the primary relation of a child to its mother. Endo-psychical structure with all its intricacies, grows out of the mother-child dyad. The *common element* between them, therefore, is the life-giving nature of a primary relationship and its fundamental importance for every subsequent dimension of human personhood. (Price, p. 11)

In both fields, therefore, the essence of human personhood grows out of interpersonal encounter with an "other." For object relations psychology (especially as developed by Fairbairn) the primary object of study is the mother-child relationship. For Barth's theology, the primary object of study is God's own interpersonal identity (as Father, Son, and Holy Spirit) and the reflection of that identity in human interpersonal relationships (seen paradigmatically in the male-female relationship as the *imago Dei*). While it is theology's task to reflect on the I-thou relationship between human beings and God, both theology and object relations psychology are interested in a person's relationship to self and others. Price suggests that though they approach the study of this interpersonal reality with very different methods and for different purposes, they come to conclusions that in striking ways are closely analogous.

Price argues powerfully that those scholars who find Barth irrelevant to dialogue with the social-scientific disciplines have misunderstood Barth and have dismissed him prematurely. Price surmises that many of these mistaken assessments of Barth are based on readings of his early dialectical theology and do not take his mature theology (i.e., the *Church Dogmatics*) into account (Price, p. 6). A careful reading of volume III/2, for instance, such as that done by Price himself, puts to rest the often touted idea that Barth neglects the human dimension. The other frequent criticism, that Barth separates nature and grace so radically that there is no way to place his theology into conversation with other disciplines, is refuted not by mere argument alone but by the substance of the book:[20] Price succeeds in showing how Barth's mature theology already engages in sophisticated interdisciplinary dialogue. Price himself extends the dialogue even further, drawing careful analogies between his theological anthropology and object relations psychology, a field that, presumably, never received much attention from Barth himself.

Before comparing these two fields of thought, however, Price deals at length with the philosophical and theological context of Barth's work. He examines basic issues in Enlightenment philosophy (especially Kant and Hegel) and post-Enlightenment theology (especially Schleiermacher and Kierkegaard). He indicates the kind of intellectual problems Barth inherited from each of these thinkers and traces the solutions Barth proposed. He also shows how Barth criti-

---

20. For example, see the essay by William R. Rogers in which he states that a position such as Barth's is "incapable of generating much significant dialogue. It belies both the coherence of reality and the universe of scholarship" ("The Dynamics of Psychology and Religion: Teaching in a Dialogical Field," unpublished paper presented at the American Academy of Religion, San Francisco, December 1977, p. 9).

cally appropriated various ideas from them in a manner that proved fruitful for his mature theology. While Price's argument is carefully crafted and richly suggestive, we must, for reasons of space, forgo summarizing them here. Although substantively contributing to his own argument, it lies outside the scope of our own interest in the material parallels he draws between Barth and object relations psychology.

After examining the historical theoretical context of Barth's theology, Price devotes a long chapter to the core of Barth's theological anthropology. He outlines virtually the entire volume III/2 with a focus on themes that are most pertinent to his eventual comparison with themes in psychology.

Price highlights the distinctiveness of Barth's theological method by contrasting it with another contemporary theologian, Wolfhart Pannenberg, who argues not from dogmatic presuppositions but from the findings of various anthropological disciplines. He proposes a starting point that is more "neutral" than that of Barth, a place where theology can share the presuppositions of the human sciences, and then proceeds to build upon common themes. Barth, however, rejects the idea of any such neutral ground, opting rather for the open declaration of his presuppositions that are based on what God's Word reveals. No amount of observation of the finite world will ever reach the infinite, according to Barth. Price reminds us that this is precisely the kind of argument "from below to above" that Barth rejected.[21]

Price discusses Barth's depiction of our real humanity as *Mitmenschlichkeit,* or being-in-encounter, carefully showing how the *imago Dei* is interpreted by Barth as relational in essence. What makes us truly human is our relationship to God and to one another. Our being-in-relationship with one another is a reflection on the human plane of God's own trinitarian being-in-relationship: the Father who loves the Son through the Spirit throughout eternity. In God's Word, we learn of our human destiny to become God's covenant partner, to live in a primary relationship with God as mediated through Christ. Price discusses Barth's critical appropriation of being-in-encounter, the relationship of an 'I' to a 'thou,' and outlines Barth's formulation

---

21. Price, p. 170. For a discussion of the methodological implications of Barth's theology, see Chapters Three and Four of this book.

of the fourfold basic form of humanity. He concludes the chapter with detailed reflections on the *imago Dei* as seen in sexual polarity (humanity created as male and female in the image of God) and on Barth's unitary anthropology of the human person as soul and body.

In his exposition of these ideas, Price is especially careful to show how Barth's theological anthropology is developed along trinitarian lines. He writes:

> A careful reading of this important volume of the *Dogmatics* [III/2] reveals that Barth's anthropology is interpreted foremost in terms of the triune God. It can hardly be stated more clearly than Barth has already put it himself, that just as God is a being in relation with Himself as Father and Son in the Spirit, so the human essence is reflected in the being of the man Jesus: a man who lived his life in encounter with God and others. . . . Human essence, then, is relational. It is being in encounter. . . . There is therefore no human being who is isolated, static, or purely individual. Isolation from God and others is the essence of brokenness and sin. (Price, p. 233)

While the relationship to God is primary for Barth, the person's essence is also constituted by his or her relationships to others, self, and time. When theological anthropology focuses on the relationship to self and others, it asks questions that other disciplines also consider. Price wants to ask what analogies might be drawn between the findings of one of these disciplines, object relations psychology, and Barth's anthropology.

In his chapter on object relations psychology, Price first traces the development of Freud's thought from a mechanical model to an instinctual (or organic) model and finally to a truly interpersonal model of being human. He shows how at each stage of his thinking Freud was challenged to move beyond the scientific reductionism of his own age (and his own intellectual propensities), which sought to explain human phenomena along the lines of Newtonian physics. In order adequately to explain humans, Freud's thought had to evolve into an interpersonal theory. With the formulation of the oedipal theory in his mature thought, Freud was moving toward such an understanding. Object relations theory after Freud built upon these latter developments.

Price especially appreciates Fairbairn's critical evaluation of Freud's libido theory. Unlike Freud, Fairbairn did not see libido as primarily pleasure seeking. The goal of this fundamental drive was not pleasure but a human person. As Fairbairn puts it: *"The ultimate goal of libido is the object."*[22] For Fairbairn, "the instincts are never an end in themselves, but always a means of expressing or repressing an object relationship" (Price, p. 281). According to Price's reading of him, Fairbairn succeeds in shifting psychology from an organic model to a dynamic, interpersonal model. No longer is the person seen as an instinct-driven organism seeking pleasure and satisfaction but rather as a human being seeking meaningful relationships.

For object relations psychology, human experience is always interpersonal experience. John Macmurray, a philosopher whose work focused on the interpersonal dimensions of human experience and on whom Price draws at length, writes: "Human experience is, in principle, shared experience; human life, even in its most individual elements, is a common life; and human behavior carries always, in its inherent structure, a reference to the personal Other. . . . The unit of the personal is not the 'I,' but the 'You and I.' "[23] This quotation from Macmurray calls to mind Barth's conception of human personhood as being-in-encounter, an 'I' with a 'thou' in interpersonal relatedness. For Barth, the source of reality is the interpersonal reality of the triune God. Human beings reflect God's image as they exist in authentic human encounter with each other.

Price draws on contemporary discussions in the philosophy of science to develop his dialogue in a rather sophisticated manner. As mentioned, he first traces Freud's development from a mechanical, to an organic, to an interpersonal model of human beings. At each stage of development, Freud shows greater openness toward more comprehensive understandings of human relationships. While Freud himself apparently never relinquished his desire to be able to reduce psychology to the "lower" sciences (such as physics or chemistry),

22. Ronald Fairbairn, *Psychoanalytic Studies of the Personality* (London: Tavistock, 1952), p. 31; quoted in Price, p. 280.
23. John Macmurray, *Persons in Relation* (London: Faber and Faber 1961), pp. 58-59; quoted in Price, p. 306.

postcritical philosophy of science suggests a model in which each level of explanation is upwardly open to understandings at higher levels. Price clarifies his own interdisciplinary model as one in which knowledge is seen as a kind of stratified hierarchy, where each discipline opens out upwardly to more comprehensive explanations, but which cannot be reduced to lower levels of explanation. Thus any mechanical or organic model by itself would be judged inadequate. For human beings are people with willful intentions and histories and are not mere organisms. The findings of Macmurray are, according to Price, in "implicit agreement with the post-critical philosophy of science, under the influence of Polanyi, who affirms a stratified structure, or hierarchy, of intelligible reality in which each successive level of inquiry is open upwards into wider and more comprehensive systems of knowledge, but are not reducible downwards" (Price, p. 304). Such an understanding is developed further in Price's dialogue with theology. Theological knowledge, according to this model, should be seen as the discipline at the top of the hierarchy of stratified knowledge. It could thus not legitimately be reduced downward into psychology any more than psychology could be reduced to physics or chemistry.

Thus, while object relations psychology shows the foundation of the human psyche to be the personal love of the parent that nurtures and sustains the human infant, Barth's theology shows how it is divine love that is the foundation of human love. One can never arrive at a conception of divine love by examining human love, but if, through revelation, one begins with an understanding of divine love, one can then see analogies between it and human love. This is precisely what Price does.

Price draws one such analogy between the spiritual insight from 1 John, which says that "perfect love casts out fear," and from the psychological insight of Fairbairn that hate and fear arise not from a "death instinct" but as a result of poor personal relationships. Whenever there is continual or recurring frustration or deprivation, the child will defend against its longing for connection with the parent through hate, fear, or aggression. Fear, then, is seen not as something in its own right but as the absence of love. "Love is the positive motivation to communicate, while fear is its negative" (Price, p. 308). "Fear . . . presupposes love and is subordinate to it."[24] While human love is

24. Macmurray, pp. 66-67; quoted in Price, p. 306.

always imperfect, the Bible points to an unseen level of reality in which God's love casts out all fear. Analogies to the spiritual insight can thus be drawn in the psychological sphere, indicating the close connection between the presence of love and the absence of fear. For object relations psychology (at least insofar as Fairbairn and Macmurray are representative of this view) as for Barth, essential personhood is in interpersonal communion, whereas the turning away from the other is evidence of brokenness: of bad object relations in psychology and of sin in theology. Neither sin nor aggression is seen as "normal" but, rather, as a symptom of a rupture in fundamental relationships.

The similarities that Price highlights between Barth and object relations psychology may be summarized as follows.

First, both Barth and Fairbairn reject mechanical and organic models of human being as inadequate to the truly interpersonal reality of human being.

Second, both Barth and Fairbairn are interested in developing a unitary anthropology. For Barth, the Spirit unites the human being as an embodied soul and besouled body. For Fairbairn the person is a psychosomatic unity. The ego is an integrated whole that becomes split only through inadequate parenting.

Third, both Barth and Fairbairn are holistic and reject compartmentalization of the human being. Each sees the person as a dynamic and integrated whole.

Fourth, aggression and sin are, therefore, seen as "abnormal." They arise from a condition of fallenness and brokenness. For Barth, to turn away from God is to lose our real humanity. For Fairbairn, aggression arises when our normal sphere of relationships is threatened.

Finally, human beings are meant to live in interpersonal relatedness. For Barth, our very being derives from our relationship to God. Our need of God will also be reflected in the creaturely sphere in our relationships with one another. For Fairbairn, human beings are fundamentally and irreducibly object seeking.

The differences between Barth and Fairbairn have to do with their object of study, their method, and their consequent differences of perspective. When Barth speaks of human interpersonal relationships, it is always in a derivative and secondary way. His primary focus is on the reality of the triune God as revealed in Christ, then on the human creature in relation to God, and finally on human's relationships with each other as they reflect (or fail to reflect) God's image. Fairbairn's focus is on the empirically observable and describable relationship that develops between the mother and her child as a paradigmatic instance of human love. Human love cannot be equated with divine love, yet it may reflect it. It is an image of divine love. Thus object relations psychology provides a "material illustration" of the human "capacity for interpersonal communion" which is the *imago Dei* (Price, p. 319).

For both Barth and Fairbairn, a person's interpersonal history with others is constitutive of who they are. For Barth, a person's very being is defined by his or her encounters with God and derivatively with other human beings. For Fairbairn, one's interpersonal relationships, one's history with the people whom one introjects into one's own psyche, are the very building blocks of the self, hence also constitutive of one's being. For both, interpersonal history is that "in which the being of one person can actually affect the being of another at the deepest ontological level. There is a mutual shaping of one another in the moment of encounter such that there is a mutual exchange of personal form and content, of energy and structure" (Price, p. 325). History, then, is not the mere motion of organisms; history is truly dynamic, a term that implies human intention and choice in all movement or action.

Another similarity that Price indicates between Barth and Fairbairn is in their understanding of knowledge. Both conceive of knowledge as interpersonal at its foundation. For the object relations psychologist, "all cognition stems from recognition" (Price, p. 357). The infant's relationship with its mother is the interpersonal matrix out of which perception and cognition grow. All later cognition rests upon (and depends upon) the mother having first bonded with the infant, talked to and cuddled it, giving the child a reliable relational context in which to grow. The child's first rudimentary awareness of the world occurs in the initial process of learning to differentiate between the self and the personal other.

Analogously for Barth, knowledge is also object related. Just as all later cognition is built upon the primary mother-infant bond, so with Barth our knowledge of the common things of the world depends upon our relationship with God. For as both source and goal of human knowledge, God is known as ordinary objects mediate knowledge of the Divine. As Barth writes:

Human beings may sense and think many things, but fundamentally the perceiving human self is the God-perceiving self. It is true, of course, that the other which is perceived is not identical with God, and that human beings continually perceive other things as well as God. But when the Bible speaks of the perceiving human self, there is nothing else which it is important or necessary for the human self to perceive. Human beings perceive . . . particular things. . . . But these are important and necessary for human beings only because God does not usually meet them immediately but mediately in his works, deeds and ordinances, and because the history of God's traffic with them takes place in the sphere of the created world and of the world of objects distinct from God. (III/2, 402 rev.; quoted in Price, p. 360)

As Price aptly summarizes the comparison between the two, "For those who are open to God in faith, all the knowledge of other objects mediates the knowledge of God himself. This is analogous to the affirmation of Macmurray, in view of object relations, that all cognition stems from recognition" (Price, pp. 359-60).

In his final chapter, Price deepens the dialogue between Barth and object relations psychology, showing how both Barth and Fairbairn reject materialism and idealism for an open-ended realism. Both the psychologist and the theologian seek to describe their object of study, and neither claims to be exhaustive. In the realm of interpersonal relationships each is open to learning from the other. As an example of a question fruitfully approached from the perspective of both disciplines, Price asks about the origins of aggression and hate in the mother-infant dyad. One question that eventually arises among psychologists, he observes, has to do with the internalization of a "bad" object. Is the "bad" mother internalized by the child because the child has projected hate onto her, or is she objectively an inadequate parent? Who is to blame, the mother or the child? Price comments:

When pressed up against certain theoretical impasses, such as: "Where do bad object relations originate from — neglectful mothers or angry children?" psychoanalytical theory has already begun an implicit dialogue with the theologian. Would not the psychologist here benefit from an explicit cross-disciplinary dialogue with those whose task it is to talk about the nature of the Fall, guilt, sin, atonement and forgiveness? (Price, p. 372)

The question of ultimate origins cannot be answered within a psychoanalytic frame of reference, for as Dorothy Martyn indicates in her article on psychoanalysis as parable, each generation inherits both the strengths and the deficits of the preceding generation, back through time to prehistory.[25] The very question calls to mind the biblical story of the man who was born blind. "Who sinned," the disciples asked Jesus, "this man or his parents, that he was born blind?" Even Jesus did not attempt to answer the question directly but, rather, deflected it by focusing instead on God's healing purposes for him. Jesus answered, "It was not that this man sinned or his parents, but that the works of God might be made manifest in him" (John 9:2-3). The origins of sin and evil thus remain a mystery to be answered by grace and forgiveness, not a problem of where to place blame.

There are also places, Price observes, where theology can learn from the insights of object relations psychology. Thus psychological studies can provide certain "material parallels" to dogmatic findings. Again, focusing on the question of original sin, Price suggests that object relations psychology provides a more satisfying response to the question of how sin is transmitted from one generation to the next than those usually encountered in theology. Augustine, for example, suggested that sin was transmitted biologically through the human seed. Would not an object relations description of the introjection of one's parents be a far more adequate explanation for this mysterious phenomenon? While not equating the Fall with bad object relations, Price does argue persuasively for an analogical relationship between them.

After a discussion of Schleiermacher's "feeling of absolute dependence" from the perspective of early childhood object relations, Price concludes with an extended conversation between Barth and object relations psychology about human sexuality. For both, he says, sexuality is "central to human personhood." Barth's interpretation of the *imago Dei* in terms of gender differentiation makes sexuality "determinative in providing both the structure and motivation for interpersonal en-

25. Martyn, "A Child and Adam," p. 278.

counter" (Price, p. 382). Although the focus of object relations theory tends to be more on infantile sexuality than that of adult male-female relationships, the same could be said of it. For both Barth and Fairbairn, sexuality is defined broadly and includes the wholeness of both people in the relationship. For Barth, the spiritual nature of sexuality is apparent when it reflects "the covenant character of God's own covenant-love" (Price, p. 388). Sexual relations are seen as instances of self-giving to a particular person with whom one is involved in a committed relationship of mutual service and love. Sexuality is "demonized" when the other is a mere object of libidinal desire and where the covenant-love of God is not reflected. The other person is depersonalized, robbed of his or her humanity. "Deliverance from such non-human sexuality," Barth writes, "can be effected only by a reintegration from the heart's core by love and fellowship" (III/4, 137; quoted in Price, p. 389).

Similarly, according to Fairbairn, the bond between the particular mother and her particular child is of paramount importance. The child needs to be loved and nurtured as this individual person by his or her own parent. Fairbairn writes, "Frustration of his desire to be loved as a person and to have his love accepted is the greatest trauma that a child can experience."[26] Thus, says Price, the "fundamental building block" of the human psyche is not libido but the interpersonal relationship (Price, p. 389).

For Barth, the mystery of sin is the mystery of our broken relationship with God. Sin, for Barth, is a kind of fall into non-being. Human beings are restored to wholeness through the restoration of their vital relationship to God. Similarly, in object relations psychology, one is restored through the intervention of a "good object." Without the relational presence of a person who can be internalized as good, loving, and trustworthy, psychological healing is not possible. In Fairbairn's terms, "the appeal of a good object is an indispensable factor in promoting a dissolution of the cathexis of internalized bad objects."[27] For both theology and psychology, then, Price comments, "the curative power of a good relationship cannot be underestimated. Establishing a relationship with a good object, it would seem, is the *sine qua non* of human wholeness, and the only path to healing the 'sinsick soul'" (Price,

26. Fairbairn, pp. 39-40; quoted in Price, p. 389.
27. Fairbairn, p. 74; quoted in Price, p. 393.

p. 394). This insight is, of course, at the heart of the practice of pastoral counseling, where the pastoral counselor seeks to become not only a trustworthy "good object" to the counselee but also a reflection, however fragmentary, of the goodness and trustworthiness of God. "We are called to become for others," concludes Price, "what God has become for us: a healing presence" (Price, p. 398).

The significance of Price's book, one might say in conclusion, is in the clarity he brings to his theoretical task. He is careful in his presentation both of Barth's ideas and also Fairbairn's. He is a close reader of primary texts and seeks at the same time to understand the broad historical context in which each theorist works. Thus, he places Barth's perspective in its philosophical and theological setting and Fairbairn's in relation to Freud and other psychological theorists of his time, indicating the precise questions each of them were addressing in their respective contexts.

For the pastoral counselor seeking to bring bilingual fluency to the pastoral counseling task, Price is especially helpful because of his methodological clarity. He is clear about the boundaries between the disciplines he is studying, and while he does not separate or divide them artificially, neither does he confuse them or try to integrate them into one voice. Instead, he draws a number of insightful analogies between them, clearly delineating both the similarities and dissimilarities between the two modes of discourse. Because he conceives of the relationship between the fields as one of "stratified hierarchy" where one cannot reduce the concerns of theology to psychological concepts, he helps the pastoral counselor to conceive how the two disciplines might properly be related. Psychological questions, for the believer, are thus placed in their broadest theological context. By showing the close analogies that can be drawn between Barth and object relations psychology, Price succeeds, in my opinion, in his goal of helping provide a more adequate anthropology for the church today.

Conclusion

As we have seen, each of the authors that bring Barth into dialogue with psychology or counseling has a particular way of framing the issues each wants to address. Guthrie, a theologian, shows how Barth's theological anthropology might help a pastoral counselor employ a Reformed doctrine of human beings in the practice of pastoral counseling. Although he uses no case studies, he does model the kind of careful theological reflection needed by the pastoral counselor who wishes to be theologically fluent.

Martyn, by contrast, excels in using the case study to illumine her central theoretical questions. Moving skillfully between vivid example and well-formulated questions of psychological theory, she draws her conclusions and then submits them to theological scrutiny by means of Barth's reflections on the perfections of God. She thus demonstrates how to use Barth's theology in a way that is consistent with his own methodological decision to develop an anthropology on the basis of the doctrine of God. While neither she nor Guthrie reflects directly on the interdisciplinary implications of Barth's theology, both of them work accurately and creatively on the basis of its presuppositions.

Oden raises questions similar to Martyn's, especially those pertaining to the issue of therapeutic effectiveness. It seems somewhat curious, however, that although Oden reflects on Barth's method at length and advocates its use, his own way of proceeding does not always reflect an accurate understanding of its implications. Although he seems to appreciate Barth's concern for the distinctiveness of theology as a discipline, as evidenced in his giving such clear and sustained attention to a discussion of the *analogia fidei,* he himself tends to confuse psychological and theological modes of thought, especially when he speaks of the "theology" of Carl Rogers. Although Oden explicitly discourages the use of theological language in the counseling setting, and in that way is not so helpful to the pastoral counselor who seeks bilingual fluency, he does develop some creative and illuminating analogies between his understanding of the gospel and Rogers's marks of therapeutic effectiveness, reflections that a pastoral counselor could use to assess the compatibility between various psychological and theological conceptions.

Finally, Price brings admirable clarity to the very questions of method that Oden's comments tend to obscure. In creating a carefully constructed dialogue between the two disciplines, Price develops some interdisciplinary implications of Barth's theology, neither separating psychology artificially from theology nor confusing one discipline's vocabulary and method with the other. By drawing on contemporary discussions in the philosophy of science, Price also orders the two disciplines in a particular way. The concept of "stratified hierarchy," which he uses, suggests that while each academic or scientific discipline is upwardly open to more comprehensive systems of knowledge, it cannot legitimately be reduced downward. Thus psychology is conceived as being appropriately understood within a larger theological framework and theology is conceived as not being reducible to psychology. While Price, as a student of theology, does not use case studies, his work is of great value to the pastoral counselor who wants to understand some of the complex issues about how to relate these two disciplines on a theoretical plane from a Barthian perspective.

This book shares some common concerns with each of the authors surveyed. Like Guthrie, I hope to demonstrate what it means to bring a theological perspective to pastoral counseling. I will do so by drawing, as he did, on many of Barth's distinctive formulations, but unlike Guthrie I will also use a case study approach to exemplify what I am proposing. Reflecting on a clinical case, both psychologically and theologically, is the element common to my study and Martyn's. However, I will also make explicit the pattern that governs the relationship between theology and psychology, something Martyn leaves implicit. Developing a method for relating psychological and theological material is the interest that my discussion holds in common with both Oden and Price. In some respects Oden is clear about how to relate the two disciplines, but as he proceeds he fails to abide by his own best insights and ends up confusing the reader. Price, on the other hand, represents exemplary clarity on the methodological question, but he restricts his use of the pattern by which the two disciplines are interrelated to the theoretical level. My own project, by contrast, is interested in exploring this pattern not only in its theoretical but also in its practical implications for pastoral counseling.

Since none of these authors is a practicing pastoral counselor, none of them is asking the particular question on which I will focus: How would the relationship between theology and psychology be understood by a pastoral counselor who works from a Barthian perspective? While each author offers some important clues, none of them has asked explicitly about the underlying pattern that would govern the relationship between the two disciplines in pastoral counseling. It is to this question that we now turn.

CHAPTER THREE

The Chalcedonian Pattern:
A Barthian Approach to Method

AS NOTED in the previous chapter, several authors have attempted to bring Barth's theology into dialogue with counseling and depth psychology. Each one had a unique set of questions for the interdisciplinary conversation between the two fields. In this chapter the question of special interest to this study will now be addressed: How would the relationship between theology and psychology be understood by a pastoral counselor who works from a Barthian perspective?

The proposal to be explored here is that the relationship between the two disciplines would be seen as governed by the "Chalcedonian pattern." Originally devised in the fifth century to sort through various christological controversies and to guide the church in its understanding of Jesus Christ as both human and divine, this complex pattern has been identified as a characteristic structure in Barth's thought. Since the defining terms of the pattern, as Barth uses it, are formal rather than material, they can be applied to a wide range of doctrinal or substantive questions. Here the pattern will be extended to encompass a set of interdisciplinary questions not examined by Barth himself.

This chapter falls into three sections. In section one the Chalcedonian pattern itself will be presented. Its features will be outlined and two examples of its application in Barth's theology will be indicated. By examining Barth's interpretation of the story of Jesus' healing of the paralytic, it will then be possible to raise the question of the relationship between the concepts of "healing" and "forgiveness." An analogy will then be developed between "the sinner" and "the victim."

The second section focuses on theoretical proposals about how theology and psychology are related. From a Barthian standpoint, the Chalcedonian pattern will be shown to offer significant categories of discernment and assessment. Three different proposals will be discussed, each representing an approach that the pattern would rule out. The purpose of the critique is to demonstrate that the pattern is useful at the theoretical level for thinking critically about such proposals. Each of the three approaches ruled out will be shown to pay insufficient attention to a different formal aspect of the pattern.

The third section turns to questions of practical application. By examining two hypothetical clinical examples, the Chalcedonian pattern is shown to help in sorting through the various psychological and theological issues at stake.

The Chalcedonian Pattern

The Council of Chalcedon in A.D. 451 was an ecumenical assembly that defined how the divine and human natures of Jesus Christ were to be conceived in the teaching of the church. The Council declared that the person of Christ was to be understood as "complete in deity and complete in humanity" and that his two natures were related "without separation or division" and yet also "without confusion or change."[1] According to Barth's interpretation of Chalcedon, Jesus' divine and human natures, each present in a complete or unabridged way, were to be understood not only as related without separation or division and without confusion or change but also with conceptual priority assigned to the divine over the human nature. While the divine and human natures of Christ remained conceptually distinct and were not to be confused with one another, they also could not be separated or divided from each other. They constituted the identity of Jesus Christ only as they occurred in differentiated unity. For example, as interpreted by Barth, one could not say that only the human nature

---

1. The Chalcedonian definition can be found in *The Oecumenical Documents of the Faith,* ed. T. H. Bindley and F. W. Green (London: Methuen and Company, 1950), and in *The Creeds of Christendom,* vol. 2, ed. Philip Schaff (New York: Harper and Row, 1931).

of Jesus suffered and died on the cross or that only the divine nature attained victory over death. In order to be able to save us from sin, Jesus had to be a divine-human unity in every aspect of his life. Even so, only when the divinity of Jesus is assigned precedence over his humanity does Barth regard the relationship between them as properly conceived.

The Chalcedonian pattern thus has to do with the complex and mysterious relationship between the divine and human natures of Christ. In his account of this relationship, Barth always took pains to emphasize the unity, the integrity, and the ordering of the two natures. Although unified in a single person, coexisting and coinherent, the divine and human natures of Christ each retained its own basic integrity. Furthermore, though inseparably unified in the history in which Jesus Christ was who he was, they still displayed the ordering of their two different levels, so to speak, with the divine level having the priority. Even with this precedence, however, Jesus' divine nature did not swallow up or diminish his human nature. He was not divine without also being fully human, or human without also being fully divine, for at one and the same time he was fully both. His human nature had its own inviolable integrity, which was not diminished or changed by the presence of his divine nature. As understood by Barth, the ordering between the two may be said to exhibit a pattern of asymmetry as opposed to hierarchy because, as Hunsinger indicates, "the two natures are not conceived as ordered according to a scale whereby they would differ only in degree" (cf. III/3, 104). Instead, they are "conceived as asymmetrically related, for they share no common measure or standard of measurement. Although there is a divine priority and human subsequence, their asymmetry allows a conception which avoids hierarchical domination in favor of a *mutual ordering in freedom*."[2]

It is important to note that the concept of asymmetry, as stipulated by the Chalcedonian pattern, introduces a significant modification into the idea of the pastoral counselor as someone who has acquired "bilingual" competencies in psychological and theological modes of discourse. Taken by itself, the idea of being "bilingual"

2. George Hunsinger, *How to Read Karl Barth: The Shape of His Theology* (New York: Oxford University Press, 1991), pp. 286-87 n. 1.

would imply a situation of "symmetry" because two different languages (like French and English) can be thought of as being materially equivalent to one another so that (in general) one can translate freely forth and back between them without any loss in meaning. The stipulation of asymmetry, however, implies that no such material equivalence exists between theology and psychology, for their essential subject matters are fundamentally different. Thus although the pastoral counselor who has acquired competency in both fields of discourse can move forth and back between them, he or she takes care not to translate theological into psychological categories or vice versa. Instead, theological and psychological modes of discourse are conceived as existing on different levels. Even when areas overlap (as in the theological doctrine of human nature vis-à-vis a psychological anthropology), only analogies not equivalences can be drawn between them. The Chalcedonian pattern is thus understood as the framework that governs the possibilities and limits of being "bilingual."

"It is probably safe to say," writes Hunsinger, "that no one in the history of theology ever possessed a more deeply imbued Chalcedonian imagination" than Karl Barth.[3] One example of how the Chalcedonian pattern functions as an underlying thought-form in Barth's theology can be seen in his discussion of the relationship between the body and the soul. Barth distinguishes between the body and the soul, arguing that they are ineffaceably different. At the same time, he also holds that they cannot be conceptually separated or divided from one another. Thus he speaks of an "embodied soul" and a "besouled body" (III/2, 327). One cannot heal the soul without also being concerned with the body and vice versa. Yet, in the conceptual ordering of this differentiated unity, the soul is first and the body is second. In speaking of Jesus' full humanity, Barth states that "his body is the body of his soul, not *vice versa*" (III/2, 339). A human being is the soul of his or her body as established by God. He or she is (and here is the Chalcedonian pattern) "soul and body totally and simultaneously, in indissoluble differentiation, inseparable unity and indestructible order" (III/2, 437).

The same formal pattern may also be seen to underlie Barth's

3. Hunsinger, p. 85.

conceptions of the relationship between God's grace and human gratitude, or between God's command and human obedience, or between
God's promises and human faith. In particular, in each case the same
sort of asymmetrical pattern seems to emerge. For in each of these
instances, as understood by Barth, God's activity is precedent and the
human response is subsequent. In the mysterious encounter between
divine and human freedom, God's freedom is not conditioned by the
freedom of the human creature, whereas the creature's freedom is
entirely dependent on the sovereign initiative of God. God does not
coerce or manipulate the human response, and yet the free response
of human gratitude is actualized solely by grace. In any such particular
encounter, faith will not perceive divine grace at the expense of human
freedom, or human freedom at the expense of divine grace. Although
they are conceptually distinguishable from one another, and although
each retains its own basic integrity, yet they are unified as they occur
in a single event. The divine action, though distinct from the human
response, has conceptual priority over it. The concepts of human
gratitude, obedience, and faith are logically subsequent to the concepts
of divine grace, command, and promise. While there is no single
standard of measurement by which the divine and human actions may
be compared, the free human response is seen to be dependent upon
God's prior action alone.

The three features of the Chalcedonian pattern, as used in any
number of different contexts, can thus be summarized as the "indissoluble differentiation," the "inseparable unity," and the "indestructible order" (III/2, 437) of two particular terms (often but not always
divine and human). "Indissoluble differentiation" means that they are
related without confusion or change. "Inseparable unity" means that
they coincide in an occurrence without separation or division. And
"indestructible order" means that in and with their differentiated
unity, the two are asymmetrically related, with the one term having
logical precedence over the other. The two terms are thus differentiated, unified, and ordered in a particular way.

With this pattern in mind, Barth's commentary on Jesus' healing
of the paralytic can be examined. When Jesus first says to the paralytic,
"My son, your sins are forgiven" (Mark 2:5), the scribes react with
shock that Jesus apparently regards himself as one with authority to
forgive sins. Jesus then says to them:

"Why do you question thus in your hearts? Which is easier, to say to the paralytic, 'Your sins are forgiven,' or to say 'Rise, take up your pallet and walk'? But that you may know that the Son of man has authority on earth to forgive sins" — he said to the paralytic — "I say to you, rise, take up your pallet and go home." And he rose, and immediately took up the pallet and went out before them all; so that they were all amazed and glorified God, saying, "We never saw anything like this!" (Mark 2:8b-12)

Barth interprets the relationship between healing and forgiveness in this story as a relationship between "the sign" and "the thing signified." Healing is presented as a sign of Jesus' lordship. It points to his divine power to forgive sins. Healing and forgiveness are thus seen to occur in a differentiated unity; they are not identical, yet they cannot in this instance be separated from each other. As Barth understands the relationship between them, the power to forgive sins is shown to be conceptually prior to and independent of the act of healing. In a pithy summary of the logic of the concepts implicit in the passage, Barth states, "The forgiveness of sins is manifestly the thing signified, while the healing is the sign, quite inseparable from, but very significantly related to, this thing signified, yet neither identical with it, nor a condition of it" (I/2, 189).

Forgiveness of sins is seen as clearly differentiated from healing, though they both occur in a single event. Interpreted as a "sign," the healing is placed within the larger context of a theological claim about Jesus' identity as one who has divine authority and power. While the healing can be conceived in some sense as independent of that to which it points, in the actual depiction of the event it is shown to have a kind of subordinate or subsequent status to the thing it signifies, namely, Jesus' divine power of forgiveness. Moreover, although the healing points to the forgiveness, the forgiveness, as interpreted by Barth, is neither identical with nor conditioned by the healing.

All three aspects of the Chalcedonian pattern — the *unity* of forgiveness and healing, the clear *differentiation* between them, and the *asymmetrical* order of their relation — are all present in his interpretation of the story. Healing and forgiveness are seen to occur in a differentiated unity. They occur together (unity), yet each remains distinct (differentiation), and the divine power to forgive sins is understood as conceptually prior to and independent of the act of healing (ordering). The healing points as a sign to the forgiveness in a way that the forgiveness does not in turn point to the healing. The divine act of forgiveness is seen as being free and unconditioned, while the healing is seen as existing in the service of Jesus' power to forgive sins. The concepts are so ordered that the forgiveness is logically prior and the healing is logically subsequent.

What exactly does it mean to speak of "logical precedence" and "logical subsequence"? Logical priority or precedence, according to the philosopher W. F. R. Hardie, pertains to the question of "priority in definition." "A is logically prior to B," he writes, "when the definition of B mentions A, but the definition of A does not mention B."[4] Salvation would be logically prior to healing, therefore, when the definition of healing mentioned salvation but the definition of salvation did not mention healing. For Barth, healing would be conceived as properly ordered within a context determined by salvation. For healing occurs as a "sign" or "parable" that points to salvation. There is thus a sense in which, from the perspective of faith, healing is understood to be ultimately ordered in relation to salvation. That healing as such is still relatively independent of salvation, however, is suggested by the obvious fact that psychologists, medical doctors, or other healers can proceed quite competently in their work without necessarily having a concept of salvation. The kind of definitional or logical priority that we are speaking of, therefore, clearly has to do with the arrangement of therapeutic concepts in relation to theological beliefs. From a Barthian perspective, the significance of healing is logically subsequent to salvation because although salvation does not necessarily point to healing, healing can be defined as ultimately pointing to salvation.[5] This observation will have far-reaching implications for developing a Barthian approach to interdisciplinary relationships between theology and psychology.

The formal logic of this kind of asymmetrical ordering can be further elaborated as follows:

4. W. F. R. Hardie, *Aristotle's Ethical Theory* (Oxford: Clarendon, 1968), p. 52.
5. Although the focus here has shifted from "forgiveness" to "salvation," I assume that the former can be taken as a synecdoche for the latter.

A conceptual account of X is an account of what we mean, understand, and intend ourselves to be talking about, when we talk or think
about X. If X is not correctly thus accounted for in terms of Y, then
X is conceptually independent of Y; if Y is accounted for in terms of
X, where X is not in turn accounted for in terms of Y, then X is
both conceptually prior to and independent of Y.[6]

This pattern suggests how theological and psychological concepts can
be brought into formal relationship from a Barthian standpoint. Following Hurley's definition, we could say that theological concepts like
salvation would be conceptually independent of psychological concepts like healing. Similarly, psychological concepts like healing would
also in some sense be conceptually independent of theological concepts like salvation. This conceptual independence of the two from
each other would reflect the "indissoluble differentiation" between
them.

When healing and salvation are conceived in relation to each other,
however, as in the story of the paralytic, then it is the healing whose
significance is accounted for in terms of salvation (or, in this instance,
of divine forgiveness), but not the reverse. Salvation does not acquire
its significance from the healing. Its significance is logically prior to
and independent of the healing. As Barth says, it is neither identical
with the healing nor conditioned by it. The significance of the forgiveness would be found on a different level of reality than that of
the healing. For the concept of the forgiveness of sins pertains directly
and primarily to our relationship to God in a way that healing does
not.

The concept of healing, from a Barthian standpoint, would thus
be seen to have both a relative independence of, and yet also a final
dependence on, the concept of salvation as establishing its ultimate
context of significance. On the one hand, in speaking of healing in its
more proximate aspects, so to speak, as an event or process that occurs
within the world, it would not also be necessary to speak of salvation.
Conceptually an occurrence of healing would stand on its own to that
extent. In its ultimate aspects, on the other hand, as it is seen in relation
to salvation from the perspective of faith, the significance of healing

6. S. L. Hurley, *Natural Reasons: Personality and Polity* (New York: Oxford University Press, 1989), p. 10; cited in Hunsinger, pp. 286-87 n. 1.

would be defined as logically subsequent to and dependent on something beyond itself. Conceptually the occurrence would not stand on its own but would be placed within a larger context of theological significance. To generalize from the pattern as set forth, therefore, it could be said from a Barthian standpoint that although psychological categories are both logically independent of *and* dependent on theological categories in different ways, theological categories are by definition both logically prior to and independent of psychological categories with respect to their significance.

It is important to note that what is at stake here are logical relationships that pertain to *concepts*. We are speaking of theological and psychological concepts, not directly of theological and psychological *realities*. In reality, there is no reason why these factors may not all come together at one time. The paralytic, for example, was both forgiven and healed in a single event or sequence of events, and his healing was understood to be significant both for its own sake and yet also for the sake of its analogy to forgiveness. Any particular event may have both psychological and spiritual or theological aspects at the same time. The presence of the former aspects would not invalidate the significance of the latter, nor would the presence of the latter aspects invalidate the significance of the former. Although they could be conceptually differentiated, they could not finally be separated or divided from one another. At one level the psychological aspects would be significant for their own sake while at another level they would be significant within a larger pattern of meaning. The spiritual or theological aspects, on the other hand, would be significant in themselves as well as for the way in which they would establish the larger pattern of meaning within which the psychological aspects were ordered.

Bearing these distinctions in mind, we may now turn to an issue of long-standing significance in the interdisciplinary discussion between theology and psychology, namely, how to think about the relationship between "salvation" and "health" or between "sin" and "neurosis." These two sets of concepts, each developed according to its own field of discourse, have terms that have typically been correlated with each other as if they were on the same plane, either merely intuitively or with some methodological sophistication, by a variety of thinkers over the last fifty years. Thus, for example, in *Psychotherapy and a Christian*

View of Man, a ground-breaking book on interdisciplinary dialogue, David E. Roberts concluded:

> In this book I have attempted to show that some of the basic concepts of psychotherapy are correlative with the human side of events which Christian doctrine interprets. Insofar as I have succeeded it follows that the therapist's description of bondage to inner conflict should be incorporated in the doctrine of sin, and his description of healing (through the release of involuntary changes which occur in a personal relationship of trust and acceptance) should be incorporated in the doctrine of grace.[7]

One cannot read this statement from a Barthian standpoint without wondering whether a more precise way might be found of formulating the relationship between theological and psychological concepts. Roberts appears to be operating with a "method of correlation" (perhaps broadly Tillichian), a method that seems to imply a "symmetrical" relationship between psychology and theology. On the other hand, when he suggests that the psychological concepts should be "incorporated" into a theological framework, he could be read as suggesting that the two disciplines are asymmetrically related. As will be shown, the Chalcedonian pattern offers a more precise vocabulary for discriminating these complex relationships.

If healing and forgiveness are differentiated, unified, and ordered asymmetrically, as Barth proposes in his discussion of the healing of the paralytic, what might be said along the same lines about how to relate the concepts of "sin" and "neurosis"?[8] Consider the chart on page 71.[9]

By definition, the concept of sin is essentially a *universal* category, while both the victimized and their victimizers belong to *particular* and mutually exclusive groups. While "all have sinned and fall short of

---

7. David E. Roberts, *Psychotherapy and a Christian View of Man* (New York: Scribners, 1950), p. 153.

8. The category of victimization is used here rather than the older term "neurosis," focusing thus on the unfavorable environmental (especially familial) conditions that foster "neurotic" as opposed to healthy development.

9. This chart is adapted from material in an unpublished lecture by George Hunsinger, "The Sinner and the Victim in Barth's Eschatology."

Sinner	**Victim** *(of childhood abuse or deprivation)*
1. Universal category. ("All have sinned and fall short of the glory of God.")	1. Particular category. (Not all children have "good-enough" parenting.)
2. The sinner qua sinner is culpable.	2. The victim qua victim is innocent.
3. An "essential" characteristic.	3. A "non-essential" or "accidental" characteristic.
4. A theological category. Discerned as such only by faith.	4. A psychoanalytic or family-systems category. Empirically describable.
5. Only God can save from sin.	5. Human effort may bring healing or improvement.
6. Sin fosters illusion. People actively complicit in sin.	6. Victimization has potential to foster insight. Victims complicit only by adapting to dysfunctional system.
7. Salvation is an essentially eternal resolution.	7. Healing is an essentially this-worldly resolution.

the glory of God" (Rom. 3:23), not all are victims of childhood abuse or deprivation. While neither victimizer nor victimized are free of sin, it is obvious that the actual manifestations of their sin would in some ways be quite different in form.

Second, sin is always a matter of personal culpability and responsibility. We are responsible for the sin we commit. As sinners, we *undertake* evil. On the other hand, a victim of injustice (qua victim) is always one who *undergoes* evil. By definition, he or she is an *innocent* victim.

Third, sin is a category that in some sense describes an "essential" characteristic of human being. That is, according to the traditional conception of sin to which Barth subscribes, and which he finds attested by Scripture, sin entails a corruption of the whole person to the very core. In biblical language, it is a disposition of the "heart." By contrast, the category of victimization indicates an "accidental" or "non-essential" characteristic. It is something imposed from without. It is not as such in any sense a corruption of the person, nor is it a disposition of the heart. It is, rather, a violation of the whole person as that person is created and affirmed by God.

Fourth, sin is an essentially theological category. It is primarily a description of our broken and hostile relationship to God. It only secondarily pertains to relationships between human beings and then only as they are understood through the primary God-relationship. Victimization, on the other hand, as here being considered, is primarily a psychosocial category. Strictly speaking, sin can be perceived and described as such only on the basis of faith, only by the truth of divine revelation. Victimization, by contrast, is empirically describable by psychoanalytic or family-systems analysis and is based on a truth of rational perception.

Fifth, again according to the traditional conception that Barth finds attested by Scripture, bondage to sin is not something the sinner can possibly overcome by his or her own effort, whereas the bondage of the abused or deprived person is possibly overcome by taking concrete steps toward his or her own healing. Salvation from sin is beyond one's human power to obtain; only God can save from sin. By contrast, human effort can make all the difference in working toward psychological or emotional healing.

Sixth, sin fosters illusion or what the Bible calls "blindness." By its very nature, sin hides and obfuscates its true reality. Sinners are always as such involved in self-justification, by which they remain in denial and blind to their sin. They are thus actively complicit in their sin and culpable in their ignorance. By contrast, victims become complicit in their own victimization only as they are indoctrinated by the dysfunctional family environment in which they live. No ignorance of their actual condition is in this sense culpable. The process of healing fosters insight, as the person learns to work toward his or her own empowerment.

Seventh, salvation is the solution to the problem of sin. Through sin, whose weightiness cannot be underestimated, we are placed in eternal jeopardy. Just as our sin has ultimate consequences unless God intervenes on our behalf, so does that divine intervention or salvation also promise a significance that extends beyond history. Salvation is essentially the promise and the reality of sharing in the eternal life of God. By contrast, emotional healing is a this-worldly solution to an essentially this-worldly problem. It is something to be realized on earth within history. However desirable or imperative it may be in its own way, healing is historically relative in a way that salvation is not.

The Chalcedonian pattern, which has functioned implicitly in the ordering of these two sets of concepts, may now be explicitly stated. First, the concepts of "sinner" and "victim" are clearly differentiated from each other. The plight of the sinner is substantially different from that of the victim so that the two should not be confused with each other. Each concept pertains to a different web of interrelated concepts forming the contextual whole of which it is a part and in which it finds its proper meaning.

When viewed from a Barthian perspective, however, the two concepts can also be placed in a kind of unity. That is, the plight of the victim and that of the sinner need not be separated or divided from each other, even though they must be differentiated. For the healing of the victim can be interpreted theologically as a sign of salvation, even as salvation can be interpreted as that which is signified or attested theologically by the healing of the victim. The healing that takes place on one level, so to speak, points to the salvation promised on another, more ultimate level. Whenever genuine human need is met, it can be interpreted by faith as a sign of God's promise and readiness to remove all forms of human distress. The neediness of the creature, whether in the form of sin or in the form of innocent victimization, ultimately moves God to mercy. The removal of any form of human distress can thus be interpreted as a parable of God's grace insofar as it points beyond itself to God's gracious will to bring salvation to God's creatures. As forms of distress, the plight of the victim and that of the sinner are not to be separated from one another, for the healing of the one stands as a sign for the saving of the other.

At this point, however, an important distinction needs to be introduced. When used to describe this analogy, the formal idea of "inseparable unity" is not unambiguous. For the term can indicate either a necessary or a contingent relation. In Barth's discussion of body and soul, from which the term has been taken, the relationship would seem to be a necessary one. In any living human being body and soul always occur together so that there is no body without the soul and no soul without the body. That is why Barth can speak of a besouled body and an embodied soul. Body and soul always occur together because by definition neither can exist without the other.

When we turn to human neediness and well-being, on the other hand, in their psychological and theological forms, the possibilities would seem to be more complex. Healing and salvation, for example, are not inseparable by definition, for each can be adequately defined without direct reference to the other. Nor are they always inseparable in experience here and now, for it would seem that healing can be experienced without forgiveness, and forgiveness without healing, even though there are also cases where the two may be closely intertwined. However, as Barth's discussion of the healing of the paralytic shows, the grace of God seems to promise that different forms of human well-being like healing and forgiveness are ultimately inseparable. Nevertheless, the relationship between them seems to involve elements of contingency not found in a case like that between body and soul. For although neither finally exists without the other, they do not always occur together in experience here and now (or at least not always clearly and directly). Therefore, when the formal idea of "inseparable unity" is applied to the kind of relationship proposed between psychological and theological concepts, the "inseparability" in question must be understood as allowing for a flexible set of complex relations. For from a Barthian standpoint, the unity between matters like healing and salvation is essentially analogical, contingent, and eschatological in form.

Finally, the relationship between healing as the sign and salvation as the thing signified is not only analogical but also asymmetrical. Although healing points to salvation, the relationship is not reversible, as though salvation would also point in the same sense to healing. The relationship would be symmetrical (and therefore reversible) only if the two were essentially or materially equivalent. But from a Barthian standpoint "healing" and "salvation" are not so equivalent, for they occur on two different levels and indicate two different contexts of meaning. Whereas the significance of the one is temporal, the significance of the other is eternal; whereas the one is penultimate, the other is ultimate. The relationship of signifier to signified cannot be reversed without effacing this important difference in levels. The theological significance of salvation can be stated without reference to healing, but the theological significance of healing cannot be stated without reference to salvation. The significance of salvation as the ultimate term is thus independent of that of healing as the penultimate term, but the relationship is irreversible, for the significance of the penultimate depends on that of the ultimate. The significance of the one (salvation) is logically prior to that of the other (healing). Salvation thus sets the terms within which to think of healing but not (as the asymmetry requires us to add) the reverse.

Uses of the Chalcedonian Pattern: Theory

How might the formal features of the Chalcedonian pattern — unity, integrity, and asymmetry — be usefully applied to the conversation between theology and psychology that forms the theoretical context for the work of a pastoral counselor? The pattern arguably provides a method for analyzing existing proposals about how to understand the relevant interdisciplinary relationships. In light of the pattern, certain critical questions about any such proposal would arise. Does the proposal recognize, for example, the "indissoluble differentiation" between the two fields? Does it allow each discipline to define its own boundaries, to secure its own self-defined integrity, to proceed with the investigation of its own subject matter according to the methods that are appropriate to the discipline? Moreover, in clearly distinguishing between the disciplines, does the proposal also allow for the possibility of their "inseparable unity" from a theological point of view? Does the proposal allow that in practice a theological or spiritual perspective cannot always be neatly separated from psychological considerations or vice-versa? Finally, does the proposal recognize and appreciate the "indestructible order" between the two disciplines? Does it allow that a certain asymmetry exists between them by virtue of their respective subject matters existing on different levels? Does the proposal, therefore, see how the psychological concepts are properly understood within a larger theological frame of reference rather than the reverse? Does it see that the two sets of concepts cannot be systematically correlated with one another because such correlation implies that they exist on the same level?

It might be noted that in my previous discussion the formal features of the Chalcedonian pattern have already been in the background. In Chapter Two, the pattern was used implicitly to sort through the contributions of four thinkers who draw upon Barth in a dialogue with psychology and counseling.[10] The pattern will now be brought into the forefront by explicitly showing its usefulness as an analytical tool. In undertaking such an analysis, it will be important to use the categories to illuminate what is at stake in any given proposal itself. By offering categories of discernment, the pattern can help not only to illumine basic presuppositions but also lines of thought that may be underdeveloped or confused. The categories are not for the purpose of fitting the various proposals into preconceived molds but, rather, for clarifying the issues analytically from a Barthian perspective.

Three thinkers will be examined. First, in order to illustrate problems of "separation" or "division," the thought of Eduard Thurneysen will be examined. Second, to exemplify issues of "confusion" or "change," a work by Edward Edinger will be assessed. Finally, a short essay by Tillich will be studied in order to explore questions related to the asymmetrical ordering of the concepts.

10. Dorothy Martyn, for example, can be interpreted as using the Chalcedonian pattern implicitly when, in her case studies, she relates theological and psychoanalytic concepts. First, she avoids confusing them with one another. Each set of concepts is seen as having its own legitimate sphere of inquiry and basic integrity, proceeding with methods appropriate to its own subject matter. Theology is not translated into psychological categories, nor is psychology theologized. Second, theological and psychological conceptions are not separated or divided from each other. The source of power that enabled the children to grow in the therapeutic situation is examined both psychoanalytically and theologically. Finally, the asymmetrical order of their significance is respected. Human love is seen as secondary and derivative, a kind of attestation or "mediation" of the prior love of God. Her psychoanalytic concepts, while retaining their own integrity and distinctness, are understood within a larger context. Martyn's work thus exemplifies an underlying formal pattern: psychological and theological perspectives are brought to bear in a way that shows their distinctive integrity, their conceptual unity, and their asymmetrical order.

Without Separation or Division:
Critique of Thurneysen

Eduard Thurneysen (1888–1974), a Swiss Protestant pastor and lifelong friend of Karl Barth, wrote a book entitled *A Theology of Pastoral Care* that is often criticized for making a strict dichotomy between psychotherapy and pastoral care. The persistence of this criticism suggests that he may finally separate and divide the two fields from each other. Thomas Oden, for example, accuses Thurneysen of "two-sphere thinking" in which he bifurcates "reality into sacred and secular healing."[11] Thurneysen is an important thinker to consider, particularly because he is commonly associated with Barth, as one who applied many of Barth's insights to the field of practical theology. (Thurneysen was professor of practical theology at the University of Basel from 1927 to 1959.)

When Thurneysen's discussion of the relationship between theological and psychological concepts is considered, all three features of the Chalcedonian pattern can be clearly seen. Perhaps because of Barth's marked influence on his thinking, Thurneysen himself is fairly clear about the pattern's formal shape, which in certain places seems to be the hidden thread guiding his thought. Consider, for example, the following passage, in which the formal issues are implicitly set forth:

> When the physician speaks of neurosis and the pastor speaks of sin, do these connote the same thing? Is it only a matter of different words? Certainly not! The physician and the pastor have not only a different vocabulary but a different subject. True, both illness and the sin of the patient are displayed in one and the same scene (man's inner being, his soul), but the one is to be distinguished from the other. Each belongs to its own order: the neurosis to the immanent and natural, sin to the transcendent. Sin is something *toto genere* other than neurosis. Each, however, is related to the other; they are correlated in the way characteristic for the biblical understanding of man. The pastor understands this correlation to mean that the illness called neurosis by the physician is a symptom of that deep disturbance of

11. See Thomas Oden, *Contemporary Theology and Psychotherapy* (Philadelphia: Westminster, 1967), p. 74.

life which has taken place between God and man. This disturbance is something in itself; it is different from a neurosis.[12]

Thurneysen carefully distinguishes between theological and psychological concepts in a way that reflects the Chalcedonian pattern. The "indissoluble differentiation" between them is indicated by the basic thrust of the entire passage but particularly in such phrases as "different vocabulary," a "different subject," "one is to be distinguished from the other," and "*toto genere* other." At the same time, however, it can be seen that he also explicitly acknowledges their close relation. "Both illness and the sin of the patient," he observes, "are displayed in one and the same scene." Their inseparability in the soul of the person is thus acknowledged. Finally, they are seen to have been placed in an asymmetrical relation to each other. Neurosis is placed in an immanent order, sin in a transcendent order. Neurosis is understood as a symptom of sin. This point would seem to be related to Barth's observation about healing being the "sign" of forgiveness as "that which is signified." Here neurosis is the "symptom" of sin as its ultimate "source" or "cause." Yet just as forgiveness, from a Barthian standpoint, is neither identical to healing nor conditioned by it, so also would sin be neither identical with neurosis nor conditioned by it. And just as healing typically has proximate sources or causes, so also would neurosis. In both cases, therefore, the overall pattern of relationship would be asymmetrical.

The emphasis on the "indissoluble differentiation" between theology and psychology, which is seen so clearly in this paragraph, is pervasive throughout the book. One might fairly ask whether this emphasis does not sometimes obscure the "inseparability" that is also required by the logic of the Chalcedonian pattern. Consider the following remarks, for example, "Pastoral care is a discipline of its own, unexchangeably distinct and different from psychology and psychotherapy." Although both psychological and physical healing may result from the work of pastoral care, such healing is understood by Thurneysen to be "*entirely different* from the release and solving of psychic

---

12. Eduard Thurneysen, *A Theology of Pastoral Care* (Richmond, Va.: John Knox, 1962), p. 226. Subsequent references will be given parenthetically in the text.

conflicts brought about by psychological, psychiatric methods." This fundamental difference in result is integrally connected for Thurneysen with the fundamental difference in purpose between the two activities. The purpose of psychotherapy, according to Thurneysen, is to help people resolve their psychic conflicts, while the purpose of pastoral care "is and remains proclamation of the Word to the individual and neither can nor should be anything else" (Thurneysen, p. 201).

Thurneysen conceives of the pastoral counseling task as one of applying the Word of God to individuals in their particular life situation. Psychology is seen to be needed as an auxiliary tool to help pastors become knowledgeable about the kinds of human situations into which the Word must be spoken. Thurneysen thus recommends a thorough study of psychology to pastors.

> [Pastors need to avail themselves] of a knowledge of a human being's inner life in as exact, methodical and comprehensive a way as is possible. . . . Pastoral care needs psychology as its outstanding auxiliary. We cannot know enough about human beings, and, consequently, may not be expert enough in the methods and perceptions which psychology and psychotherapy use in the investigation and treatment of human beings. Hence the relationship of psychology to pastoral care may be defined as that of an *auxiliary science*. (Thurneysen, pp. 201-2, rev.)

Knowledge of human psychology is understood to be needed so that the word of forgiveness may be spoken concretely to individuals in their particular life circumstances.

The pastor, however, *uses* the tools of psychology in a way that is understood to be quite different from their use by a psychotherapist. The psychotherapist uses them directly to help resolve psychic conflicts and heal neurosis. The pastor is concerned, however, not with neurosis but with a deeper disturbance, that of sin. Sin is understood to be the ground out of which neurosis emerges but as something quite distinct from neurosis. Because the pastor is more focused on sin than on neurosis, he or she brings other tools to the counseling task, tools that would immediately be seen to be out of place in the psychotherapist's office. Thurneysen can again be seen to draw a sharp contrast between the two activities:

If we compare the analytic conversation with the pastoral conversation we find that they are *toto genere* and unexchangeably different. In contrast to the psychoanalytic conversation, the pastoral conversation proceeds in strict and fundamental dependence on Holy Scripture. Prayer is an indispensable ingredient. These are sufficient marks of its distinctiveness. (Thurneysen, p. 245)

While Thurneysen seems to have a clear grasp of the formal issues, one wonders whether he doesn't finally emphasize the "indissoluble differentiation" and the "asymmetrical order" at the expense of the relative "inseparability" of the two disciplines. Can sin and neurosis really be so sharply separated from each other in practice? If neurosis is a symptom or sign of sin, in actuality don't they always occur somehow together? Sin, of course, is something quite different from neurosis, but if, from the standpoint of faith, as Thurneysen himself says, neurosis is ultimately grounded in sin and cannot be theologically understood apart from a conception of sin, then isn't it necessary to think of them as occurring in some kind of unity? Further, how can the healing of psychic conflict be *totally different* from the healing that occurs through the Word of forgiveness, if that healing includes the restoration of psychic health in some measure? Even if one were to agree that the pastoral conversation proceeds along essentially different lines from the psychoanalytic conversation, especially in its dependence upon Scripture and prayer, does it necessarily follow that the healing that emerges from such conversation is *entirely different* from the healing that arises out of psychoanalytic conversation? Even if it were significantly different, how could it be entirely different if sin and neurosis both occupy the heart, the central core of a person? The two must certainly be distinguished from one another, but can they really be so utterly separate in theory and practice as Thurneysen seems to indicate?

In his zeal for giving the Word of God precedence, and for basing pastoral conversation solely on the Word, Thurneysen finally leaves little room for the "inseparability" of theology and psychology in the practice of pastoral counseling. In arguing for proclamation as the sole task of pastoral care, he seems to be divorcing forgiveness as the thing signified from healing as that which signifies it. He leaves virtually no room for psychology to contribute its own unique resources toward the healing of the individual. The proper task of pastoral care, argues Thurneysen,

> is and remains the proclamation of the Word of God which is the one thing which is necessary. But can proclamation, can the Word of God, can the forgiveness of sins, be the one thing necessary if man's life is secretly or openly, wholly or partially, nourished from other sources and therefore also interpreted and understood on the basis of them? If this assumption prevails, and the understanding of man in modern psychology suggests it rather insistently, the pastoral counselor will be tempted to turn to these other sources and to expect salvation and help from them. He will then no longer use psychology as a necessary auxiliary science; rather, he will begin to practice pastoral care as an auxiliary to the norm of psychology. (Thurneysen, pp. 213-14)

Although Thurneysen professes that his concern is one of properly ordering the two disciplines (so that theology has conceptual precedence and psychological concepts are placed into a larger theological framework), doesn't he finally allow too little space for the distinctive contribution of psychology? Even if his basic point were granted, that the proclamation of the Word of God is the one thing necessary for salvation, it would not thereby follow that other kinds of help are not also needed. Human life *is* nourished from other, more proximate sources as well; it *is* interpreted and understood on the basis of these other sources, and these facts pose no real threat to theology or to the proclamation of the Word. While salvation is naturally not to be expected from these other sources, it is surely not illegitimate to expect genuine help from them in important respects. There are countless situations where the needed remedy is not directly the proclamation of forgiveness but, rather, insight and understanding of one's psychological condition. In any concrete instance, moreover, forgiveness and healing are deeply entwined; they may not always be so sharply separated from each other without doing violence to the "inseparable unity" of the person who needs both salvation from sin and healing of emotional wounds.

Thurneysen overstates the distinction between the two disciplines because he is concerned not with the dangers of "separation" or "division" but, rather, with those of "confusion" or "change." His argument is perhaps best understood if it is seen within a polemical context. Thurneysen was sharply critical of what he called "psycho-logical counsel in religious garb" (Thurneysen, p. 214); in turn he was frequently criticized, especially in American circles of pastoral care and counseling. (Oden, for example, finds Thurneysen's thought to be "burdened by an unnecessary cynicism toward all secular heal-ing."[13]) The basic attitude toward Thurneysen found in American circles is summarized in an encyclopedia article on Protestant pastoral theology. "Eduard Thurneysen, the principal advocate of Barthian pastoral theology on the continent, is little known and generally dis-liked by American pastoral care leaders, who have tended to view him as the antithesis of the clinical tradition."[14] The heart of Thurneysen's concern is perhaps best understood as a polemic against those who confuse properly theological with essentially psychological concepts. The thrust of this polemic is evident in passages like the following:

> Everything is turned around. Instead of the Word of God, psycho-logical considerations take first place. The words of faith, insofar as they are still used, are stripped of their own content and become mere symbolic concepts which are applied to the investigation of purely psychic facts. "Sin" becomes a symbol for the entanglement of man in neurotic fixation; "forgiveness" another word for the inner release and liberation sought in the psychotherapeutic process of healing; "prayer" a remedy for the recovery of self-confidence. (Thurneysen, p. 214)

It is Thurneysen's effort to counter this kind of illegitimate "trans-lation" of properly theological concepts into essentially psychological ones that makes him sound so anti-psychological. His polemical stance against an illegitimate use of psychology tends to render his own actual affirmation of psychology mute. When he says "true pastoral care takes a positive stand toward a scientifically-oriented psychotherapy" (Thurneysen, p. 240), he is not believed, because in other contexts he seems to devalue the legitimate contribution of psychology toward

---

13. Oden, *Contemporary Theology and Psychotherapy,* p. 73.

14. J. R. Burck and R. J. Hunter, "Protestant Pastoral Theology" in *Dictionary of Pastoral Care and Counseling,* ed. Rodney J. Hunter (Nashville: Abingdon, 1990), p. 868. Is it possible that Thurneysen is partly responsible for the pervasive anti-Barthian sentiment that exists in American circles of pastoral care and counseling?

the healing of individuals. In his passion for giving the task of proc-lamation precedence, Thurneysen tends to allow no real place for psychology to stand in its own right, to be a discipline that contributes in an essential way to the task of the pastoral counselor. In stressing the "indissoluble differentiation" between the two disciplines, Thur-neysen fails to account adequately for the possibility that in practice forgiveness and healing may occur in "inseparable unity." For al-though in principle forgiveness can occur without healing and healing without forgiveness, in practice the two may well be closely bound up with one another for any particular individual; and in any case the grace of God would seem ultimately to promise both in such a way that healing stands in analogical unity with forgiveness, as Barth's discussion of the healing of the paralytic shows.

Without Confusion or Change: Critique of Edinger

Edward Edinger, a prominent Jungian analyst and thinker, has inter-preted Jung's ideas in such a way as to suggest that Edinger himself confuses the distinctive language of theology with that of depth psy-chology. While Thurneysen can be said at times to discount the "in-separable unity" between the two worlds of discourse, Edinger might be said to discount the "indissoluble differentiation" between them. In fact, one might say that Edinger systematically collapses all mean-ingful distinctions between properly theological concepts and the lan-guage of depth psychology, interpreting the former by means of the latter. While some critics have leveled this charge at Jung himself, Jung may arguably be regarded as at least more ambiguous than Edinger, sometimes seeming to collapse the two worlds of discourse, while at other times keeping them adequately distinct.[15] Although Edinger

15. For example, commenting on his book *Answer to Job,* Jung says, "I deliberately chose this form because I wanted to avoid the impression that I had any idea of announcing an 'eternal truth.' The book does not pretend to be anything but the voice or question of a single individual." To which Edinger replies, "The fact is that he *does* announce an eternal truth and I think he knew it." See C. G. Jung, *Answer to Job* (Princeton: Princeton University Press, 1973), prefatory note; cited in Edward F. Edinger, "Depth Psychology as the New Dispensation," *Quadrant* 12 (Winter 1979): 7-8.

strongly exemplifies the type of confusion I wish to illustrate, not all Jungians, it should be noted, interpret or use Jung's thought as Edinger does. Despite the reductive interpretations of Jungians like Edinger, there would seem to be no good reason why a pastoral counselor could not have a Jungian orientation in psychology and a Barthian orientation in theology. A Barthian use of the Chalcedonian pattern would simply allow Jungian psychology to function on its own level without letting it either confuse itself with theology or transmute theology into psychology.[16]

At first glance, it seems that Edinger wants to propose an analogical relationship between the language of faith and the language of analytical psychology, for he begins his chapter on "Christ as Paradigm of the Individuating Ego" with these words: "The image of Christ and the rich network of symbolism which has gathered around Him, provide many parallels to the individuation process."[17] Individuation, as the concept has been developed by Jung, so Edinger seems to argue, will be shown in various ways to be similar to what Christians mean when they speak of the image of Christ. But in his next statement, Edinger makes a much larger claim than one of analogy, for he continues, "In fact when the Christian myth is examined carefully in the light of analytical psychology, the conclusion is inescapable that the underlying meaning of Christianity *is* the quest for individuation" (Edinger, *Ego and Archetype,* p. 131; emphasis added). Edinger thus effectively reduces the "underlying meaning of Christianity" to a core concept in a system of psychological thought. Jung's concept of individuation, defined by Edinger as "a process in which the ego becomes increasingly aware of its origin from and dependence upon the archetypal psyche" (Edinger, *Ego and Archetype,* p. xiii), becomes the overarching category by which distinctively biblical and theological language is then interpreted and absorbed. From a Barthian standpoint, one would say that Edinger does not adequately distinguish the

16. For clearly drawn distinctions between the disciplines of theology and depth psychology from a Jungian (though non-Barthian) standpoint, see, for example, Ann Belford Ulanov, *The Feminine in Jungian Psychology and in Christian Theology* (Evanston: Northwestern University Press, 1971), pp. 5-12.

17. Edward F. Edinger, *Ego and Archetype: Individuation and the Religious Function of the Psyche* (New York: G. P. Putnam's Sons, 1972), p. 131. Subsequent references will be given parenthetically in the text.

one field of discourse from the other. By collapsing the theological into the psychological, he does not respect their ostensibly different subject matters. Although avoiding the pitfall of separation or division, he falls into the pit of confusion or change.

With great ingenuity, Edinger systematically translates what he calls the "Christian myth" into the language and concepts of analytical psychology. Thus, for example, he interprets various sayings of Jesus in light of concepts developed by modern psychology. Two brief examples may suffice. Edinger sees Jesus' comment about the speck of sawdust in the brother's eye without recognizing the plank in one's own to be an apt formulation of the idea of psychological projection, that is, the phenomenon by which one sees one's own negative quality in another person while remaining completely unaware that the dreaded character trait really belongs to oneself. Or again, Edinger recognizes Jesus' psychological acuity when he sees him as warning against the dangers of identifying psychologically with one's parents or family. Because the process of individuation requires that one first radically separate one's sense of personal identity from one's family of origin, Edinger considers this saying of Jesus to be particularly important: "I have not come to bring peace, but a sword. For I have come to set a man against his father, and a daughter against her mother" (Matt. 10:34-35; Edinger, *Ego and Archetype,* p. 133).

Following Jung's example of interpreting Christ's sayings subjectively, that is, as reflecting an autonomous psychological process, Edinger proceeds to reinterpret the Beatitudes psychologically. "Seen in this light," he says, "Jesus' teachings become a kind of manual for promoting the individuation process" (Edinger, *Ego and Archetype,* p. 136). Two examples will suffice to indicate the direction of Edinger's thought. The beatitude, "Blessed are the pure in heart, for they shall see God" (Matt. 5:8), is interpreted to mean that those who are conscious and who are thus not identified with various unconscious contents (either in the inner world or projected onto the outer world) are fortunate, because they are open to experiencing the Self, or the very center of the personality. Again, in discussing "Blessed are the peacemakers, for they shall be called the sons of God" (Matt. 5:9), Edinger comments, "It is the appropriate role of the ego to mediate between the opposing parties of an intrapsychic conflict. If the ego identifies with one side of the conflict, no resolution to wholeness is possible" (Edinger, *Ego and Archetype,* p. 137). Thus the ego is seen as the peacemaker, as one who intercedes on behalf of both sides of the conflict. In doing so, it acts in the interest of the whole of the personality, or in Jung's terminology, the Self. Thus, according to Edinger, one might aptly describe the ego as a "son of God."

It does not take long to become familiar with Edinger's reductive strategy. The Self is seen as the psychological equivalent of God. The non-inflated ego, that is, one that does not identify with unconscious contents, is seen as blessed because it is only by avoiding inflation that one can continue in the process of individuation. The kingdom of heaven is interpreted to mean "contact with the archetypal psyche and its healing, life-giving images" (Edinger, *Ego and Archetype,* p. 138). Subjectively interpreted, loving one's enemy means to love oneself, especially that aspect of oneself that one is ashamed of, the inferior shadow side. The lost coin (or the lost sheep) represents that part of the personality that has been repressed. It is seen to be of such great value precisely because it is the very part needed by the Self to become whole.[18]

If Edinger had proposed these interpretations of Scripture as psychological analogies or parallels to a properly theological or spiritual process, he might have been able to elucidate the text from a psychological perspective while still differentiating between psychological and theological discourse. But Edinger explicitly disallows the latter by considering it to be guilty of committing what he calls the "concretistic fallacy." He writes:

> In the concretistic fallacy . . . the individual is unable to distinguish symbols of the archetypal psyche from concrete, external reality. Inner symbolical images are experienced as being real, external facts. . . . The same fallacy is at work in those religious believers who misunderstand symbolic religious images to refer to literal concrete facts. (Edinger, *Ego and Archetype,* p. 111)

Christian symbols, in other words, actually refer, according to Edinger, to inner psychic processes, not to external realities or historical events. Thus Christ is understood to be an instance of the universal archetype of the dying and rising god.

18. For Edinger's full discussion, see *Ego and Archetype,* pp. 131-56.

One is guilty of the concretistic fallacy if one understands the historical rabbi, Jesus of Nazareth, to be the Christ or the incarnate Word of God. Properly understood, according to Edinger, Jesus should be seen as one who exemplifies the archetypal process of individuation, an inner symbolic and psychic process, which has been projected onto Jesus, the human being, by believers. Thus believers are regarded by Edinger as people who are "contained" in the Christian myth. "Containment is an unconscious phenomenon of psychic identification," he writes. "One can be contained in a religion just as he can be contained in a family or other collective group."[19] According to Edinger, to be contained in this way is not even to have begun the process of individuation, for one is destined always to remain at a collective level.

> This is inevitable in an individual for whom the archetypal psyche remains contained in a religious faith. In that case the archetypes are understood as metaphysical entities and have not yet appeared as *psychic* reality. For such a person psychic images can have only personal reference and religious images, at least the images of one's own religion, can have only metaphysical reference.[20]

If one considers the "hallmark of individuation" to be, as Edinger does, the "differentiation of the individual psyche from its containment in the collective psyche,"[21] one would consider conventional religious believers not yet to have discovered the true (psychological) meaning of their putative theological convictions. They see these truths as pertaining to independent spiritual realities and do not or not yet see their true psychic meaning. By contrast, those who interpret Jung as Edinger does find in his psychology of the unconscious a new dispensation. "The new psychological dispensation finds man's relation to God in the individual's relation to the unconscious."[22]

By translating theological and biblical concepts without remainder into psychological categories, Edinger may be seen to confuse theological and psychological discourse. Rather than seeing individuation

19. Edinger, "Depth Psychology," p. 6.
20. Edinger, "Depth Psychology," p. 17.
21. Edinger, "Depth Psychology," p. 21.
22. Edinger, "Depth Psychology," p. 24.

as a psychological parallel or analogy to a spiritual or theological reality, he systematically translates theological meanings into anthropological or psychological meanings. From the perspective of the Chalcedonian pattern as used by Barth, Edinger stands out as one who consistently fails to appreciate the "indissoluble differentiation" between theological and psychological discourse.

Asymmetrical Order: Critique of Tillich

In an essay entitled "The Relation of Religion and Health," Paul Tillich inquires about how properly to order the respective concepts of health and salvation with the question, "What is the place of health in the frame of the idea of salvation?"[23] By formulating the question in this manner, Tillich's answer might be expected to exemplify the third feature of the Chalcedonian pattern, for the question in this form might well point beyond a symmetrical ordering of the two concepts. By asking how one concept ("health") is to be understood within the framework of another ("salvation"), the question at least suggests the possibility that the relation between them might be asymmetrical. The contours of Tillich's answer will be traced as it is developed in this particular text.[24]

Tillich's answer is intriguing, for at first he seems to reverse the potential asymmetry of the original question by placing salvation within the frame of the idea of healing, while he then later seems to identify the two as having the same essential content. Even when he seems to equate the two concepts, however, they remain conceptually distinct and are not collapsed into one another. For that reason his thought can better be used to explore the question of "asymmetrical order" than that of "confusion" or "change." For the distinctive fea-

23. Paul Tillich, *The Meaning of Health: The Relation of Religion and Health* (Richmond, Calif.: North Atlantic Books, 1981), p. 13. Subsequent references will be given parenthetically in the text.

24. Because my purpose in this section is more to exemplify the use of the Chalcedonian pattern as an analytical tool than it is comprehensively to criticize the thought of any particular individual, my comments will be limited primarily to this particular text and should not necessarily be taken as applying to Tillich's thought as a whole.

ture about Tillich's thought seems to lie precisely in the *symmetrical* way in which he orders the diverse concepts of theology and psychology.

Tillich begins by arguing that the church has lost touch with the biblical meaning of salvation. Originally salvation was not defined narrowly as the eventual spiritual destiny of this or that particular Christian, he argues, but was understood rather to be "a cosmic event: the *world* is saved" (Tillich, *Meaning of Health,* p. 13). When salvation is understood in this widest sense, "healing is not only included in [salvation]," but "salvation can be described as the act of cosmic healing" (Tillich, *Meaning of Health,* p. 14). Here Tillich seems to stand the asymmetrical order on its head, giving a kind of conceptual priority to healing, into which framework the concept of salvation is placed. Accordingly, Tillich states, "Salvation is basically and essentially healing; the re-establishment of a whole that was broken, disrupted, disintegrated" (Tillich, *Meaning of Health,* p. 14).

Any perceived asymmetry — of health seen within a framework of salvation, or the reverse, salvation seen within the framework of healing — is essentially nullified, however, when Tillich proceeds explicitly to identify the two concepts. He says, "Most interesting and important for the relation — *more exactly the identity* — between healing and salvation is the mythological interpretation of the psychic disruptions in man" (Tillich, *Meaning of Health,* p. 15; emphasis added). He goes on to amplify this claim of a basic identity between healing and salvation by reflecting on the meaning of Jesus as *soter,* which, he remarks, literally means healer. "The identity of healing and salvation," writes Tillich, "is nowhere clearer than in Asclepius, except perhaps in Jesus of Nazareth. . . . In the Gospel of Mark, Jesus is, first of all, the healer, because the coming of the Kingdom of God implies the appearance of an irresistible healing power." Salvation as cosmic healing also includes victory over demonic forces. "Thus the healing of mental illness is the most crucial proof of salvation" (Tillich, *Meaning of Health,* p. 17). Healing as salvation is also understood as conquering cosmic guilt and disease and its underlying cause, sin, and finally even death itself. Sin is understood as "willful separation" and salvation as reconciliation with oneself, God, others, and nature (Tillich, *Meaning of Health,* pp. 17-18).

Healing and salvation are both seen as having a temporal and an eternal aspect. Tillich explicitly rejects the notion of healing being assigned to the temporal order and salvation to the eternal. Cosmic disease and cosmic healing are seen as virtual equivalents to the universal fall and universal redemption. "The eternal fulfillment is actual in the fragmentary fulfillment in time and space," he writes. "Healing as well as salvation are temporal and, at the same time are eternal. Healing acquires the significance of the eternal, and salvation the actuality of the temporal" (Tillich, *Meaning of Health,* p. 21).

With so much emphasis on the (dialectical) identity between salvation and healing, Tillich can clearly be seen to recognize an "inseparable unity" between the two. The questions of "indissoluble differentiation" and "indestructible order" remain more problematic, however. Tillich does seem to differentiate healing and salvation but apparently only for the purpose of negating the significance of any real or final distinctions between them. In a certain sense, one might say that Tillich elevates the concept of healing from the realm of the physical and the psychological into the directly theological realm. As the concept of healing is thus elevated, it is conceptually placed on the same level as salvation and can thus enter into a kind of reciprocal relation with it. At the same time, the particularly Christian understanding of salvation, at least from a Barthian perspective, seems to be lost. In fact, Tillich does not seem to be dealing with salvation as a distinctively Christian concept. He freely draws on Indian and Greek myths, for example, as well as on Christian symbolism to substantiate his view of the relationship between salvation and healing. Thus he shows how, in a variety of sacred texts, the universe has fallen into cosmic disorder and disease and stands in need of the healing that is finally its salvation.

It is, however, the distinctively *Christian* concept of salvation, at least as Barth understands it, that logically requires an asymmetrical relation between the concepts of healing and salvation. From a Barthian perspective, healing would be seen as the restoration of a person to his or her full created being, whereas salvation would be seen as the sublation or dialectical transformation of created being, as its *Aufhebung* or cancellation but also preservation and elevation into eternal life with God. Salvation by definition is not a possibility proper to creaturely beings as such. It utterly exceeds any creaturely capacity, as Barth sees it, coming to the creature from God alone. "Salvation," writes Barth, "is more than being."

> Salvation is fulfillment, the supreme, sufficient, definitive and inde-structible fulfillment of being. Salvation is the perfect being which is not proper to created being as such but is still future. Created being as such needs salvation, but does not have it: it can only look forward to it. To that extent, salvation is its *eschaton*. Salvation, fulfillment, perfect being means — and this is what created being does not have in itself — being which has a part in the being of God, from which and to which it is: not a divinized being but a being which is hidden in God, and in that sense (distinct from God and secondary) eternal being. Since salvation is not proper to created being as such, it can only come to it, and since it consists in participation in the being of God, it can come only from God. (IV/1, 8)

From this passage one can see that for Barth salvation and healing are not two different names for one and the same reality or two forms of one and the same content. However much they may intersect in actuality (such as when healing becomes a kind of secondary or deriva-tive "sign" of salvation), they remain conceptually distinct. Their content is analogous but not identical. The structure of created being is the context in which we are to understand healing. But salvation comes to the creature utterly from outside this structure, from God. "The love of God," writes Barth, "always throws a bridge over a crevasse" (II/1, 278). This crevasse may be interpreted as both the ontological and the sinful divide that lies between God and the human creature and that can be crossed by God alone.

Tillich's thought, on the other hand, doesn't require this concep-tual asymmetry because Tillich typically posits a fundamental con-junction between God and the world at the point where Barth sees a fundamental disjunction. The ontological divide posited by Barth is the infinite qualitative difference between God's eternal being and the creature's finite being, just as the sinful divide is that between God's holy being and the creature's sinful being. Although Tillich acknowl-edges that through sin human beings are separated from God, crea-turely being nevertheless continues to participate in divine being, regardless of however transcendent God may also be conceived to be.

Human beings by nature participate in the ground of being. Tillich writes, "Everything finite participates in being-itself and its infinity. Otherwise it would not have the power of being."[25] Being itself (God) is conceived as the "power inherent in everything, the power of resisting nonbeing."[26]

Even though Tillich states that "Being itself infinitely transcends every finite being" and that there is an "absolute break" between the finite and the infinite, God's being and human being are still mutually implicated in his thought in a way that they could never be for Barth. Tillich writes, for example, that "God is eternally creative" in the sense that "through himself he creates the world and through the world himself."[27] The world and God are here conceived as being conceptually interdependent and symmetrically related. God is in some sense understood to need the world in order to "create himself," just as the world needs God in order to be created. There is thus a kind of reciprocity and mutuality between God and the world according to Tillich's conception that does not correspond to Barth's asymmetrical conception.

For Barth, God does not create the world "through himself" but, rather, creates the world ex nihilo. Nor does God create "through the world himself." For Barth, God does not need the world in order to be God; God is complete and self-sufficient (the Father loves the Son and the Son the Father, in the unity of the Holy Spirit throughout eternity). Yet, God in sovereign freedom chooses not to be God apart from the world. God chooses to enter the realm of created being in Jesus Christ in order to reconcile the world to God.

> God chooses not to be God without us. He creates the world in absolute freedom for the sake of his covenant with humankind. The relationship between God and the world is thus grounded *entirely* in the unconditioned freedom of God. It is not *in any sense* grounded in some condition inherent in the world or in creaturely being itself. It might thus be said that Barth posits an ontological break between

25. Tillich, *Systematic Theology*, vol. 1 (Chicago: University of Chicago Press, 1951), p. 237.

26. Tillich, *Systematic Theology*, vol. 1, p. 236.

27. Tillich, *Systematic Theology*, vol. 2 (Chicago: University of Chicago Press, 1957), p. 147.

God and the world which is nevertheless encompassed, transcended, and overcome by the mystery of divine freedom for the sake of divine love.[28]

The asymmetry in the relation between God and the world rests finally, for Barth, on God's sovereign freedom, which by definition is not conditioned by anything creaturely or anything given in the structure of being or reality. The kind of symmetry between God and the world that Tillich posits would be seen by Barth as an "order of being" that logically functions in a significant sense as an "order of necessity," an order that would finally be seen to condition the freedom and grace of God.

For Barth the relation between theology and psychology would be fundamentally different from that between any two disciplines that pertain essentially to creaturely realities per se. For theology essentially pertains not only to creaturely realities but also to the reality of God. According to Barth, psychological concepts could not possibly exist on the same level as theological concepts because psychology by definition pertains only to a creaturely level of reality. For Barth there is a specificity to theological content which has no anthropological or psychological counterpart and to which psychological concepts as such have no access. They cannot, therefore, be seen as being in some sense interchangeable with concepts that describe only creaturely reality. The concrete content of the gospel and the distinctively *theological* claims it is making by definition cannot be understood in psychological terms (or historical, sociological, or physical terms either, for that matter).[29] The disciplines that describe creaturely reality logically function at a different level because they are not also trying to make the kind of claims about ultimate reality that Christian theology makes. "What other word speaks of the covenant between God and the human race?" asks Barth.

What other of its character as the work of God, and indeed of the effective and omnipotent grace of God on the basis of eternal love

28. George Hunsinger, "A Note on Barth and Tillich," unpublished essay.

29. "If this saving reality is what is at stake, then no method — historical-critical, psychological, phenomenological, or any other — can get at it. What method can reveal when, in our words and actions and in the events of this world, *God* acts to save?" Christopher Morse, "The Future of Karl Barth's Theology," *dialog* 20 (Winter 1981): 12.

and election? What other of the fulfillment of this covenant in the humiliation of God and the exaltation of the human race? What other of a comprehensive justification of the human race by God and sanctification for it? What other of the fact that this reconciliation of God with the human race and the human race with God is no mere idea but a once-for-all event? . . . What other is directed so concretely to each and every human being? (IV/3, 107-8 rev.)

The concrete content of the gospel is not accessible as such by disciplines other than theology because they are not, and by definition cannot be, making specifically theological claims, claims that arise out of this "singular and unrepeatable history" of God with humanity, claims grounded not in universal structures of being but in the particular actions and unique freedom of God.[30]

For Tillich, by contrast, spiritual or theological reality is just one dimension of reality among others. It is not conceived to be logically on a different plane. Tillich explicitly says, for example:

When I spoke of dimensions of life, there was implied a rejection of the phrase "levels of life." This must now be made explicit. Man should not be considered as a composite of several levels, such as body, soul, spirit, but as a multidimensional unity. I use the metaphor "dimension" in order to indicate that the different qualities of life in man are present within each other and do not lie alongside or above each other. . . . In each dimension all the others are present. (Tillich, *Meaning of Health*, pp. 53-54)

Tillich then discusses the mechanical, chemical, biological, psychological, and spiritual dimensions, showing how each of them interpenetrates the others. Although the spiritual reality is understood to be "decisive for all the preceding dimensions," it is not logically on a different level, at least not in the same sense as in Barth. For even Spirit, with a capital *S,* which is understood to transcend the ordinary creaturely spirit, is defined as "the presence of what concerns us ultimately, the ground of our being and meaning" (Tillich, *Meaning of Health*, p. 57). This "ground" is thus more like a universal structure than like what Barth means when he refers to God as a "genuine

---

30. Hunsinger, "A Note on Barth and Tillich."

Counterpart" who is "a true other," who is a "real outside and beyond," who has "a specific will," who "accomplishes a specific act,"
and who "speaks a specific word" (III/4, 479).

For Tillich, then, healing and salvation are understood to participate in a kind of "mutual within-each-otherness of the dimensions"
(Tillich, *Meaning of Health,* p. 59). This can finally be seen to be quite
different from Barth's conception of the asymmetrical order between
divine and human reality and, consequently, between divine salvation
and more proximate events of healing that point to salvation analogically and are understood by faith within the context of that unique
salvation.

By examining various theoretical proposals about how psychology
and theology are related, this section has sought to demonstrate the
usefulness of the Chalcedonian pattern as an analytical tool. An assessment of three different proposals has made it possible to bring out
the significance of each of the pattern's three defining terms. First,
the importance of not separating or dividing the two realms of discourse was emphasized in relation to the work of Eduard Thurneysen,
who, in his zeal to distinguish them, failed to account adequately for
the nature of their conceptual unity. Next, the importance of not
confusing the two or changing them into one another was emphasized
in relation to the proposals of Edward Edinger, who systematically
translated and reduced distinctly theological meanings into psychological meanings, thus failing to observe the "indissoluble differentiation" between them. Finally, the significance of their asymmetrical ordering was developed in relation to Paul Tillich's essay, which
was shown, by contrast, to order psychological and theological concepts symmetrically. The alternative being propounded here, however,
is one where psychology and theology are seen to be related in an
ordered and differentiated conceptual unity. Both realms of discourse
are allowed to remain distinct in their own right, while psychological
concepts are interpreted as being related analogically and asymmetrically to theological concepts. In this relationship the analogical aspect
accounts for their conceptual unity, and the asymmetrical aspect accounts for their conceptual ordering.

Uses of the Chalcedonian Pattern: Practice

How might an understanding of the Chalcedonian pattern be brought to bear on clinical issues in the therapeutic setting? Is it important for the pastoral counselor to be able to differentiate between psychological and spiritual issues, to perceive the possibility of their underlying unity when interpreting the counselee's material, and to discern the priority of the spiritual over the psychological? While the pastoral counselor's skill in both psychological and theological interpretation might be acknowledged as crucial, how important is it in actual practice also to understand the kinds of logical relations that obtain between them from the perspective presented here? What kinds of applications of the pattern might be made in practice?

The practical consequences of a pastoral counselor's ability to distinguish among these modes of discourse, neither to confuse them with one another, nor to separate them from one another, and yet also to understand the spiritual reality as the overarching context into which psychological judgments are finally placed, is indicated in a passage of Shirley Guthrie's already cited in Chapter Two. Guthrie writes:

> Pastoral counseling acknowledges that God wills and gives human freedom. . . . It is true, for instance, that sinful human beings cannot simply "decide" to love God with their whole being, but they can at least go to church, or talk to people (including the counselor), or read a book (including the Bible) in order to find out who the God is who promises and gives freedom. It is true that they cannot "decide" to be loving and just, but they can risk the personal encounters and social contexts in which love and justice can happen. . . . None of these small steps toward freedom are a guarantee that freedom will come. None of them force the hand or buy the favor or earn the help of the God whose sovereign grace alone can set people free from their self-contradiction. But Christian pastoral counselors will encourage these small steps nevertheless.[31]

In this passage Guthrie distinguishes between theological and psychological concepts, perceives their underlying theological unity,

---

31. Shirley C. Guthrie, Jr., "Pastoral Counseling, Trinitarian Theology, and Christian Anthropology," *Interpretation* 33 (1979): 140-41.

and indicates the asymmetrical relationship between them. He begins with the assertion that "Pastoral counseling acknowledges that God wills and gives human freedom."[32] This statement can be seen as a theological comment about the asymmetrical relationship between divine grace and human freedom. Divine grace is understood as the overarching context in which human freedom is actualized. If it were not for God's prior decision to will human freedom before God, no such freedom would be possible.

Guthrie then proceeds to state that, "It is true, for instance, that sinful human beings cannot simply 'decide' to love God with their whole being." To think that one *could* just "decide" to love God with one's whole being would be an example of a confusion between theological and psychological conceptions. It may be recalled that as we distinguished the concept of "sinner" from that of "victim," we noted that on the one hand, "only God can save from sin," while on the other, "human effort may bring healing or improvement." While it would be a confusion for a person to think that he or she could simply decide to love God wholeheartedly (and thus to be virtually without sin), there are nevertheless a number of things that he or she might do toward healing and growth: go to church, read a book, ask questions, or risk personal encounters.

Only if the person were radically to divide his or her self-conception of a sinner from the self-conception of a victim would the person suppose that there was nothing he or she could do on his or her own behalf. For going to church or reading the Bible might become the occasion or the event in which God actually speaks to the person, in which real freedom to love God actually occurs. Or it might not. Guthrie acknowledges that none of these small steps guarantees that God will also act, for God's action is not under human control.

But when God does so act, it is within the events of ordinary human reality, which can also be described empirically and therefore psychologically. Faith's perception of God's action cannot, of course, be described as such psychologically, but the ordinary human decisions and actions done within the context of everyday reality can. From a Barthian standpoint, any such complex occurrence can be viewed as having both a visible (psychological) dimension in the human being's

---

32. Guthrie, p. 140.

decisions and actions and, yet, also an invisible dimension in God's action, as perceived and attested by faith.

The hypothetical counselee in Guthrie's example, then, would misunderstand the *asymmetrical order* by thinking that human actions or decisions could coerce or manipulate God into giving the freedom to become the kind of person he or she wishes to become. The counselee would misunderstand the underlying *unity* of spiritual and psychological reality by deciding that there is nothing to do on his or her own behalf and complacently waited for God to change his or her life. And finally, the counselee would misunderstand the basic *distinctions* between psychological and theological concepts by thinking that it would be possible just to "decide" to be loving and just or to love God wholeheartedly. It seems obvious that if the pastoral counselor were not clear about these interdisciplinary relationships, the interested counselee could easily become confused about where to exert his or her will and freedom and where simply to trust God.

To take another example of the practical importance of the pastoral counselor's ability to maintain clarity about the relationship between these two modes of discourse, let us consider the therapeutic process of a woman's recovery from childhood incest with a parent. As we recall the distinctions made between the concepts of "sinner" and "victim," we remember the statements that "the sinner qua sinner is culpable" and that "the victim qua victim is innocent." As a victim of childhood sexual abuse, the woman qua victim is innocent. The category of innocence is understood here as an empirical description of the woman's psychosocial reality as a child. It was her parents' responsibility to protect her from harm; rather than protecting her, however, they perpetrated terrible abuse. No matter what the particular dynamics in the family were, the child by definition was an innocent victim and the parents were culpable.

Speaking theologically, however, one cannot speak meaningfully of innocence. Each human being in relation to God is mysteriously entangled in a web of sin. In her status as a fallen creature, this woman, like all others, is culpable and utterly dependent upon God's grace and forgiveness.

What might be an example of confusing these two conceptions? One example of confusion might be for the woman to blame herself for having been sexually abused. She would confuse her status as a victim with her status as a sinner and blame herself for the evil that was perpetrated upon her. She would confuse the evil she underwent as a child with the evil she undertakes as a woman. Because both have the potential to immerse her in feelings of shame, defilement, and unworthiness, she may confuse them with each other.

Indeed, it is common for a sexually abused girl to protect her parents by assuming that she somehow "brought it upon herself." As she grows into adulthood, she may defend against the pain and terror of the abuse, insofar as it is conscious at all, by minimizing or rationalizing the extent of her parents' culpability. She thus may fall into a stance of self-blame as a way to protect the idealized parent. She may, for example, feel guilty or berate herself over adult sensations of sexual pleasure. Insofar as they are associated with the childhood incest, they seem to be "proof" of her own culpability.

But as Alice Miller, the Swiss psychoanalyst who has studied patterns of intergenerational abuse, has shown, the woman's very healing would depend upon her being able to place the blame where it belongs: squarely on the perpetrator of the abuse. In *Banished Knowledge* she writes, "Anyone who is not allowed to *condemn outright* what is evil, perfidious, vile, perverse, and mendacious will always be lacking in orientation and compelled blindly to repeat his own experiences."[33] Miller describes how the destructive cycle of abuse will unfortunately be repeated in one form or another unless or until it becomes conscious. For, as Miller shows so lucidly, repressed memories push toward conscious realization through the compulsion to repeat. Only as the repression is lifted and as the woman consciously suffers the emotions that accompany the remembered trauma would she be released from the compulsion blindly to repeat her past in one way or another.

If a pastoral counselor does not, in effect, help the woman to distinguish her status as a victim from her status as a sinner, she may unwittingly retard the therapeutic process. If, for example, the pastoral counselor were to focus on her common status as a fallen creature as a way to urge reconciliation with the estranged parents, the counselor may only reinforce repression and could possibly undercut the entire therapeutic process. The woman's justified anger at her parents would

33. Alice Miller, *Banished Knowledge* (New York: Doubleday, 1990), pp. 132-33.

possibly become submerged (repressed again) if she were to perceive a moral demand being made by the pastoral counselor for reconciliation. Writing as one who has apparently seen much harm done in this way, Miller is quite sharp in her criticism of what she regards as "the traditional values of morality and religion."[34]

> If a person is not allowed to acknowledge the newly awakening anger — because, of course, he has already forgiven his parents during therapy — the person is in danger of transferring these feelings to others. Since, to me, therapy means a sensory, emotional and mental discovery of the long-repressed truth, *I regard the moral demand for reconciliation with parents as an inevitable blocking and paralyzing of the therapeutic process.*[35]

Only as the pastoral counselor focused on her counselee's status as an innocent victim could she be helped to come to terms emotionally with the trauma of her past. Clearly distinguishing between her counselee's status of victim and that of sinner would in such a case be a matter not of remote academic interest but of urgent therapeutic need.

What might be an example of separation or division in this hypothetical example? While the pastoral counselor needs to help the woman distinguish her status of victim from her status of sinner, the woman is, from a theological perspective, both a sinner in her relationship to God and a victim in her psychosocial reality. While it is important that she cease to blame herself neurotically for things that clearly lie outside her responsibility, it would also be important for her to come to terms at some point with her actual sins. Compulsive self-blame can sometimes be an unconscious strategy for avoiding one's true sins.[36] One way of separating or dividing the two, then, would be for the woman to see herself only as a victim and never as a sinner. Such a strategy could conceivably lock her into an infantile position of never learning to take responsibility for herself. Everything

34. Miller, p. 133.
35. Miller, p. 154.
36. See Ann Belford Ulanov, *The Wisdom of the Psyche* (Cambridge, Mass.: Cowley, 1988), chap. 2, "The Devil's Trick," for a helpful distinction between what she calls "the false cross" of neurotic suffering, which leads nowhere, and "the real cross," whose suffering "opens to remorse, reparation, resurrection" (p. 38).

would be blamed on the parent (or on the past abuse), and the woman's responsibility for her own life would be evaded.

As the therapeutic process unfolds, the woman may at some point have her own real sins to face and confess. There may come a time when she will see how the repression of her early trauma may have compelled her to act in self-destructive or harmful ways. She may even come to see how she has repeated patterns where she has victimized others, even as she herself was victimized. As the weight of her sins bears down upon her, it is important for her not to separate her understanding of herself as a victim from that of herself as a sinner. For she may come to recognize herself to be trapped in the same web of sin, in the same situation of "corporate wrongness,"[37] that had caught her parents before her. Not in any sense excusing her parents' unconscionable actions, the woman may nevertheless recognize that she stands, *theologically,* on the same plane as they. Like them, she, too, stands in need of God's mercy and forgiveness. While patterns of abuse and neglect as they are handed down from one generation to the next are not the equivalent of sin, one begins to understand their inseparability from a theological perspective.

Dorothy Martyn captures this relationship aptly when she writes,

> If one spends a bit of time with the mother, in an attitude of listening, it becomes quickly manifest that the mother did not willfully deprive her child; the difficulty lay in the fact that she, too, for various reasons, was deprived, in her turn, of "good-enough mothering and father-ing." She herself had not found nurture at a mother's breast, and therefore had little nurture to offer her child. She also was brought up by a mother and father who likewise had little to give because they also had been brought up by parents who had little to give. . . . Psychological distress in itself is not erasable because there is no way to start over. We are caught in an infinite series of mirrors in which repetition of man's error is inevitable because internalization from one's relational matrix is axiomatic.[38]

37. Dorothy Martyn, "A Child and Adam: A Parable of the Two Ages," *Journal of Religion and Health* 16 (1977): 279.
38. Martyn, p. 278.

The kind of perception evident in this passage reveals the connection between one's status as a victim and one's status as a sinner, showing especially how one's own victimization tragically sets one up, so to speak, for victimizing others. The distortions in interpersonal relationships, which are describable through empirical observation, arise out of a matrix of human sin and cannot be understood theologically apart from a concept of sin.

An understanding of the connection between the woman's status as victim and that of sinner leads a person of faith at times to the question of forgiveness and reconciliation. If the woman herself desires reconciliation as an outgrowth of her own healing process, it emerges not as a moral demand on the part of the counselor, which would only impede the therapeutic process, but as a gift from God. Here we may recognize the third feature of the Chalcedonian pattern, the asymmetrical order between divine and human action. True forgiveness and reconciliation do not happen as a response to a moral demand. They emerge, rather, from a healed and grateful heart, from one who already knows herself to have received God's forgiveness. To conceive of forgiveness as a psychological possibility or as a moral demand is to misconceive it. But if one understands the asymmetrical order between divine and human activity, one sees that the possibility for forgiveness and reconciliation arises not from willed effort but, rather, only from God's prior action of mercy, forgiveness, and healing. The pastoral counselor who understands the order of these events would perhaps be less likely to inflict forgiveness as a moral demand on the counselee, responding instead to the counselee's desire to forgive only as it grows out of the inner healing that has already occurred.

Practically as well as theoretically, then, understanding how to apply the Chalcedonian pattern to psychological and theological concepts is an important skill for the pastoral counselor. Being able to sort through the issues, to discern which language to speak and why, to keep them conceptually distinguished and ordered, but not to divorce them from one another in one's interpretation: all these skills are seen to be important in practice as well as in theory.

Conclusion

This chapter has uncovered the explicit pattern in Barth's thought that may be used to relate theological and psychological concepts. The two sets of concepts have been shown to have their own "indissoluble differentiation;" they are seen as distinct concepts which belong to their own respective disciplines and which have a kind of irreducible integrity within their own context. They are not to be confused with each other; theological concepts are not to be changed into psychological ones nor vice versa. At the same time they are not to be separated or divided from each other. In any interpretation of mundane events, from a theological point of view, both spiritual and psychological phenomena may be seen to be present. Any particular event may be perceived from two distinct perspectives. For psychological and theological or spiritual phenomena, though they may co-exist in and with one another, are still to be clearly differentiated. From a Barthian standpoint, the two perspectives presuppose that psychological and spiritual phenomena, though converging, reflect essentially different levels of reality. Theological interpretation is understood to have a kind of logical precedence over the psychological as its ultimate context for understanding, even as psychological interpretation, though relatively independent in itself, holds a status of subsequence within that context. From a theological perspective, the two forms of interpretation are thus asymmetrically related.

The three aspects of the Chalcedonian pattern — differentiation, unity, and order — were then used as a tool to analyze the thought of three thinkers who have ventured to relate the concerns of theology and psychology: Eduard Thurneysen, Edward Edinger, and Paul Tillich. My aim was to show their usefulness as categories of discernment and to bring out some of the distinctive features of a Barthian method for conducting interdisciplinary dialogue.

The same formal features of the pattern were then used as categories of discernment to reflect on pastoral counseling practice. A passage from Shirley Guthrie was considered in which the formal pattern is seen to help clarify the psychological and theological issues at stake when pondering the reality of human freedom in relation to divine grace. The distinctions made had definite implications for practice. A hypothetical case of a woman healing from childhood incest was then developed as a way to highlight the importance of the pastoral counselor's ability to distinguish between modes of discourse, neither confusing them nor dividing them, while yet perceiving the priority of the spiritual over the psychological.

CHAPTER FOUR

God Representation and Knowledge of God: Methods and Norms

HOW MIGHT a "bilingual" pastoral counselor, as one who brings both theological and psychological competencies to the interpretive task, view the counselee's relationship to God? That is to say, what would it mean to bring such a distinctively dual focus to the question of any particular individual's unique relationship with God? Here, too, the particular features of the Chalcedonian pattern would apply. A person's belief in God may be viewed from both a psychoanalytic and a theological perspective even though, existentially speaking, the two dimensions merge or coalesce for the believer. For the sake of methodological clarity the two perspectives may be differentiated, showing how each discipline thinks about belief in God according to its own normative frame of reference. Each discipline is conceived here as having the freedom to define its own boundaries and to investigate its subject matter in a manner appropriate to its own discipline. In this chapter the question of differing methods and norms of psychoanalysis and theology (from a Barthian perspective) will be applied to the formation of a person's God representation. A psychoanalytic description of how one internalizes and develops an unconscious image of God will be presented along with a Barthian theological understanding of how one acquires knowledge of God. Psychoanalytic method and Barth's theological method will be differentiated from each other, showing how each is appropriate to its own object of study. A normative understanding of the God representation from the perspective of the two different disciplines — broadly conceived as "psychological functionality" on the one hand and "theo-

105

logical adequacy" on the other — will then be introduced. These norms will be brought into relationship with each other by exploring the logically possible ways they can be related. The close interweaving of psychological and theological issues will then be explored in a number of hypothetical pastoral counseling situations. The purpose of the chapter is thus to focus more closely on differentiating the methods and norms appropriate to each discipline and to do so in relation to an issue central to pastoral counseling, namely, how a person comes to know and "image" God.

Rizzuto's Psychoanalytic Study: Representation of God

Ana-Maria Rizzuto, a psychiatrist with expertise in object-relations psychology (and a Roman Catholic laywoman), has written a book, *The Birth of the Living God: A Psychoanalytic Study,*[1] which has been hailed as a classic in the field.[2] The book is a systematic investigation of the psychological origins, development, and functions of a person's belief in God. In this section attention will be given to Rizzuto's psychoanalytic method and her basic theoretical assumptions. Her argument will be placed particularly in relation to Freud, upon whose insights she builds but from whom she departs at significant junctures.

Rizzuto uses Freud's basic psychoanalytic framework (discarding his more controversial anthropological speculations) as she traces the formation, epigenetic development, and subsequent transformation of an individual's God representation. Like Freud, she locates the source of an individual's private image of God in the relationship to primary objects, that is, to one's significant others from early childhood, especially one's parents. She argues that a child creatively pieces "God" together out of fantasies about and experiences with these emotionally significant people. An internal psychic image or repre-

1. Ana-Maria Rizzuto, *The Birth of the Living God: A Psychoanalytic Study* (Chicago: University of Chicago Press, 1979).
2. See reviews by Merle R. Jordan, *Journal of Pastoral Care* 35 (March 1981): 69-70; and C. D. Hackett, *Journal of Religion and Health* 20 (Fall 1981): 254-55.

sentation of God is formed from the *prima materia* of a child's hopes, fears, and longings as they are imaginatively interwoven with some of the actual characteristics of those in the family of origin. Such a God representation is used throughout life to provide psychological stability and equilibrium, a minimum of relatedness to others, particularly those people who contributed to the formation of the God image, and a sense of self-esteem and hope.[3]

Rizzuto studied twenty people, ten men and ten women, from a broad spectrum of diagnostic categories and types of background. They took part in the study without their knowledge, perceiving the questionnaires and biographical interviews to be a normal part of the psychiatric care of the institution where they were hospitalized.

Rizzuto designed two parallel questionnaires: one with questions about the patient's family of origin and another with complementary questions about God, both designed to elicit basic attitudes and feelings. Each patient also drew a picture of his or her family as well as a picture of God. Rizzuto's working hypothesis was that there would be a close correlation between a person's internalized primary objects and his or her unconscious picture of God. The data collected enabled her systematically to correlate these two sets of feelings, images, and attitudes. Whenever there emerged a noted difference between the internalized images, Rizzuto would hypothesize about the various defense mechanisms that might account for the discrepancy. In addition to the questionnaires and drawings, each person was asked to describe his or her entire life history (on tape), emphasizing each stage of development and important turning points, including religious experiences. Specific questions were asked about the person's relationship to God and any changes in it that had taken place over the course of a lifetime.

In her interpretation of the data, Rizzuto employed Freud's basic psychoanalytic framework. "God" was seen to be a creation of the human mind, an illusory image created by the child out of the "simple warp and woof of everyday life" (Rizzuto, p. 5). After tracing the life histories of individuals in a concrete and detailed manner, Rizzuto found she could support Freud's fundamental conclusion that "it is

---

3. Rizzuto, pp. 89, 199, and 202. Subsequent references will be given parenthetically in the text.

out of this matrix of facts and fantasies, wishes, hopes and fears, in the exchanges with those incredible beings called parents that the image of God is concocted" (Rizzuto, p. 7). While Freud saw the father as the prototype for one's picture of God, Rizzuto found that the mother and sometimes grandparents and siblings were just as consistently used as sources for the God representation. Indeed, her study showed that frequently the mother, not the father, was the primary source (Rizzuto, p. 44). Significantly, the role of fantasy — the child's wishes and fears toward the parents — was found to be as important as, if not more important than, the actual objective characteristics of the parents.

Rizzuto also disagrees with Freud's contention that one's God image is forever fixed at the oedipal stage. She argues that individuals frequently rework and reelaborate their God images throughout life, particularly at times of crisis in personal psychological development. Only in cases of definite pathology does the God image become fixed at a single stage. Rizzuto finds Freud inconsistent on this point, for he explicitly states that a person's relation to God "depends on his relation to his father in the flesh and oscillates and changes along with that relation."[4] But if one can achieve a mature relation with one's father (or parents), Rizzuto reasons, it follows logically that one should also be able to achieve a mature relationship with God. A relationship with God need not always be, as Freud saw it, a childish dependence on an all-powerful paternal deity.

Just as psychoanalysis provides an opportunity for reworking one's internal objects, for redescribing the past such that a new relation is achieved with parents and other significant people, so similar opportunities exist for reworking the God image. Ritual, for example, is not seen necessarily as a sign of unresolved repetition compulsion but as a source of real renewal, an opportunity to gain a new relationship with one's internal objects (Rizzuto, p. 181). Religious belief, argues Rizzuto in opposition to Freud, is not necessarily a sign of immaturity any more than non-belief is a sign of health.[5] One can just as easily

---

4. Sigmund Freud, *Totem and Taboo,* ed. James Strachey (New York: Norton, 1950), p. 147; quoted by Rizzuto, p. 24.

5. Rizzuto, p. 202. See also p. 47, where she writes: "The religious person . . . does not experience God as a symbol or sign but as a living being, whose communica-

be a mature believer or an immature non-believer. Since all who have passed beyond the oedipal state of development have at least a rudimentary God representation, according to Rizzuto, it follows that lack of belief is no less in need of explanation than belief.

Rizzuto emphasizes the active, creative role that individuals play in relation to their internalized objects. She observes that the objects themselves do not *do* anything; they do not persecute, comfort, threaten, or love the person, as metaphorical language about them suggests. The internalized objects are living presences within a person only insofar as that person remembers, fantasizes, and interacts with them. Rizzuto draws on the contributions of various object-relations theorists to describe more precisely the scope of the process at work.

> Object relations are a particular case of more encompassing processes: representing, remembering, fantasizing, interpreting and integrating experiences with others through defensive and adaptive maneuvers. . . . The process of representing objects and oneself provide "the material framework for all mentation, including the ego's adaptive and defensive functions" (Moore and Fine, 1968). . . . "The consequence of this process is that any single corner of our bodies, any of our impulses, any of our encounters with any aspect of reality is object-related" (Kestenberg, 1971).[6]

Despite the all-encompassing scope of the process of relating to one's internal objects, the objects themselves are not hypostatized, changeless "things"; they change as the individual grows and develops and comes to use them in new ways. The process of psychoanalysis with its technique of free association, which allows repressions to be lifted, is an example of how traumatic memories can be seen and understood in a new light and the past can be reinterpreted. In this process the internal object itself actually changes. Rizzuto gives an example of a woman who carefully describes a past event and concludes: "Well, although that was a terrible experience, I realize now that my mother did not mean to hurt

---

tion the believer interprets. The believer, in spite of the uncommon nature of the relation, is not psychotic, or even necessarily neurotic. He or she may be an emotionally mature person."

6. Rizzuto, pp. 76-77.

me" (Rizzuto, p. 80). This woman's internalized image of her mother will henceforth be less persecuting, less hurtful. Both the object and its relation to the self have changed.

In this example the woman's self-representation would also change as the internalized picture of her mother changes. Her sense of self would be less victimized, less of a cowering child waiting for her mother to hurt her again. As the internal object changes through reworking, so would the woman's perception and picture of herself. While a change in any internal object would have effects on one's self-representation, the relation between one's self and one's God representation is especially close and intimate, Rizzuto notes, for God is the one being said to know the self as it really is. As such, God occupies a unique position in the psyche, not identified with the self, though intimately connected with it, nor identified with one's primary objects, though in constant relationship with them. It is this unique position as a bridge between the self as it really is and one's emotionally significant others that enables the God representation to further psychic equilibrium and stability.

> If the relevant objects of everyday life are a source of pain, God may be used, through complex modification of his representation, to comfort and supply hope. If they are accepting and supportive, God may be used to displace ambivalence and angry feelings, or as a target for disturbing and forbidden libidinal longings. This use of the God representation for regulation and modulation of object and related self-representations begins in childhood, continues throughout life, and finds its final and critical potentialities at death. (Rizzuto, pp. 88-89)

In line with general psychoanalytic theory concerning the critical role of unconscious images, Rizzuto emphasizes the central importance of unconscious God representations as opposed to conscious conceptual thought about God. While belief itself is a conscious process, she argues, its motivating, emotionally compelling roots lie in the unconscious (Rizzuto, pp. 201-2). It is how the unconscious picture of God is used that is finally the decisive factor in bringing about belief or non-belief. The picture of God, based on one's imaginative internalization of one's primary objects, either lends itself to belief or not depending on the individual's concrete needs. Rizzuto comments that some people have a strong need to deny God's existence because their unconscious image of God is so threatening and potentially shattering to their psychic equilibrium. Conscious processes, such as formal religious education, abstract theological reasoning, and other forms of secondary process thought may have a definite effect on the individual's conscious religious affiliation and commitments, but, according to Rizzuto, they contribute nothing essential to emotional involvement with God (Rizzuto, pp. 48, 200). The distinction between primary and secondary process thought is responsible for Rizzuto's basic contention that it is the unconscious God image that is the living God, that is, the God who has the emotional transformational power in the person's inner psychic world. The mere concept of God by itself is seen as largely irrelevant psychologically. "Emotionally . . . it adds nothing" (Rizzuto, p. 200).

Actual belief in God is dependent upon its psychic function; if it furthers psychic health and stability, an individual will generally adopt the internal God image as an object of belief. Rizzuto concludes:

> I propose that *belief in God* or its absence depends upon whether or not a *conscious 'identity of experience'* can be established between the God representation of a given developmental moment and the object and self-representations needed to maintain a sense of self which provides at least a minimum of relatedness and hope. (Rizzuto, p. 202)

Drawing upon D. W. Winnicott's imaginative conceptualization of transitional phenomena, Rizzuto describes the God representation as an illusory transitional object that functions to promote psychic health and meaning. According to Winnicott, transitional phenomena are neither solely external nor solely internal to the self but belong to "an intermediate area of experiencing to which inner reality and external life both contribute."[7] The actual objective reality of the child's mother, father, and other significant people would be the external factors that contribute to making the God representation, while the child's needs, wishes, and desires would be the contributing internal factors. Winnicott wants to preserve an area of experiencing that he

---

7. D. W. Winnicott, *Playing and Reality* (New York: Basic Books, 1971), p. 2. Subsequent references will be given parenthetically in the text.

believes is inherent in art and religion in adult life, an area of "illusory experience" exempt from the normal requirement of reality testing (Winnicott, p. 3). A transitional object must show some kind of vitality or reality of its own; it is not a hallucination, but neither is it a real objective other since it carries so much of the child's inner psychic reality (Winnicott, p. 5). Transitional phenomena manifest themselves in the area between pure fantasy (primary creativity) and pure objective reality (object perception based on reality testing), easing the strain of relating inner and outer reality (Winnicott, p. 11).

Contrary to Freud, who would urge us to renounce any object incapable of being subjected to reality testing, Rizzuto argues for the essential place of "illusion" in psychic life. "Illusory transmutation of reality . . . is the indispensable and unavoidable process all of us *must* go through if we are to grow normally and acquire psychic meaning and substance" (Rizzuto, p. 228). Rizzuto differentiates her use of the term "illusion" from its use in ordinary or everyday language, where "illusory" is understood to be antithetical to "reality." She argues that in the transitional space "illusory and real dimensions of experience interpenetrate each other to such an extent that they cannot be teased apart without destroying what is essential in the experience" (Rizzuto, p. 227). Illusion, in this sense, is closely akin to the ordinary meaning of the word imagination, with the important qualification that one engages in illusory transmutation of reality because of pressing psychological wishes and needs. "Man is always playing with reality either to create himself through illusory anticipation, to sustain himself through illusory reshaping of what does not seem bearable, or simply to fool himself through illusory distortion of what he does not like." Rizzuto does not consider such reshaping of reality to be pathological except in those cases where it "goes beyond immediate need" (Rizzuto, p. 228).

In summary, Rizzuto proceeded on the hypothesis that there is a close correlation between an individual's internalized primary objects and his or her unconscious picture of God. To test this hypothesis, she collected significant historical data concerning the counselees' interpersonal relationships and coupled it with their ideas and feelings about God. She then correlated the two, using the explanatory model of defense mechanisms (for example, denial, reaction formation, displacement, repression, etc.) as a way to understand those cases where the God images were different from the parental images. She found a definite correlation and developed further hypotheses about how the God representation functions toward stable interpersonal relationships in adult life, particularly in relation to those people who originally contributed to the formation of the God image. She concludes that we must assign a positive value to the role of illusion in psychic life, since we all inevitably transform reality in accordance with our wishes and needs and since this imaginative transformation gives us psychic depth and meaning.

Barth's Theological Method: Knowledge of God

The question of how a person comes to know God is, of course, approached very differently by Barth than by Rizzuto. While Rizzuto is interested in the various human phenomena that contribute to a person's forming an unconscious image of God (and that finally affect the person's conscious "belief" or "unbelief" in decisive ways), Barth does not approach the subject empirically or phenomenologically. He does not raise the question of an unconscious representation of God. Indeed, even our conscious images of God are in themselves theologically uninteresting to Barth; they would become significant only as God acts to make them truly reflective of his identity. While Rizzuto's focus is on the intricacies of psychic introjection and projection, Barth is concerned to find a way to ground human knowledge of God in God alone.

It is important to notice the different kinds of questions Rizzuto and Barth are asking. Although they are both ostensibly addressing the question of "belief in God," they do so from within widely different frameworks of meaning. Rizzuto's questions do not concern Barth qua theologian, nor do Barth's questions concern Rizzuto qua psychoanalyst. They are oriented toward their material differently, because each is investigating "belief" in a way appropriate to his or her own discipline. Yet, both sets of questions concern the pastoral counselor as one who is called to think about case material from both frames of reference. Differentiating theological and psychological methods and norms from each other and learning to ask questions that are appropriate to each discipline are important skills to acquire for the pastoral counselor who needs to be fluent in both realms of discourse.

As we turn to Barth we should note that Barth understood his task to be a "dogmatic" rather than an "apologetic" one. He took theology to be an attempt to clarify and redescribe the meaning of Christian concepts but not to demonstrate their truth on neutral grounds. That is to say, Barth did not believe it was possible to specify external or independent criteria by which one could supposedly confirm the reality of one's faith or that of others. He, therefore, deliberately avoided any kind of supposedly normative empirical or phenomenological description of how one might come to faith. It seemed self-evident to him that God could use anything in creation as a witness to himself and that there was thus no one single kind of event or process by which God necessarily encounters us. "God may speak to us," he writes, "through Russian communism or a flute concerto, a blossoming shrub or a dead dog. We shall do well to listen to him if he really does so" (I/1, 60). No particular kind of psychological or spiritual experience, in other words, is necessary to have faith in God. Faith may arise and grow under adverse circumstances (as when a child is neglected or abused by its parents) or under favorable circumstances (as when a child grows up feeling loved and accepted in the midst of a believing community). Neither "good-enough" parenting or lack of it, nor any other particular set of circumstances, should be understood as a condition necessary to bring about faith.

Regardless of its experiential or psychological correlates, the condition for the possibility of knowing God, Barth argued, is to be grounded in God alone, not in any kind of human experience, whether conscious or unconscious. In this section we will explore why such a view was so important to Barth. The distinctive features of his theological method, particularly as they relate to psychoanalytic method, can be brought out by examining his response to Ludwig Feuerbach. For in many ways Feuerbach anticipated Freud's radical criticism of religion. Although he developed his ideas differently, Freud would surely have agreed with Feuerbach's basic contention that "theology is anthropology." Feuerbach argued that the real object of theological language was not God but human beings:

> The object which we call in Greek, *Theos,* in our language, God, there expresses itself nothing other than the nature of man. . . . Every god is a being of the imagination, an image and in fact an image of man, but an image which man places over against himself and imagines as an independent being.[8]

Put in psychoanalytical terms, at the heart of Feuerbach's critique is an implicit theory of "projection," that is, the act of unconsciously attributing to another what is really a characteristic of the self. Human beings, by this account, project images of their own nature and being into the unknown and call it "God." The basic assumption that religious images are the result of unconscious projection is one developed by Freud and assumed by Rizzuto.[9]

In order to understand Barth's response to Feuerbach, it will be important to keep in mind Feuerbach's implicit distinction between religion and theology. Religion, for Feuerbach, was a form of false consciousness. It involved the formation of images that were projections of genuine anthropological content in disguised and alienated form. He described the objects of our religious consciousness as "something in the imagination only, but in truth, in reality, nothing."[10] Religious consciousness, in other words, was based upon an illusion, and first-order religious utterances were manifestly untrue. Theology, on the other hand, he regarded as the systematization of religious illusion. Whereas he saw latent (that is, anthropological) truth behind the manifest untruth in statements of immediate religious consciousness, he could only regard theology, a second-order reflective discipline, as a mode of thought that transformed illusion into nonsense. Roughly speaking, in other words, he tended to regard religion from the standpoint of truth and theology from the standpoint of meaning or meaninglessness. In either case, the only valid content he could allow was strictly anthropological.

8. Ludwig Feuerbach, *Das Wesen der Religion* (Lectures 3 & 20, 1848), as quoted in II/1, 292.

9. For example, Rizzuto speaks in one instance of the Devil being "psychologically unnecessary as an existing being. There is nothing to be projected onto mythological reality" (p. 173).

10. Feuerbach, *The Essence of Christianity* (New York: Harper and Brothers, 1957), p. xl.

In responding to Feuerbach, Barth focused more on Feuerbach's question regarding theological meaning than he did on the question about religious truth. He was fond of quoting Feuerbach's statement that "theology long ago became anthropology."[11] Barth, that is to say, took most seriously Feuerbach's challenge to the internal logic of second-order theological schemes. He embraced Feuerbach as a shrewd commentator on the logical vulnerability or untenability of modern theological projects. For by starting with anthropological premises, as so much modern theology seemed to do, it seemed clear to Barth as to Feuerbach that the result could finally only be anthropological conclusions regardless of their theological form. Therefore, Barth adopted as his own project the attempt to construct a theological scheme whose internal logic could not possibly be subject to Feuerbach's critique. Only by starting with strictly theological premises, as received by God's self-revelation in Jesus Christ, could one end up with theological statements whose logic was not reversible and hence whose content was not reducible to anthropology.[12]

If the basis for one's theological statements were found in the projection of images onto the unknown, one could logically reduce those God images, as Feuerbach did, to mere anthropological truths. As anthropological truths, they might not be insignificant; indeed Rizzuto and others have argued that it is precisely as statements about human beings that they derive their importance. But Barth wanted to say something about God, that is, about God's objective identity, and not simply about human projections or human images of God. Barth says, for example, that "Biblical faith lives upon the objectivity of God. . . . It stands or falls with the fact that it is faith in God" (II/1, 13). If one had a basis for speaking about God's actual objective identity, then one's statements about God would not be reducible to statements about human subjectivity. But how does

---

11. Barth, "An Introductory Essay," in Feuerbach, *Essence of Christianity,* p. xix.

12. With regard to the question of religious truth, by the way, Barth did not try to answer Feuerbach directly, because he believed that the living God was perfectly capable of being convincing through God's own self-witness in counterpoint to and along with the faithful proclamation of the church. No rational attempt to prove the truth of Christian religious self-consciousness was therefore either appropriate or necessary. God, as Barth repeatedly insisted, can be known by God alone.

Barth suppose he can make statements about God's objective identity?

It is an axiom of Barth's theology that God is no different in relation to us than he is in himself. Otherwise, God's act of self-revelation would not truly be revelation, that is, it would not disclose God's actual identity. If God in himself is no different from God in relation to us, then we can draw logical inferences about God's actual, objective identity based upon how God is in relation to us. So, for example, if through reading and studying Scripture (the written witness to God's self-revelation as received and transmitted by the church) we discern that God is loving and free in his relation to us, we can then go on to affirm that God is loving and free in himself. This inference is based on the order of discovery. We come to know or discover God as God is in relation to us. Obviously, we cannot know God in any other way. But through that knowledge we can make statements about God's identity apart from us.

Barth then takes the conclusion that God is loving and free in himself and turns it into his premise. Since God in himself is loving and free, God is able to be the same in relation to us. Stated more technically, the condition for the possibility of God's being loving and free in relation to us is precisely that God is loving and free in himself. Barth's premise thus follows the order of being rather than the order of discovery. God as he is in himself thereby becomes the ground of any true statements we might make about God as God is in relation to us. If the ground of our statements about God is thus found in God and not in human experience, then at the formal level Feuerbach's objection to theological language has been overcome.[13] That is

13. Barth is well aware of the magnitude of the "if" clause. If the ground of our statements about God is thus found in God, then we indeed have a basis for theological language that is able to overcome Feuerbach's objections. But a great deal, of course, depends on that "if." If our statements about God are *not* after all grounded in God, then Feuerbach is right; we are at bottom not speaking of God at all but only of ourselves. Barth writes: "It could so easily be an empty movement of thought, that is to say, if, in the movement which regards the knowledge of God, we are really alone and not occupied with God at all but only with ourselves, absolutizing our own nature and being, projecting it onto the infinite, setting up a reflection of our own glory. Carried through in this way, the movement of thought is empty because it is without object. It is a mere game. As far as concerns the knowledge of God it is pure self-deception" (II/1, 71 rev.).

to say, the logic of Barth's theology is such that statements about God cannot logically be reduced to statements about human beings, because the condition for the possibility of God's self-revelation is not conceived as anthropological (for example, not the depths of human self-consciousness, the structure of world history, or some other experiential phenomenon). Therefore, the condition that makes it possible for us to speak about God would ultimately reside in (and only in) God's free decision to reveal to us who God is.

We can now see why Barth is so emphatic in his rejection of the *analogia entis* (analogy of being). The concept of God's freedom is Barth's primary way of designating the divinity of God, in other words, that which makes God to be God. Consequently, the concept of God's freedom is intimately connected with the concept of God's otherness. The idea of *analogia entis* assumes some sort of structure or similarity between God and the created world such that by pondering some creaturely structure one can get some idea of what God is like. No act of self-revelation would be needed for this kind of reasoning to occur, for God would be known and understood by analogy to that which can be rationally discovered about human nature or the wider world. This would be precisely the movement from below to above that Barth's theology disallows and that would be susceptible to the force of Feuerbach's critique (that is, that our notions about God are disguised notions about humanity projected into the unknown).

But Barth rejects the *analogia entis* for other reasons as well. He argues, for example, that the *analogia entis* cannot be justified in light of what the biblical witness says about God's holiness and human sin. How, he asks, could the holy and eternal God attested by Scripture be thought to share a common ontological structure with sinful and finite human beings? Instead of common ground, do we not rather find a gaping chasm between God and humanity, most especially by the facts of sin and death? Barth asks:

> Will not this being of ours be given over to death? Will it not be so questioned that we can be sure only of its not being? And where then is the comparability between his Creator-being and our creature-being, between his holy being and our sinful being, between his eternal being and our temporal being? (II/1, 83)

For Barth the concept of *analogia entis* fails to appreciate the real status of human nature as created and fallen. It fails to acknowledge the radicalness of human sin that only God's grace can overcome.

Barth's emphasis on grace alone means that grace has to create the possibility for us to know God. Instead of the *analogia entis* Barth argues for the *analogia fidei* (analogy of faith). When faith is understood as the human response to God's prior action of grace, then the analogy takes place between two events — the event of God's gracious self-revelation and the event of human faith in response. The correspondence is not, as in the case of the *analogia entis,* between two structures of being but, rather, between two actions, namely, the divine initiative and the human response. Because sin is by definition precisely the human incapacity to affirm God's grace, but because grace is by definition precisely that divine action that overcomes our human incapacity and elicits, invites, and commands our free response, it is in this radical and mysterious sense that the condition for the possibility for our knowing God is grounded in the freedom of divine grace alone.

The knowledge of God as received by faith is understood to be secondary and derivative in the sense that it rests on the foundation of God's own self-knowledge. God is always the subject who knows himself before he is ever known as an object by us. He knows himself (the Father knows the Son, and the Son the Father, in the unity of the Holy Spirit) immediately. But we know God only through a medium, that is, the worldly medium by which God's revelation reaches us. Barth makes an important distinction between God's primary and secondary objectivity. God's primary objectivity is based on the fact that "God is first and foremost objective to himself" (II/1, 16). Apart from us, in God's eternal being as Father, Son, and Holy Spirit, God knows himself. God is manifest in secondary objectivity, on the other hand, when he chooses as a free gift to make himself known to the creature. He makes himself known by using objects in the creaturely sphere to represent him and bear witness to him.

> He is not objective directly, but indirectly, not in the naked sense but clothed under the sign and veil of other objects different from himself. . . . It is in, with and under the sign and veil of these other objects that we believe in God, and know him and pray to him. (II/1, 16)

The creaturely realities that represent God do not thereby cease to be themselves; they do not in any sense become identical with God, but they are used by God to bear witness to himself.[14]

Because God reveals himself through creaturely realities different from himself, God runs the risk of our misunderstanding him. We do not, indeed cannot, know God in the immediate way that he knows himself (primary objectivity), yet we do really know God in the mediated way that he gives himself to be known (secondary objectivity). Because God gives himself to be known in this indirect and mediated way, his self-revelation always entails a kind of concealment or hiddenness. Human beings may see the creaturely signs of God's grace but fail to see the reality of God in, through, and under the signs. "God exposes himself, so to speak, to the danger that human beings will know the work and sign but not himself through the medium of the work or sign" (II/1, 55 rev.).

Knowledge of God is, therefore, always the knowledge of faith, not of sight. Only by faith can a human being perceive the glory of God in the crucified humanity of Jesus. Apart from faith such a perception appears foolish or even outrageous. God is hidden in the very act of revelation. The creaturely object chosen by God to be the medium of God's self-disclosure always functions at the same time as a veil. Even in the incarnation, the quintessential revelation, where God unites with the human nature of Jesus to reveal his deepest identity, there is the danger that we will fail to understand, that God will remain hidden, and that all we will see is the terrible suffering of an isolated human being from Nazareth. Because we experience God's works and signs and not God, we remain subject to all the dangers and ambiguities inherent in subject-object relationships. Barth writes, "Even our faith as such belongs to the veiling and limitation of revelation. Our knowledge of faith itself is the knowledge of God in his hiddenness. It is indirect and mediate, not immediate knowledge" (II/1, 57).

God's primary objectivity (God as he is in himself) is the condition for the possibility of his secondary objectivity (God as he is in relation to us). Knowing God depends not upon us but upon God, upon God's

---

14. For example, concrete events in the life of Israel, the burning bush that Moses beheld, the call of Abraham, the covenant with Noah, etc. See II/1, 19.

free decision to reveal himself. Faith depends upon God's prior action of grace. Barth writes: "Everything depends on the fact that God does not cease to bear witness to himself. What would become of this knowledge if it were not continually renewed and re-established by its object?" (II/1, 23-24). It is in this sense that Barth can say that "God is known by God alone." Human beings have no capacity for faith apart from God's self-revealing grace. The human capacity to know God "cannot finally be grounded in itself" (II/1, 65) but must be grounded in God.

Definitions: Theological Adequacy and Psychological Functionality

Rizzuto's psychoanalytic method, based on a clinical study of observable data, is self-consciously "phenomenological" in the sense that it deals with material susceptible of psycho-social explanation and description.[15] The theory she creates on the basis of her observations is limited to understanding the phenomena of human images of God and the thoughts and feelings that accompany these images.[16] Rizzuto's work does not represent a theory about God or about knowledge of God as an extrapsychic or transcendent and objective reality. Rizzuto is clear about the limits of her method. Insisting that hers is "not a book on religion" (Rizzuto, pp. 3, 177), she also writes:

> Questions about the actual existence of God do not pertain here. My method enables me to deal only with psychic experiences. Logic does not permit me to go beyond a psychological level of inference. . . . As a researcher I will not make pronouncements appropriate for philosophers and theologians. My only obligation is to respect the phenomenon and its pristine manifestations. (Rizzuto, p. 4)

15. I am using the term "phenomenological" in the ordinary sense of the word and not in the technical sense referring to the philosophical movement of phenomenology.

16. "Theory is a tool, a shorthand, a vocabulary, to identify an aspect of human perception for oneself and for others. It does not create entities whether they are called self or God. Theory provides a way of talking about observable phenomena in order to understand them" (Rizzuto, p. 11).

Barth's theological method, on the other hand, based on the biblical witness to God's self-revelation in Jesus Christ, is self-consciously theological in the sense that it deals with material that extends or lies beyond the limits of ordinary experience. Although God may choose to reveal himself through ordinary human phenomena such as Rizzuto describes, one cannot perceive or know about such a revelation merely on the basis of the phenomena themselves. Such a perception or insight comes from beyond what is intrinsic to the phenomena or experience — in particular, from God's grace. Even the biblical witness is a mere human book (a phenomenon to be studied) apart from the transcendent work of the Holy Spirit awakening faith in the reader.

Given such manifestly divergent basic assumptions, frames of reference, and purposes, how might the concerns of Barth and Rizzuto perhaps be brought into conceptual relationship? Both Barth and Rizzuto are concerned about belief in God, but can it be said that they are concerned about the same thing? Are they describing the same thing (belief in God) merely from two different perspectives or are they describing two different things altogether? Rizzuto's findings on the psychic origin and function of the God representation could be an accurate description of the kind of historical or developmental process human beings happen to go through, but, by virtue of its limited or delimited methodological orientation, it cannot tell us the extent to which this process might actually have anything to do with God, when God is understood to be the transcendent God of the biblical witness. Only theology can do that on the basis of faith.[17]

One way to relate Barth's and Rizzuto's concerns would be to

17. "Psychology, philosophy and theology may all be concerned with the same phenomenon, such as a particular belief or a particular ritual, but they ask different questions about the phenomenon. Psychological analysis is concerned with the psychological development and the function of the belief or ritual. Theology is concerned with the correspondence between the belief or ritual and . . . such criteria as the will of God and other norms of faith. The answers to the psychological questions do not necessarily imply or presuppose answers to the philosophical or theological questions. Even a thorough assessment of the psychological history and functions of a particular belief carries no ordinary implications for the 'truth' or 'faithfulness' of the belief; these still must be ascertained by the criteria appropriate to philosophy and theology" (James E. Dittes, "Religion: Psychological Study," in *International Encyclopedia of the Social Sciences,* vol. 13, ed. David L. Sills [New York: Macmillan and the Free Press, 1968], p. 416).

focus on their implicit or explicit normative frameworks. A central though implicit norm in Rizzuto's study is that of psychological functionality. Does the God representation enable the individual to maintain emotional equilibrium and balance? Does it help stabilize one's sense of self and one's interpersonal relationships? Does it provide a source of meaning, security, and self-esteem? A central norm for Barth would be that of theological adequacy. Does the God representation conform to the picture of God in Christ as given in the New Testament? Under what circumstances might God use a person's God representation to convey real knowledge of God? What is the relationship between a theologically adequate God representation and God's gift of faith?

Clearly, at least from a Barthian perspective, one would have to say that the norms of psychological functionality and those of theological adequacy of a God representation are two quite different matters. It is theoretically possible, for instance, that a God representation might be demonstrably functional in terms of preserving an individual's psychic balance but still have little to do with the God revealed in the Bible. A psychologist might accurately describe the entire process of creating and transforming a God representation for the purpose of furthering psychic health, but this process would not necessarily say anything about the theological adequacy of the resulting images. The theologian's question might be, what possible relationships can exist between any given God representation and the picture of God given in the witness of Scripture? Logically speaking, any particular God image could be either psychologically functional or dysfunctional as well as either theologically adequate or inadequate. I now want to explore the possible range of options suggested by these distinctions, but my terms must first be defined more precisely.

How Would Barth Test Theological Adequacy?

The first criterion of adequacy for any particular God representation would, in Barth's theology, be its congruence with the image of Christ as the true image of God. Barth's christological concentration requires that the various pictures of God in the Bible be interpreted in light of the Christ-event. An example of how Barth takes this material as a key to theological adequacy appears in his argument that God is distinguished from all false gods by his act of self-humiliation. Although Lord, God becomes servant. Although eternal, God becomes subject to human flesh and, therefore, to human time and suffering. In Jesus Christ God humbles himself and becomes human, taking on our sin and suffering on our behalf and for our sakes. False gods, by contrast, it is argued, are never satisfied to serve but strive mightily to glorify themselves. They are all "reflections of a false and all-too-human self exaltation. They are lords who cannot and will not be servants, who are therefore no true lords, whose being is not a truly divine being" (II/1, 25). Because by faith Christians proclaim that God's deepest identity is disclosed in the incarnation, death, and resurrection of Jesus Christ, the biblical stories about him are the source of their knowledge of God's true image. One basic theological question about any given God representation would, therefore, be to what degree it corresponds to or is congruent with that picture as given by the New Testament.

From this point of view, a second criterion of theological adequacy would be that no human God representation can possibly be adequate in itself, not even the most biblical or christological. Like the human beings who created them, our God representations as such remain *simul iustus et peccator* and, therefore, need in some sense to be justified by grace alone. If God is known through God alone, it is God's activity and not our own that makes knowledge of God possible. Our God representations may perhaps approximate God's identity closely. We may perhaps have an internalized image of God that has been shaped by a profound engagement with Scripture, that has been further refined through prayer and Christian fellowship, and that has been tested beyond all these by doubt and suffering. This God representation may even perhaps be operative on deep unconscious levels, motivating and moving us in ways that we are not fully aware. Even so, in itself, such a God representation will nonetheless fall short of God's singular identity. Revelation in Barth's sense cannot be "housed" by the human psyche or by anything human. It remains an incomprehensible event that can be received ever anew only insofar as God acts. Our human creations will always stand in need of renewal and transformation by God.

Any particular God representation, however, could conceivably act as a "little light," that is, as a genuine witness to and reflection of the great light that shines in Jesus Christ. As a little light it would function as a parable of grace. Having no independent revelatory status of its own, it would still be recognizable as light by its congruence with God's revelation in Jesus Christ. These "little lights," as Barth sometimes calls them, would in some sense be instances of God's secondary objectivity — those creaturely objects other than God that God uses to bear witness to himself despite their intrinsic inadequacy. If God can use anything in the world as a witness, including secular movements or realities unconnected with the church, then even our psychologically generated God representations might, under certain circumstances, turn out to be one of those little lights or parables of grace. But according to Barth, the church would be able to see and understand it as such only in light of what is known of God through Scripture. To the extent that our internalized God representations are actually incongruent with the image of God as given in Scripture, they cannot be said to reflect reliable knowledge of God. But to the extent that they do turn out to be congruent, our psychologically derived God representations could be accorded the status of "witnesses," that is, instances in some sense of God's secondary objectivity (and, therefore, not merely psychologically derived). But this could be discerned only from the standpoint of faith as informed by Scripture (IV/3, 110-53).[18]

On Barthian premises, in other words, it should not be impossible for God to work through ordinary human parents in such a way that for all their limitations they become parables of grace for the child. The children of such parents might, through the normal psychic processes of object introjection and projection, internalize an unconscious picture of God not entirely dissimilar to what one finds in the New Testament. To extend the earlier example regarding the humility and servanthood of God, such parents might to some extent be wise and loving. Despite their objective power and authority, they would nonetheless at times give selflessly to their children and serve them humbly. To one degree or another, they might then consciously or

18. For a detailed discussion of this passage in Barth, see George Hunsinger on "Secular Parables of the Truth" in *How to Read Karl Barth: The Shape of His Theology* (New York: Oxford University Press, 1991), pp. 234-80.

unconsciously become genuine witnesses to God's grace, true little lights. They might thus directly or indirectly impart genuine knowledge of God — not ultimately, Barth might add, through their own action but through God's. Barth might remind us, however, that no matter how wise or loving the human parents, they would nonetheless in their own way be subject to the reality and power of sin and would, therefore, inevitably fall short of adequately reflecting God's real identity. Any picture created in this way in the child would, like all internalized pictures of God, necessarily stand in need of ongoing transformation by grace.

How Would Rizzuto Test Psychological Functionality?

A functional God representation would, on Rizzuto's premises, be one that is psychically useful for the total personality. At its best it would provide a vital "source of self-esteem, love and feelings of security" (Rizzuto, p. 32). Its primary function, according to Rizzuto, is in keeping the individual's sense of self in balance through its intimate connection to primary objects — both internal and external (Rizzuto, p. 52). That is to say, the God representation functions to enable one to relate both to one's internalized objects and to the external people with whom one is in relationship. For example, if one's mother were experienced as wholly loving and giving, the God representation might be used as an object to receive one's hidden ambivalence or the aggressive impulses that felt unacceptable in relation to the mother. In this instance the God representation would enable the person to maintain the internal image of the mother as all loving and also to stay in relation to the actual objective mother. Here one might suspect that the external mother had an emotional need to be seen in this way and deflected the child's aggressive impulses. It is the God representation that would enable the child to maintain its internal balance and external relationship by compensating for extremely one-sided attitudes as they have developed in relation to the mother.

The God representation can function in both an adaptive and a defensive manner. In some cases what gets projected onto God are all those characteristics that are impossible to deal with in the parent (through the defense mechanism of displacement). In the previous example, anger and aggression were not accepted in the parent-child relationship and so were displaced onto God. In other cases "God" might become the opposite of everything the parent represents (through the defense mechanism of reaction-formation). For example, a man may have an emotional need to see God as infinitely compassionate precisely because his father was emotionally cold and distant. Such a maneuver could be seen as defensive because it serves to protect the son from the pain of never having known "fatherly compassion." But it might also function in an adaptive manner because the representation would provide him with the image of a good father, which in turn might enable him to relate positively to male authority figures, giving him a sense of possibility and hope. The crucial point is that each person works out his or her own way of putting "God" together based on emotional needs. Clearly, there are as many possibilities for God's identity as there are people who form God representations. One can readily see that through the defense mechanisms of denial, reaction-formation, idealization, and displacement alone, any number of possibilities could evolve. Even siblings with the same parents and home environment could produce vastly different God representations, though perhaps many of the same important emotional themes would be present in their respective pictures.

A functional God representation would be one that is capable of being reworked and transformed throughout the course of life. With each new developmental stage or life crisis, the needs of the individual change. Therefore the God representation would also need to change to keep the dynamic balance of the self. Rizzuto imaginatively engages Erikson's developmental scheme from infancy to old age by reflecting upon what kind of God representation might lead to belief or unbelief at each stage (Rizzuto, pp. 206-7). For instance, at the level of trust versus mistrust (oral stage) a positive God representation would be developed on the basis of a person's experience of being tenderly but securely held, fed, and nurtured and in which there was adequate mirroring by the parent figure. A God representation leading to unbelief would be developed where the individual has experienced an absence of holding, feeding, and caring and where there was little experience of being reflected by another. An absence rather than a presence would be the decisive factor. (Of course, through the defense mechanisms of denial or reaction-formation the person might "believe in God" all the more tenaciously.) Rizzuto traces the changes that might take place in the God representation over time as various stages become of paramount developmental importance (for example, autonomy, initiative, identity, intimacy, generativity, etc.).

What, then, would be a "dysfunctional" God representation? A dysfunctional God representation would be one that undermines the person's sense of self-esteem, bringing about personal insecurity and feelings of anxiety and hopelessness. In some cases the development of the God representation becomes fixed at an early stage in such a way as to render it dysfunctional. (Rizzuto suggests that Freud himself halted the elaboration of his God representation at age two, a process which, she says, "prevented him from reaching the depth of maturity in that area of human experience he achieved in others"; Rizzuto, p. 229.) In these cases the God representation is usually repressed and is prevented from further elaboration because it is too painful or anxiety-provoking for one to acknowledge consciously. Rizzuto comments that "the God representation may become so incompatible for psychic balance that it cannot function naturally as a transitional object; along with aspects of oneself that have become consciously unbearable, it may have to be repressed" (Rizzuto, p. 202). A repressed God representation might provide some temporary measure of stability, but in the long run it could grow in destructive power by not being in relationship with the person's conscious, acting, feeling ego. Such an inner split would be particularly dangerous during life crises when the God representation is activated.

One difficulty in describing a dysfunctional God representation lies in the fact that any God representation, no matter how apparently dysfunctional, does serve some crucial emotional need and is, therefore, in some way vitally functional. At first glance it might appear that a person's God representation only causes great upheavals of terror or intense feelings of guilt or shame. Surely such an image of God would seem to be dysfunctional. But if one were to look at the precise function of the image for the entire personality, one might find that even such a picture of God functions meaningfully. In a vivid and poignant example, Rizzuto describes a woman whose central emotional need was to protect her idealized image of her mother

(Rizzuto, chap. 9). The image preserved her deepest hope that one day her mother would love her. She was thus completely unconscious of how much she feared her mother. This fear seemed to be displaced onto God. "God" thereby became a terrifying and unapproachable figure. If one were to look only at the God representation, one could not imagine how it could in any way be functional. Although apparently dysfunctional in the extreme, it nevertheless functioned to preserve her picture of her mother as one who was loving, even though she never demonstrated that love to her daughter.

Even an apparently dysfunctional God representation may thus provide a measure of homeostasis in the personality. If the person has neurotic needs, the God representation may function homeostatically to preserve patterns that are neurotic. From the point of view of psychic health, the God representation is dysfunctional, but from the point of view of securing a precarious emotional balance, it may provide a crucial function for the personality.

To sum up, it is apparent that, from a Barthian standpoint, questions about the theological adequacy of our God representations can be answered only within a theological framework and that questions about their psychic function are quite distinct. Three criteria have been identified by which theological adequacy (as so understood) might be tested. First, any God representation would need to be interpreted in light of the Christ-event. Second, our God representations, no matter how congruent with Scripture, would nevertheless stand in continual need of renewal by God. Finally, our God representations could conceivably be used by God as witnesses to God in a kind of "parable of grace." But their assessment would be possible only from the standpoint of faith as informed by Scripture.

As explained by Rizzuto, on the other hand, a God representation may be found to be psychologically functional whenever it provides the individual with a source of self-esteem, love, and security. A well-functioning God representation is able to provide a unique kind of homeostasis by interacting symbolically with significant internalized objects. It may be used both adaptively and defensively. A psychologically functional God representation, moreover, is capable of being reworked throughout the life-cycle, keeping the self in dynamic balance as life issues change. Even an apparently dysfunctional God representation, it was shown, might serve some crucial emotional need and could thus be assessed as functional in some limited way.

Possible Relationships Between Theological and Psychological Norms: Four Classifications

If we assume that the norms of each field, psychology and theology, are derived through the methods of their own disciplines and are meaningful primarily in their own context, then how might these norms be related? It seems clear that any particular God representation could be viewed from the perspective of both disciplines respectively. For any given God representation, therefore, various possibilities would exist for relating the two sets of norms. A logical classification can be seen in the table on page 131.

1. Psychologically Functional; Theologically Adequate

For Rizzuto, a psychologically functional God representation would be one that is reshaped throughout life according to one's concrete emotional needs in the context of one's interpersonal relationships. For Barth, a theologically adequate God representation would be one that is congruent with the biblical depiction of Christ and that is actively shaped and transformed by the mysterious work of the Holy Spirit. It is conceivable that a given individual's God representation could be both psychologically functional and theologically adequate.

Rizzuto has described how one might acquire a psychologically functional God representation, but how might one acquire a God representation that was also theologically adequate? Rizzuto's description of the origin and development of the God representation focuses on the process of parental object internalization. While she acknowledges the "wider context" (for example, "family, social class, organized religion, and particular subcultures") as contributing to the shape of the God representation, her delimited psychological method does not allow her to take it into account (Rizzuto, p. 209). Hence she does not ask about the specific contribution that religious education or religious conversion (the two shaping factors most often cited by traditional

Theological Norm (Θ)

	Adequate	Inadequate
Functional	#1 Ψ Functional Θ Adequate	#2 Ψ Functional Θ Inadequate
Dysfunctional	#3 Ψ Dysfunctional Θ Adequate	#4 Ψ Dysfunctional Θ Inadequate

Psychological Norm (Ψ)

belief) might make to the final contours of the God representation. Like Freud, she assumes that the unconscious God image is largely formed before one begins formal religious training and that such education, being largely conceptual, affects only one's conscious religious commitments and not the deeper, unconscious, "living" image of God.[19] The relative absence of any significant religious education or formation among her patients is, indeed, quite striking. Some of the patients she describes seem to have had at least a tenuous connection to church or synagogue, but nothing indicates any ongoing education and important emotional involvement in a religious community.

Involvement in such a community could presumably foster the shaping and reshaping of a theologically adequate God representation. There are, theologically speaking, three ways in which such a process might take place: Christian nurture, conversion, and sanctification. By "Christian nurture," I mean the ongoing and perhaps lifelong involvement of a person in a Christian community with its web of interpersonal

---

19. "If Freud's formulation is correct, the transformation produced in the image by formal religious education can only be added to a representation of God that has already been formed. Religious education will not contribute essentially to the creation of the image" (Rizzuto, p. 9). "The concept of God is fabricated mostly at a level of secondary process thinking. This is the God of the theologians, the God whose existence or non-existence is debated by metaphysical reasoning. But this God leaves us cold" (Rizzuto, p. 48).

relationships, its reading and study of Scripture, its regular gathering for worship and fellowship, and its personal and corporate life of prayer. By "conversion," I mean a more dramatic and sudden decision to follow Christ, which comes as the result of a meaningful chain of events where God is felt to be the hidden author. By "sanctification," I mean the mysterious and transcendent work of the Holy Spirit by which Christians hope to be transformed into the image of Christ.

Central to the process of Christian nurture would be one's knowledge and internalization of Scripture. As already noted, George Lindbeck has described what it means to become a Christian as the process of becoming skilled in the language or symbol system of the Christian faith. "To become a Christian," he suggests, "involves learning the story of Israel and of Jesus well enough to interpret and to experience oneself . . . in its terms. A religion is above all an external word . . . that molds and shapes the self and its world."[20] By limiting herself to the role of parental object relations in the formation of an internal image of God, Rizzuto bypasses this "external word" and its possible role in shaping and reshaping a person's image of God.[21]

Even a very small child's imagination could be captured by the vivid images and stories of the Bible. There is no reason why these images would necessarily involve only conscious processes or just conceptual thought. On the contrary, why shouldn't biblical stories, with their emotionally charged dramas, have the potential of activating all levels of the personality, both conscious and unconscious? The psychological process of internalizing biblical images need not be a matter of abstract reasoning but could involve a process similar to that which Rizzuto describes in the introjection of parental characteristics, only what would now be introjected would be images of God as they develop in the context of the biblical story. Moreover, the Bible would not be encountered in a vacuum but in the context of significant interpersonal relationships. It is

20. George A. Lindbeck, *The Nature of Doctrine: Religion and Theology in a Postliberal Age* (Philadelphia: Fortress, 1984), p. 34.

21. The decision to ignore the texts that can shape belief is what Paul Ricoeur has judged to be "Freud's greatest shortcoming in his theory of religion." Ricoeur considers it "impossible to construct a psychoanalysis of belief apart from an interpretation and understanding of the cultural productions in which the object of belief announces itself" (Paul Ricoeur, *Freud and Philosophy: An Essay on Interpretation* [New Haven: Yale University Press, 1970], p. 544).

conceivable that these relationships might also contribute to the final shape of the God representation. Why shouldn't a continual process of projecting and introjecting images be at work as the small child is nurtured to learn the biblical story and ponder its meaning?

Even if the child's God representation were completely formed before he or she received any religious education, why shouldn't an encounter with the Bible have the potential for altering those images? One can conceive that in some cases a person would be faced with two conflicting sets of images: those based on images related to the personal parents and those based on the biblical stories.[22] The images might be similar or widely different from one another, but one supposes that the biblical themes and images that were felt to be important would, at least at first, be closely related to the significant emotional themes in the early family environment. The process of acquiring a God representation that was both psychologically functional and theologically adequate might arise out of the creative ferment of the conflicting images. Those who take seriously the biblical injunctions against idolatry would be prepared at least to question basic assumptions about God on the basis of what the Bible tells us about God's identity.

A second and closely related way in which one's image of God might possibly come to be conformed to the biblical depiction of Christ, and thus be considered theologically adequate, would be through what is sometimes called "conversion." If Christian nurture represents a model of organic change centered on, but certainly not limited to, knowledge of Scripture, then conversion represents a model of more dramatic or sudden change. Obviously in the life of faith both factors might in various ways be involved. Conversion might precede but would not thereafter substitute for nurture, and nurture could perhaps be described as an ongoing process of conversion.

---

22. Rizzuto has some astute comments on those cases where the private and "official" God are in conflict. "The individual's private and unconscious process of forming that representation, however, may not coincide with the God offered by official religion. In that case, the private and the official God provide endless potential for maladaptation and for raising family tragedies to a cosmic level." In other cases the idiosyncratic private God and the God offered by church or synagogue are more integrated. "If the private and the official God are sufficiently well-integrated, religion may also be a lasting source of self-respect and ego-syntonic replenishment for meeting human needs at any level of development" (p. 90).

Rizzuto has a fascinating discussion of "conversion experience" from a psychoanalytic point of view. She thinks of it as the "de-repression" of a previously acquired God representation that suddenly takes on a new meaning in light of emotionally significant changes in the self or the environment. In other words, the God representation has been repressed for some psychologically important reason. In the experience of conversion, the image emerges dramatically from the unconscious. The image, heretofore repressed, feels intimately familiar, based as it is on significant themes and images from early childhood. This strange familiarity is accompanied by a compulsive feeling; the image cannot be resisted. Or as Freud says and Rizzuto reiterates, "It *must* be believed" (Rizzuto, p. 51).

From a Barthian theological perspective, the hidden author of any true conversion experience (as well as of any true Christian nurture) would be the Spirit of God. Rizzuto has described conversion in a way that emphasizes its psychological function. But how would one know if the resulting image with its compelling character had anything to do with what Christians mean when they talk about conversion to Christ? From a merely phenomenological or psychological standpoint, one could not know whether any dramatic and life-enhancing change would be "conversion" in the theological sense or not. Theological assessment of the experience would have to take place over time, requiring that one take into account the congruence (or lack of it) of one's new God representation and total form of life with the biblical depiction of Christ.

"Sanctification," as the work of the Holy Spirit, would be the strictly transcendent dimension to both nurturance and conversion. If God uses ordinary human beings and concrete historical experiences to give knowledge of God, one could know this only through faith. In other words, it is only from within the circle of faith that it would make sense to speak of one's God images becoming true images of the true God. The process of sanctification, by which (among other things) one's God image came truly to reflect God and in which one's self became conformed to the image of Christ, would be a hidden process perceptible only by faith. Faith, as Barth suggests, would enable one to affirm the invisible work of God, forming and transforming one's images and thoughts about God.

> As such our images of perception, thought and words neither are nor
> can be images of God. They become this. They become truth. But
> they do not do so of themselves; they do it wholly and utterly from
> their object, not by their own capacity but by that of their object. . . .
> The capacity to know and therefore to view and conceive God cannot
> be reinterpreted as a human capacity but only understood as a divine
> gift. (II/1, 194 and 196 rev.)

In other words, a theologically adequate God representation
would come only as a wonderful, mysterious, and transcendent gift.
It would be one that undergoes a continuous process of reshaping or
transformation initiated and guided by the Holy Spirit. It would not
become or remain adequate without God's ongoing self-witness as
known and attested within the context of the ongoing practices of the
community of faith. Therefore, faith would never be something that
one simply has or possesses. It would, rather, be something continually
given anew as God acts to disclose and confirm God's identity.

It might be noted again that in his work as a dogmatic theologian,
Barth was not interested in phenomenological descriptions of the
process of coming to faith from an anthropological perspective. His
interest was rather in describing (not "explaining") from within the
circle of faith what it means to have faith in God and who God is
based on his self-revelation in Jesus Christ through the witness of
Scripture. He, therefore, would not have assumed that he and Rizzuto
could occupy some sort of "neutral territory" by which each could
disinterestedly explain the phenomenon of acquiring a God representation from their own methodological or substantive perspective. It is
not that a phenomenological account would necessarily be somehow
insufficient or problematic in itself but, rather, that any phenomenological explanation, by definition, excludes God's action, which understood properly is transcendent. Barth did not suppose that there
were no phenomenal correlates to faith. Rather, he supposed that no
such correlates had privileged status in the sense of being indispensable to faith and that all such correlates in themselves were fundamentally ambiguous when experientially confirming or demon-
strating faith. He would, therefore, have no objection in principle to
Rizzuto's phenomenological description of the psychological origins,
development, and transformation of God representations. He would,

however, consider that nothing yet had necessarily been said about God or about the divine action that makes knowledge of God possible. From Barth's perspective the attitude of faith must be assumed as the ground upon which the theologian stands and from which he or she can make comments about coming to faith and acquiring a sense of God's true identity.

2. Psychologically Functional; Theologically Inadequate

Perhaps the vast majority of Rizzuto's vivid examples would fall into this category — images of God that help one's emotional equilibrium but that have little to do with the picture of God in Christ as given by the witness of Scripture. A God representation of this sort might raise questions for both the psychologist and the theologian, but their concerns would be decidedly different. The psychologist would be concerned about the emotional health and stability of the individual. Hence the psychologist might be concerned about any attempt to impose a theologically "orthodox" standard on a person who already has a well-functioning and personally meaningful God representation. If the God image functions well, providing a sense of security and enabling one to relate to one's significant others, then why impose any other criteria of theological adequacy? Couldn't one inflict considerable emotional damage by trying to change a God representation into one more acceptable from a theological perspective? On the other hand, the theologian might be concerned that if one were to subordinate one's criteria for adequacy to one's concern for functionality, then one would become subject to unqualified relativism. Any sort of God representation would do so long as it was psychologically functional. Certainly Barth's concern for the objectivity and particular identity of God in Christ would not be adequately met by a solution that allows for just any "well-functioning" image of God. God or belief in God would in that case become a mere function of the human personality — the very conclusion Barth strove most strenuously to avoid.

Rizzuto is, in fact, concerned about the emotional damage that religious people might do in their zeal to change people's images of God into theologically more acceptable ones. She explicitly warns against intrusive efforts to change God representations that are perceived as inadequate from a theological perspective. She feels that such people may not fully appreciate the crucial emotional function that the "distorted" picture of God serves. Rizzuto considers some such efforts as tantamount to emotional violation or manipulation. She is vitally concerned that educators, pastors, and parents appreciate the concrete needs that the God representation serves. She says, "Trying to change a child's 'distorted' God into a more 'normal' one could amount to a violation and manipulation of the child's private world." In another context she warns: "If a religious zealot were to try to give this man a direct experience of God, he could, I propose, precipitate a psychotic break" (Rizzuto, p. 134). This particular individual had created a God representation based on the image of his father, a sadistic, persecuting man who repeatedly transgressed important psychic boundaries, violating his son's integral sense of self. Hence the son's atheism became an emotionally indispensable measure for giving him a sense of safety and security.

Given this sort of situation, where one has a God representation that is psychologically functional but theologically inadequate, what role might the church play in bringing about the ideal combination in which functionality is joined with adequacy? Are there cases where the two norms are destined to be in tragic conflict with each other?

Perhaps in some instances there are. The particular circumstances of a person's life might make it psychologically necessary that God be pictured in a certain theologically inadequate way. But given Barth's particular theological perspective, the church would at least be released from the kind of zealous intervention that Rizzuto fears. That is to say, if the church believes God's active self-revelation brings about transformation, then the church's role remains the more modest one of witness. The work of the church would not be understood as giving someone "a direct experience of God" but, rather, providing the conditions (insofar as is possible from the human side) for Christian nurture, conversion, and sanctification: Scripture, prayer, fellowship, worship. In, with, and under the simple act of human witness, God may bear witness to himself:

> Where between one human being and another there is real communication of the report of what took place in [Jesus Christ] and through him, he himself is there and at work, he himself makes

himself to be recognized and acknowledged. . . . He himself is present as actuality, as his own witness. (IV/1, 17 rev.)

The ministry of pastoral counseling would perhaps provide a
setting where both the psychological and theological concerns could
be respected.[23] As one trained in psychology, the pastoral counselor
could discern and appreciate the important emotional function that
the theologically "distorted" God representation plays. As one trained
in theology, the pastoral counselor would also have an appreciation
for what sorts of images correspond to or diverge from biblical images
and conceptions of God. The pastoral counselor with such a dual
focus would be equipped for the task of helping to sort out the various
images and their meanings.

One could thus use the pastoral counseling setting to examine the
counselee's expectations, wishes, and needs as they relate to the counselee's images of God. With proper care one could explicitly examine
the parallels and discontinuities that might exist between meaningful
God images and internalized parent-images. Rizzuto's implicitly reductive analysis, which assumes a direct correlation between the two
sets of images, could be illuminating in this context. By tracing the
close correlation, an individual could perhaps be led to see how he or
she has projected certain characteristics onto God, expecting from God
similar (or, through various defenses, opposite) responses to those
received from early childhood caretakers. In this way he or she might
get a sense for why "God" needs to be imaged in a particular way.

Seeing the correlations between the counselee's early childhood
experiences of primary relationships and the person's expectations of
God might bring him or her to conclude, as Freud did, that God is
simply an illusion and that one's "relationship" to God is nothing
other than a relationship to parts of the self that have not yet been
acknowledged. What one has called "God" would be nothing other
than one's projections, based on deep wishes, needs, or longings.

In other instances one might opt for a more agnostic stance concerning God's actual objective identity, saying in effect that precisely
insofar as "God" is indeed a projection, "God" carries emotional

---

23. See the review of Rizzuto's book by Ann Belford Ulanov in *Union Seminary
Quarterly Review* 36 (1981): 173-76.

clusters of meaning that need recognition. Like Rizzuto, one might not address the question of an objective God but, rather, find value in one's imaginative and meaningful "illusions" about ultimate reality.

A third possibility would be that which might lead to faith. Having seen how one's wishes and needs contribute significantly to one's image of God, one might begin to wonder about God's identity apart from one's projections. If God is not what one had expected, how can one find out what God is like? Like Barth, one might be led to ask about God's objective identity apart from any anthropological projections. One might turn to the Bible for knowledge of God based on God's own self-revelation.

While the pastoral counselor, as a minister of the church, might represent the third option, he or she could nevertheless encourage the free exploration of options one and two with any counselee. Knowing that in some sense one can never escape from one's own subjective standpoint into an objective or transcendental vantage point, the pastoral counselor also knows that a person's projections will inevitably color perceptions or images of God, no matter how biblically based. Precisely which biblical images become personally meaningful may have much to do with the deep suffering, longing, and desire of early childhood, which Rizzuto so poignantly describes. From a pastoral counseling or "bilingual" point of view, psychologically derived and biblically derived images of God can often be perceived as existing in and with one another, capable of being distinguished but not finally separable from each other.

When a person has a God representation that is psychologically functional but theologically inadequate, a dilemma arises. Should things be left just as they are, since in some sense the God image functions well, preserving emotional stability and furthering interpersonal relationships? Or should one attempt to bring about a more theologically adequate image? If one values both psychological health and the claims of biblical faith, then one will not want to forsake the norms of one field for the sake of the other but try as much as possible to remain true to both, recognizing all the while that the resolution of such dilemmas is finally beyond one's own control.

3. Psychologically Dysfunctional; Theologically Adequate

Are certain theologically adequate images of God intrinsically dysfunctional psychologically, or is it only that they sometimes happen to be used in dysfunctional ways? Psychologists of religion, among others, have often chosen certain central themes or images from Christian belief and have argued for their intrinsic dysfunctionality in the emotional development of individuals.[24] Freud, for instance, argues forcefully that the biblical image of God the Father is intrinsically dysfunctional.[25] Much of his polemic against religion was based upon the judgment that religion (that is, belief in God *as* Father) kept adults neurotic and immature. If the essence of religion were the unconscious projection of the oedipal conflict, as Freud believed, then the religious believer forever remained a child emotionally. God the Father would protect the child from feelings of helplessness in the face of evil and death in exchange for the child's devoted obedience to God's authority. The guilt the child felt over secretly wanting to usurp the father (the oedipal conflict) was dealt with obsessively, through repeated acts of confession, prayer, and penance. Such guilt was never assuaged, however, because its source in the person's instinctual wishes (sexual and aggressive) remained unconscious. The real wishes, never directly faced or acknowledged, gained in power, as repressed wishes do. Thus the believer lived in continual, anxious expectation about how to appease God. The believer never took responsibility for his or her true feelings and wishes, remaining in the position of the helpless child striving to live up to the expectations and demands of the parental authority figure.[26]

Rizzuto's investigation of people's God images led her to conclude

24. Two instances that come readily to mind are Freud's discussion of the father image and Jung on the Trinity.

25. The image of God the Father would, from Barth's perspective, have to be considered a theologically adequate image. Barth writes: "God is first of all Father. He is Father in himself, by nature and in eternity and then following on that, for us as well, his creatures" (Barth, *Dogmatics in Outline* [New York: Harper and Row, 1959], p. 43).

26. See Freud, "Obsessive Acts and Religious Practices" in *Character and Culture* (New York: Macmillan, 1963), pp. 17-26. See also Freud, *The Future of an Illusion* (New York: Doubleday, 1964).

that one cannot legitimately make such generalized statements about any image's intrinsic dysfunctionality (Rizzuto, p. 72). For one person an image of God as Father could be very functional, where for example there was a positive, mature relationship with the person's father. In another person, however, such a father-image would only exact high costs in stress and anxiety, where for example the father was more authoritarian and unyielding, as in Freud's description of the typical oedipal situation. The important factor, Rizzuto argues, is not the image itself but how the image is used in any particular, concrete situation.

Of course, neither Freud nor Rizzuto deals with the specifically biblical image of God as Father and the contribution it might make to the shaping of a person's God image. From a theological perspective, Freud's theory of the father-image could arguably be interpreted as a personification of the Law without the gospel. The father is seen to be a stern master and judge, continually threatening punishment for the child's wayward desires and behavior. Such a picture of God, the argument might run, is far removed from what the New Testament means to convey about God's identity as Father. Barth believed that if images of God "are to be heard in New Testament terms, they need to be elucidated according to the context of the New Testament message."[27] Thus Barth takes it for granted that the biblical meaning of the fatherhood of God, as seen in Jesus Christ, is actually God's fatherly goodness.

> God is Father because and insofar as Jesus Christ is his Son and he is the Father of Jesus Christ. Alongside this statement there is, as a rule, little need to lay special stress on the Father's love, goodness, grace and so forth since it contains within itself all that need be said about the character of the divine Creator and Father as the fount and origin of all good things.[28]

On the basis of his clinical experiences, Freud, apparently taking a central biblical image out of context, has drawn it into his own rather different context, drawing conclusions on the basis of premises quite foreign to the biblical description of God. Perhaps there is nothing

27. Barth, *The Christian Life* (Grand Rapids: Eerdmans, 1981), p. 58.
28. Barth, *Christian Life,* pp. 59-60.

theology and church can do to prevent such use of its ideas and images apart from showing whether an idea or image has been properly understood from its own perspective. In this way it would be possible to distinguish between use and abuse of the image of God as Father and to suggest that there is nothing intrinsic to the image itself that necessarily causes it to be used for emotionally destructive ends.

Freud's clinically based observations about the father-image may well suggest the kind of primary process or associative thinking that people sometimes bring to the reading and study of Scripture. Thus when reading about God as Father, one's own personal father might be evoked, if not consciously, then certainly unconsciously. In the process of bringing one's personal associations to the text, one's own complexes might be activated. Thus a narcissistic person might use Christian beliefs and images in a way that furthers the narcissism. A masochistic person might be drawn to selected themes (such as Christ as sacrificial victim) that reinforce fundamental feelings of vulnerability and helplessness. And so on. In this way one might find wholesale use of biblical themes and images that have definite dysfunctional effects.[29]

From the standpoint of Christian faith, one would assume that theological adequacy would promote psychological functionality in an emotionally healthy person. Christians believe that a commitment to Christ brings abundance of life but would want to interpret this "abundance" primarily from the perspective of faith, not simply in accord with contemporary canons of psychological health. In other words, the psychological concept of health would be subordinated here to the theological norm of "abundant life" (that is, by virtue of the asymmetry in the Chalcedonian pattern). Christian commitment may have more to do with shared suffering and sacrifice than with undergoing "peak experiences." One can imagine particular theologically significant images of God (such as Christ dying on the cross) as seeming starkly dysfunctional by some standards of mental health.

Pastoral counseling as a ministry of the church, however, would not want to discard a biblical image completely simply because it appeared dysfunctional in some cases as seen from some outside

29. See for example Paul Pruyser, "Narcissism in Contemporary Religion," *The Journal of Pastoral Care* 32 (1978): 219-31.

standpoint. Rather, the pastoral counselor would want to explore its unique function in the personality of a particular individual and to trace how it might be used in functional as well as dysfunctional ways. Actual instances of dysfunctionality would usually be grounds for asking whether a theological concept or image has really been properly understood, not only by an individual but perhaps at times even by theology and church. Widespread (cultural, subcultural, or communal) manifestations of theologically adequate but psychologically dysfunctional images of God would provide an occasion not only for questioning whether the image has been received as intended by the church but also for the church to question whether it has properly understood and communicated the image in accordance with Scripture.

4. Psychologically Dysfunctional; Theologically Inadequate

Even the most apparently dysfunctional God representation has the capacity, as mentioned previously, to meet some vital emotional need. The needs served, according to Rizzuto, generally have to do with enabling one to relate to one's primary objects. This positive function notwithstanding, the creation of a psychologically dysfunctional God representation can exact high emotional costs. One's feelings of hopelessness about one's family might remain entirely unconscious but, if projected onto the cosmos, can take on infinite or eternal dimensions. If one could return the focus of the problem back to the family of origin, one could sift through the concrete losses and disappointments, the hidden suffering and unfulfilled desires of the little child in the adult. One could thereby come to terms with them directly.

On the other hand, it is precisely such projection onto God that sometimes seems to enable a person to live with otherwise intolerable pain. One woman discussed by Rizzuto, for example, found it more acceptable to imagine God as indifferent or unaccepting than to imagine the same thing about her mother (Rizzuto, p. 152). Her God representation radically undermined her sense of self-esteem and kept her in a perpetual state of hopelessness about her unhappy life. She could do nothing to please God. She always felt guilty and unable to live up to God's expectations. Even such apparent dysfunctionality, however, served the deeper emotional purpose of protecting her from her true feelings about her mother.

If in this situation pastoral counseling, as a ministry of the church, were in some way to express and attest God's everlasting love and mercy, it might well be met with strenuous resistance. For the woman to accept God as loving and merciful would require a fundamental change in relation to her mother. For if God were to love and accept her, what sense could she make of her displaced rage and fear? It is possible, of course, that the rage and fear aroused by the mother might then be directed at another person or group (for example, communists, foreigners, or unbelievers).

According to Rizzuto, the woman did, in fact, resist the church's attempts to reach out to her. She refused all offers of help from a kindly priest and remained frightened of God. "The teachings of the church and actual positive experience with caring religious people," writes Rizzuto, "barely touched her God representation" (Rizzuto, p. 172). Rizzuto goes on to say:

> Her emotions were too fixed on her longings for her to . . . absent herself from her needs long enough to consider what the church had to offer. . . . [She] had arrived at the house of God with a God representation that was too painful, too fixed and too intertwined with [her] suffering for [her] to make use of it. (Rizzuto, p. 199)

Rizzuto thus clarifies some of the deeper emotional reasons why a person might actually need to resist hearing the church's proclamation. This particular woman did not seem able to afford the cost of a theologically adequate God representation. For despite its apparent extreme dysfunctionality, her image of God nevertheless served important psychological needs.

The church's attempts at providing Christian nurture failed in this case, as it might in other situations where grossly inadequate parenting brings about this kind of deeply felt suffering and where the psychological and religious issues are so inextricably intertwined with one another. The pastoral counseling relationship, as a part of the church's total ministry, might provide the kind of ongoing care needed. There, at least, the woman's longings and sufferings and her painful hopelessness about life could finally be heard. One could only hope, with all due sensitivity to the problem, that over a sufficient period of time the introjection of a new parental figure, arising through the counseling relationship, could begin to effect changes in her relationship not only to her mother but also to God.

Conclusion

What, then, are the limits and the possibilities of each method — what I have called Rizzuto's "phenomenological" method and Barth's "theological" method — in relation to one another? Both Barth and Rizzuto carefully delineate the boundaries of their own method and work self-consciously within their particular fields of discourse. Rizzuto, as noted, has developed a method that enables her to speak of observable phenomena, while Barth, on the other hand, has tried to design a method that is adequate to his particular object of study. If the object of study is the church's language about God and God's transcendent work, then, according to Barth, only a method based an transcendent categories (such as "God's self-revelation") would be adequate.[30] Both Barth and Rizzuto ask about belief in God but from widely different worlds of discourse. Rizzuto sees it as an observable psychological fact; Barth as an essential mystery that can be described only by reference to God's transcendent grace. I have assumed that these two perspectives need not be mutually exclusive and that each has a contribution to make to pastoral counseling as a ministry of the church. Yet, if any explicit boundaries can be drawn between the two fields, how might they be described?

From a Barthian theological perspective, the limits of each method might be described as follows. First, a phenomenological method is not equipped to say anything directly theological. Second, a theological method is limited in that it cannot pass direct judgment on the results of phenomenological research. I will discuss each of these points in turn.

---

30. "Understanding the nature of the object actually molds the method which will be appropriate for investigation" (Hans W. Frei, "The Doctrine of Revelation in the Thought of Karl Barth, 1909-1922, the Nature of Barth's Break with Liberalism" [unpublished dissertation, Yale University, 1956], p. 205).

First, a phenomenological method is not equipped to say anything of a directly theological nature. We have already noted Rizzuto's clear intention to stay within the boundaries of her method. Even so, her language about God in several places can be shown to be ambiguous. While she clearly intends to speak only of psychic phenomena, in a number of places she verges on making what is in effect a statement of faith, namely, that God is an objectively non-existent being. Such an impression arises precisely because of the apparently all-encompassing nature of her method. All belief in God seems to be presented as explicable in some sense within the terms of her method. Presumably even belief that supposes it has to do with a transcendent, other reality can be shown to be nothing but a rearrangement of one's internalized parental and related self-objects.

Rizzuto speaks, for example, of "the powerful reality of nonexistent objects" (Rizzuto, p. 47). She explicitly includes God in this category. By this she means to point to the undeniable psychic reality of our imaginary constructions, to the fact that poetic and artistic creations shape us and our vision of reality as much as or more than people in the flesh. Nonexistent objects — objects existing only as imaginative creations and not in any objective sense — nevertheless have psychic reality. But by relegating God to such a category, an implicit truth claim seems to have been made about God's objective nonexistence. Rizzuto writes:

> The fictive creations of our minds — those of creative artists for example — have as much regulatory potential in our psychic function as people around us "in the flesh." We have forgotten the impressive power of muses, guardian angels, heroes, Miss Liberty, Eros and Thanatos (to be Freudian), devils, the Devil and God himself. (Rizzuto, p. 47)

The obvious effect of such a comment is to place God on a par with mere imaginative creations — muses, Miss Liberty, and other such reified psychological constructs — and thus to suggest that "God" shares with them a similar sort of objective nonexistence.

At one point Rizzuto asks about "the phenomena [sic] of actual belief in God as real, existing, alive and interacting with the believer." There are cases where the religious person "does not experience God as a symbol or a sign but as a living being." She then asks, "How can we explain this phenomenon in an acceptable psychoanalytic frame of reference?" (Rizzuto, p. 49). Such acceptability is not possible, however, because by definition an acceptable psychoanalytic frame of reference excludes God as a transcendent being — or as "real, existing, alive and interacting." In her argumentation, however, all belief in God is explained as some variation on internalized parental and self object relations. Although "conscious religious experiences with God will *seem* intensely real," Rizzuto obviously implies that they are not in fact real, in the sense of pertaining to a transcendent, other reality. Closer examination, Rizzuto avers, will reveal that changes in the relevant internalized objects and sense of self are responsible for whatever "apparently inexplicable events" have occurred (Rizzuto, p. 89). Rizzuto thus appears to leave no room for the possibility of a real encounter with the living God. She appears to be making judgments about the theological status of religious experiences by suggesting they are "real" only in some psychologically significant sense. In other words, she seems to be saying that what the believer takes to be a real interaction with an existing reality called "God" is actually nothing but a particularly powerful reemergence of a parentally based, self-created, internalized object. From a Barthian theological perspective, such a judgment would constitute an arbitrary transgression of the boundaries of her psychoanalytic method (an assessment which, as previously noted, Rizzuto herself seems in principle to acknowledge).

Second, a theological method is not equipped to pass direct judgment on the results of phenomenological research. In Barth's discussions of belief in God, he speaks of faith not as a self-contained human phenomenon but as God's transcendent gift of grace. Neither grace nor faith are subject to a phenomenological description of their essence, according to Barth, for the essential ingredient, the work of the Holy Spirit, is not an observable phenomenon but a mystery "seen" only through the eyes of faith. Even Barth's theological anthropology makes a distinction between what is known about human nature on the basis of the Word of God and what is known on the basis of phenomenological observations. "Theological anthropology," writes Barth, "has not to do merely with the human being as a phenomenon but with the human being as such; not merely with human possibilities, but with human reality" (III/2, 85 rev.). Barth thus distinguishes between what he calls "real humanity" and "phenomenal humanity."

The latter is subject to scientific or empirical inquiry, while the former is known only by reference to the biblical witness. Barth takes it as axiomatic that human beings are known in their "real" or essential nature only in relation to their Creator. For it is in what they are as creatures of God and in their relation to God that their "very being and reality" is to be found (III/2, 25 rev.).

Thus Barth's theology would in principle have no grounds for denying the possible relative validity of Rizzuto's phenomenologically or descriptively based assessments and explanations. If as a trained observer Rizzuto has discovered certain patterns in God images that are closely related to internalized parental images, then Barth qua theologian would have nothing to say either in favor of or against such a hypothesis. Barth is, in fact, remarkably open toward the findings of what he calls the "exact sciences," provided only that they do not arbitrarily transgress their limits by turning their relative and delimited explanations into explanatory reductions that presume to pass judgment on questions of theological truth rather than leaving such questions open as being beyond the scope of phenomenological method in itself. His theology explicitly reserves a place for disciplined or scientific inquiry such as the kind Rizzuto has undertaken. He believes that studies of this sort provide "precise information and relevant data which can be of service in the wider investigation of human nature, and can help build up a technique for dealing with these questions" (III/2, 24 rev.).

In this chapter I have tried to keep each method distinct but also to notice areas of relationship and overlap. Thus, in discussing the genetic question — how does one come to acquire belief in God? — I have sought to allow each perspective to speak for itself, within the assumptions and procedures of its own field of discourse. For the sake of interdisciplinary discussion, each perspective is granted legitimacy in its own realm. Thus, Rizzuto's theory about the psychological origins and development of belief in God is presented in its own terms. In addition I have suggested an alternative, specifically theological description of belief in God, based on Barth's understanding of the knowledge of God. I have tried to show that the two realms of discourse are not necessarily incompatible. In, with, and under (or in some cases, perhaps, against) the psychological genesis of the God representation, Christian nurture, conversion, and sanctification might be taking place (or they might not). Judgments such as these, which can only be made on implicit or explicit theological grounds are logically distinct from questions of psychic functionality or health. Once again, while the two processes can be differentiated according to their respective spheres of discourse, they occur in and with one another in any given God representation (that is, in a differentiated unity as indicated by the Chalcedonian pattern). The same features that can be described empirically may (or may not) be seen as theologically significant.

Although distinct from one another, faith and psychic health are not necessarily incompatible. While there are claims among psychologists and psychiatrists that contend for their intrinsic incompatibility, I have suggested, following Rizzuto and Barth, that it may be more a question of the abuse of certain biblical images or concepts than their legitimate use that perpetuates certain forms of neurosis or immaturity. Anything can be used to bolster one's defensive system, including biblical images of God. Numerous variations on this theme could exist in any Christian community. The proper theological response to such abuse, I have suggested, is to take it as an opportunity for re-examining the particular article of faith or biblical image in question from a theological perspective. Has the image been properly understood in its own context? Has it been assimilated into an entirely different context (for example, the individual's needs for emotional balance) in such a way that its original intent and meaning are largely effaced? These questions of self-examination would at times need asking not only by those who hear of and internalize biblical images but also by those in the church who employ them in proclamation and witness.

Theology, at least along Barthian lines, would thus refuse to take the instrumental value of psychic functionality as a norm for itself in any final sense. The importance of faith is not that it leads (or fails to lead) to psychic health. Such a view would imply that there is some value higher than faith (namely, psychic health) that faith must serve. Faith as the free response to God's grace is, from Barth's point of view, primarily an end in itself and not merely a means to some other, more important end. The concepts of faith and psychic health are understood (by virtue of the Chalcedonian pattern) as clearly differentiated from one another. Psychological norms have their independent legitimacy within their own sphere of discourse, but when brought into relation with theological norms they are somewhat relativized. For psychological health is not understood only as an end in itself but also as a relative good within a larger context of faith. The relationship between them is thus seen to be asymmetrical, with faith setting the terms for the broader context of meaning.

Finally, I have suggested that the ministry of pastoral counseling can provide a practical setting for individual Christians and others interested to sort through various competing or conflicting images of God and their associated meanings. In that setting Rizzuto's approach, insofar as it does not become reductive, has the potential for opening vast new territory in the life of believers. Explicit connections made between experiences with and fantasies about one's parents, on the one hand, and one's expectations of God, on the other, could be extraordinarily liberating. To realize how freeing such a process can be, one has only to observe the immense relief of a single individual who, in the process of pastoral counseling, comes to see that God is not necessarily like a punitive parent.

Although such counseling is, of course, no panacea and though it is certainly no substitute for life in community — for common worship, prayer, and fellowship — it can provide a safe setting to explore various emotionally laden aspects of one's faith. Whenever one's faith in God is a living and lived reality, moving and motivating one from the heart, important psychological issues will be at stake. Unresolved issues by their very nature carry a great deal of anxiety with them. The church has few places where such deeply felt anxiety and suffering can be safely shared and explored. The kind of sorting — both theological and psychological — that occurs in the pastoral counseling relationship has the potential for bringing about both clarity and healing.

CHAPTER FIVE

Case Study: Eva and Her "Black Despairs"

WHEN PASTORAL COUNSELING is done from a Barthian theological standpoint, the Chalcedonian pattern is useful not only at the level of theory but also in the course of practice. Although theoretical clarification is important in itself, it is also indispensable for the sake of practice. The pastoral counselor who is guided by the Chalcedonian pattern at the theoretical level in relating theology and psychology will also be in a position to use the pattern in the work of pastoral counseling. The clarity afforded by the pattern at the theoretical level will facilitate the kind of complex judgments needed in counseling situations where psychological and theological materials are closely interwoven for the counselee. The purpose of this chapter is to shift attention from the more theoretical to the more practical uses of the pattern. By presenting an extended example of a case where psychological and theological questions were both explicit, the pattern's usefulness for the actual work of a "bilingual" pastoral counselor can be demonstrated.

The case to be considered is "paradigmatic" in the sense that it concerns a counselee who sought help not only at the level of psychotherapy but also at the level of guidance in the Christian faith. It is thus a case that draws fully upon the distinctive background and training of the pastoral counselor. In such cases the needs and questions of the counselee are essentially as "bilingual" as the pastoral counselor's acquired competencies. Not all counselees, of course, have explicit theological or spiritual questions. Yet, the pastoral counselor's approach to those who do not needs to be understood against the background of the more paradigmatic situation. This aspect of pastoral counselor's work will be discussed in the concluding chapters.

This chapter will consider the case of a woman who was clinically depressed and who sought psychotherapeutic help in the context of her Christian faith.[1] After presenting her condition as she herself reported it, a diagnostic evaluation will be offered. In this way it will be possible to recapitulate the experience of the pastoral counselor, who from the very outset begins to organize what is presented into various frameworks of meaning, both psychological and theological. Of course, the "raw data" has already in some sense been formed into a meaningful whole by the counselee herself, in this case reflecting a personal identity already shaped by her faith.

The chapter falls into three parts. The first part presents the case itself, the second part offers a psychological interpretation, and the final part completes the analysis with a theological interpretation. The chapter thus displays what it means to think of pastoral counseling as a work that requires dual or bilingual competencies under the guidance of the Chalcedonian pattern.

Part One. A Paradigmatic Case

Presenting the Problem

Eva came to see me because of what she called her "black despairs." She called them black because they felt so total, so obliterating, so devoid of hope, light, or space. They were annihilating in their power, like a black hole. She experienced them as a powerful void, sucking all her energy and giving nothing back. Whence they came she did not know. Why they left seemed equally mysterious. When they came, they could only be endured; all real life was suspended. In a black despair, Eva was filled with indescribable psychic pain, every bit as real as physical pain and equally as difficult to describe to one who had not felt it. She used various metaphors in an attempt to capture its essential quality. She described it as an abyss that she would claw

---

1. I am indebted to the counselee, whose name has been changed to Eva, for written permission to use this material.

her way out of, as a closed down suffocating feeling, as a descent into hell.[2]

Eva was convinced that God was offended by her black despairs. In the midst of them her soul would go dry; no images of hope would arise in prayer. At times her prayers would feel like pretense, like "going through the motions." God seemed distant, silent, a figment of her imagination. At the same time she felt she was badly disappointing God, that she should be able to "rise above it," to pull herself together and get on with her life. What good was she to God, languishing in bed all day, unable to serve God? In the grip of a black despair, Eva was able to fulfill her daily responsibilities only by driving herself inwardly. She would heap scorn upon herself, whipping herself into shape, driving herself mercilessly through her daily tasks. "What is the *matter* with you?" she'd ask herself. "Why are you always feeling sorry for yourself? Just pull yourself out of it."

Initial Reflections

Eva's choice of a pastoral counselor was based on her own preliminary self-diagnosis. She felt that she needed not only psychotherapeutic understanding but also spiritual guidance. If addressed only psychotherapeutically, the core issue as Eva saw it — that her black despairs were an offense to God — might be ignored or only inadequately addressed and almost certainly not addressed in the strictly theological terms in which it presented itself. Thus an approach that offered no theological framework for interpreting her suffering would be insufficient. At the same time, however, an approach that discounted the psychotherapeutic issues would also be insufficient. Any supposedly "pastoral" approach that merely encouraged Eva to trust in God in the midst of her despair would in this instance only paralyze her further.

---

2. "To most of those who have experienced it, the horror of depression is so overwhelming as to be quite beyond expression" (William Styron, *Darkness Visible: A Memoir of Madness* [New York: Random House, 1990], p. 83). (The book recounts his personal struggle with depression.) See also Anthony Storr's essay on "Churchill: The Man," for a moving depiction of Churchill's lifelong bout with depression, in *Churchill's Black Dog, Kafka's Mice and Other Phenomena of the Human Mind* (New York: Grove, 1965), pp. 3-51.

Eva's problem with black despairs was not an isolated symptom to be "fixed" and dispensed with. Rather it was deeply embedded in her way of understanding herself and her world. Eva's psychological difficulties seemed to be closely intertwined with her theological beliefs. Sorting through the various strands of psychological and theological meaning, examining their sources and placing them within a normative framework would all be necessary steps in the pastoral counselor's task. More was required than simply understanding the various functions of her "God representation." Such understanding would be essential but would not in itself provide the kind of help she sought. Eva also needed a partner or guide to accompany her as she sorted through certain fundamental questions of Christian faith as they related to her psychic and spiritual distress. Psychological and theological analysis each had their place. Neither the one nor the other, it seemed, could be dispensed with.

Eva, for instance, had labeled her depressive episodes sinful, an offense against God (a theological judgment). But what had such an interpretation done but perpetuate the cycle of self-condemnation that virtually guaranteed their reoccurrence (a psychoanalytic judgment)? One might surmise that her inner God representation was emotionally dysfunctional (a psychoanalytic judgment), but was it accurate or adequate within an overall understanding of God as depicted in the New Testament (a theological judgment)? Without a psychoanalytic perspective, Eva would understand little about the inner dynamics of the black despairs, how inner forces functioned to keep her, and her view of God, locked into place. Yet, without some kind of theological perspective, she would have no basis from within her religious faith by which to challenge an understanding of God that kept her immobilized in fear and pain.

Diagnostic Evaluation

Eva was middle-aged when she came to see me, a Caucasian professional woman, divorced, with no children. Her general physical health was good, though she had a history of asthma, for which she took medication. Very occasionally she experienced migraine auras. Eva was a recovering alcoholic who had been abstinent for slightly more than three years. Her depressive episodes occurred every two to four weeks, lasted one to three days, and were characterized by physical and emotional exhaustion, a pervasive feeling of "what's the use?," growing irritability, a virtual loss of her sense of humor, social isolation, and self-deprecatory attacks. From the standpoint of psychological diagnosis, Eva's symptoms corresponded to the description of dysthymic disorder. *The Diagnostic and Statistical Manual of Mental Disorders* of the American Psychiatric Association lists thirteen characteristics of dysthymic disorder. During a depressive episode, at least three symptoms need to be present. Eva characteristically exhibited all thirteen symptoms during what she called her black despairs. They are:

1. insomnia or hypersomnia
2. low energy level or chronic tiredness
3. feelings of inadequacy, loss of self-esteem, or self-deprecation
4. decreased effectiveness or productivity at school, work, or home
5. decreased attention, concentration, or ability to think clearly
6. social withdrawal
7. loss of interest in or enjoyment of pleasurable activities
8. irritability or excessive anger
9. inability to respond with apparent pleasure to praise or rewards
10. less active or talkative than usual, or feels slowed down or restless
11. pessimistic attitudes toward the future, brooding about past events, or feeling sorry for self
12. tearfulness or crying
13. recurrent thoughts of death or suicide.[3]

Also pertinent diagnostically was Eva's sixteen year history of alcoholism (now in remission) and her status as the child of an alcoholic.

Faced with this data, what might be an appropriate pastoral or theological diagnosis? My initial diagnosis, drawing on an understanding of Rizzuto and Barth (as described in Chapter Four) was formulated as an apparent "conflict between Eva's parental God representation and the New Testament image of God as confessed by faith." Implicit in

3. *Diagnostic and Statistical Manual of Mental Disorders,* 3rd ed. (Washington, D.C.: American Psychiatric Association, 1980), p. 223.

this diagnosis were at least two kinds of judgments: first a psychoanalytic judgment, that Eva's black despairs were exacerbated by the parental God representation, and second a theological judgment, that moving
toward a more theologically adequate image of God might offer relief
from certain aspects of her suffering. Let us first look at the parental
sources and possible functions of Eva's God representation as they were
discerned in the pastoral therapeutic process.

Sources of Eva's God Representation

My working hypothesis, following Rizzuto, was that Eva's internalized
representation of God was built upon her internalized parent representations. Therefore, Eva's relationship with her parents as a child
needed to be explored. The narrative as presented here took shape
over a period of months. It was not a known entity when Eva began
counseling. Indeed, it seems that much of the therapeutic benefit of
counseling was derived from the unfolding of that narrative. The
release of deeply repressed feelings and the discovery of interior images in relation to her parents seemed to provide much of the momentum that moved the therapeutic process forward. The full drama
of such a process, of course, cannot be adequately conveyed in a
summary account; Eva's narrative took shape only piece by piece, with
frequent revisions and later interpolations. Little by little an image of
her internalized parental figures emerged. Over time we sought to
apply those images to how Eva might be viewing God. During the
entire process the image she held of God was also apparently being
actively challenged and shaped through such other means inside and
outside the therapeutic process as prayer, worship, pastoral conversation, the Lord's Supper, and the study of theology and Scripture. The
entire development, in other words, took place in a much larger
context of Eva's active involvement in the life of the church.

"Mommy"

Mommy, at once desperately adored and desperately feared, had been
the powerful emotional head of Eva's childhood household. During

the first year or so the therapeutic process was more occupied with Eva's mother than with any other single person. Although her mother had been dead for nearly twenty years, Eva still seemed to be consumed with grief over her loss. She had died while middle-aged of emphysema when Eva was still a young woman and newly divorced. Eva's mother had been born to poor parents who felt they could not support their children and so placed them in an orphanage. At age eight, after six weeks in the orphanage, Eva's mother had been adopted by a wealthy, childless couple. She never saw her original family again. In adulthood she forbade any mention of them.

Throughout Eva's childhood her mother was an active alcoholic and was abusive to Eva and her older sister. In the early months of our work together, the central theme was Eva's urgent question, "How bad was it?" That is, just how bad was the emotional, physical, and spiritual abuse of her childhood home? As repressed memories emerged it gradually became clear that it had been far worse than her conscious mind had allowed. Eva eventually came to the sobering conclusion that "Mommy was the most vicious person I have ever known." Even to acknowledge such a possibility brought intense pain, for her mother was also loved, idealized, and still inadequately mourned. Nevertheless, the acknowledgment was a step toward inner healing, for with it came a release of anger and outrage over how she had been treated as a child. It was the first time that Eva had been able consciously to experience anger toward her mother without suffering days of inner, self-punishing attacks.

As part of her therapeutic process, Eva once purchased an eleven-foot metal chain complete with padlock as a palpable symbol of her bondage. On each link she had attached a card with what she called a "Mommyism," one of the abusive messages that her mother had repeatedly hurled at her. As Eva remembered them, these messages were always delivered with a scornful tone, a hateful look, and unforgettable intensity. A brief sampling from among the approximately one hundred messages follows.

- "I can't stomach you."
- "If you don't do X, we'll stop the car and leave you here."
- "I'll slap that smirk right off your face."
- "What the hell is the *matter* with you?"

- "You are beneath contempt."
- "God damn you to hell."
- "I am authority."
- "I know you better than you know yourself."
- "I'll shake you till your teeth fall out."

Any such message, delivered as they were, would obviously be a blow to a child's emerging sense of self. Yet, the impact of the entire range coming day after day with no respite seemed almost unimaginable. A small child would obviously have no way of defending herself against such an onslaught. Eva's mother would often grab hold of Eva's chin, hold it in place, and not allow her to look away for even a moment as these things were said to her. It seemed as if Eva's only recourse was to believe her mother, to internalize the denunciations as undeniable truth.

"Mommy," as Eva eventually came to see her, was a vindictive, cruel, even sadistic woman who had systematically humiliated her children. She could threaten, slap, and humiliate her daughters in a way that she could never do with any other human being, for her daughters were totally dependent upon her, believed and loved her because she was their mother, and thus could not abandon her. Mommy's voice, alive and well decades later inside Eva, showed that Eva still had not "abandoned" her mother. Eva had remained faithful to Mommy to the end of her life and beyond it.

"Daddy"

Repressed memories of Eva's father also began to emerge in the course of counseling. What struck Eva most strongly was the vehemence and constancy of her father's criticism. She felt that no matter how well she did something or how hard she tried to please him, he would find something in her behavior to criticize. Eva's father shamed and humiliated Eva not in the manner of his wife, by expressions of contempt, but rather by means of ridicule. This was especially painful during her teen years when he would complain about her sitting at home reading, while "other men's daughters" were out having fun. He was invasive with both his daughters, closely monitoring their bathroom behavior and insisting on squeezing his older daughter's facial pimples despite her active resistance. What Eva seemed to resent most, however, was that her father never stood up to her mother. She could never remember her father protecting her against her mother's onslaughts, even when she had felt that her father might be emotionally on her side.

The internalized sayings most strongly associated with Eva's father pertained to his way of stoically ignoring difficulties, repressing emotions, and forging ahead despite obvious pain in his family. Typically, he would calmly advise Eva not to "get so worked up about it." Even in the present, he might admonish her to "rise above" some difficulty or "put it behind" her. At one point he himself had tried to "rise above" his *own* difficulties by planning an escape from the family. He had left home without a word, abandoning his teenage daughters to deal with a drunk, out-of-control mother. Eva had spent hours calling the major hotels in the large city where they lived, only to learn that he had made plans to leave the next day. Apparently his daughter's call smote his conscience, for he returned home instead. For years Eva dealt with the psychic pain of her father's abandonment by telling herself that he was leaving her mother, not her, and that at least she had been old enough to be able to cope with it. Only after extensive counseling was she able to find access to the intense fear and anger she had felt about his leaving.

How might these internalized representations of Eva's parents be related to her inner image of God?

Eva's God Representation

It goes without saying that Eva's internalized parental voices were a major factor in Eva's black despairs. The self-deprecatory attacks — active hostility aimed against the self — that were a central characteristic of her black despairs came directly from her inner arsenal of "Mommyisms" and "Daddyisms."[4] Over time it became clear that

---

4. Consider, for example, Freud's technical description of the harsh superego: "In melancholia the object to which the superego's wrath applies has been taken into the ego through identification" (Freud, *The Ego and the Id* [New York: Norton, 1960],

"God," too, was on their side. God, like her mother, supposedly knew what Eva was *really* like. She was bad, sinful, falling short of what was expected, hopelessly beyond reform. God had been frequently invoked when Eva's mother needed more power to bolster up her flagging authority. Thus Eva was repeatedly enjoined to "Honor your father and mother," leaving little doubt in her mind that God supported the status quo. From Sunday school stories, Eva had learned of God as someone very wrathful, who headed up slaughtering armies. When her mother would exclaim in exasperation, "God damn you to hell," Eva could readily imagine God doing such a thing.

It seemed that "God," too, was shaking Eva "until her teeth fell out," exclaiming in exasperation, "What the hell is the *matter* with you?" Eva found herself frequently pleading for divine forgiveness, avowing her unworthiness before the Lord, and expecting God's word of judgment or wrath. She was convinced that she needed to earn God's love by proving herself worthy of it. Yet, equally as strong was her conviction that there was no possible way that she could earn it, regardless of how hard she might try. Nevertheless she had to keep trying, for she could not let go of the illusion of her power to bring about a different outcome. Maybe someday she would discover the key, the right thing to say or do that would make God love her. These clusters of attitudes and feelings obviously formed close parallels to those toward her parents.

Such a God representation seemed to stabilize deep-seated conflicts in Eva's character structure. By projecting some core characteristics of her parents onto God, Eva had a modus operandi for dealing with seemingly unmanageable conflict. One important function of Eva's God representation was to keep her justified rage at her mother and father repressed. As long as God continued to be on their side, Eva could not risk experiencing the depth of her own anger, for she

---

p. 41). Also pertinent is Fairbairn's view of the libido, which attaches itself to a bad love object (that is, one that is frustrating or depriving to the infant): "We have seen, furthermore, that libido may be attached to bad objects which have been internalized and repressed. . . . What Freud describes under the category of 'death instincts' would thus appear to represent for the most part masochistic relationships with internalized bad objects" (Fairbairn, *Psychoanalytic Studies of the Personality* [London: Tavistock, 1952], p. 79).

feared she would then alienate not only her parents but the very
Source of life itself. Now, as then, God's commandment to "honor
your father and mother" became a means by which the parental abuse
could be minimized and the pattern of denial continued. It also
enabled Eva to continue idealizing her parents at great cost to herself.
For as Eva's mother continued to bask in the sun of God's righteousness, Eva had inevitably to play the role of the debased sinner, begging
God (and her mother) for forgiveness.

No fundamental change in this system seemed possible unless a
crucial distinction could be made between the voice, authority, and
attitude of Eva's mother and those of God. Insofar as Eva's understanding of the Christian faith had been co-opted by her psychological
needs, her very faith was compromised and rendered incapable of
freeing her from the net in which she was trapped. Her understanding
of herself as a sinner only served to perpetuate an inner cycle of shame
and self-loathing, confirming the very worst about herself. Like her
parents, God was perceived to be disappointed in Eva's inability to
"pull herself up by her bootstraps." Like them, God was understood
to be sick to death of her complaints and disgusted with her sniveling
self-pity. Thus God, too, became an inner attacker, not a place of
refuge and hope.

Other Sources of Eva's God Representation

There was another side to Eva's understanding of God. Certain aspects
of her experience with God did not seem to derive from her parental
God representation. These aspects came to expression through images
that were consistently biblical in origin, yet they were not mere cognitive or intellectual constructs, for they were embedded in a deep
network of meaning in Eva's psyche, having the potential for moving
and motivating her in powerful ways. A number of biblical passages
had become a source of hope for Eva as she struggled with her
depressive episodes.

As Eva meditated on Scripture she sought to take its images of
hope to heart by copying them in calligraphy. She brought framed
words of Scripture to her therapy sessions and lay them on the floor
between us as a kind of witness to God's mercy and comfort. She

carefully copied down the verses: "Though my father and mother forsake me, the Lord will receive me" (Ps. 27:10). Another verse read, "Cast all your anxiety on him, because he cares for you" (1 Pet. 5:7). Perhaps most important was Jesus' admonition: "Take care that you do not despise one of these little ones . . . for it is not the will of my Father in heaven that one of these little ones should be lost" (Matt. 18:10, 14). As one who had been despised as a child and who had then experienced decades of feeling utterly lost, Jesus' words seemed to provide a meaningful framework for understanding the unfolding of her life. They also posed a certain challenge to the conflation of God's identity with that of her parents. For such words clearly implied that what they had done to her was not sanctioned by the will of God.

At times the conflict between these two different understandings of God — the one rooted in Eva's relationship with her parents, the other in an encounter with the Word of God — grew quite acute. Conflicting images, attitudes, and expectations seemed to coexist side by side. Sorting them out according to implicit psychological and theological norms was an ongoing part of the interpretive task.

Theological and Psychoanalytic Interpretation in Tandem: An Extended Example

By tracing a core theme in Eva's work, an unfolding process can be described where theological and psychoanalytic interpretation worked closely together over a period of several months. Although the initial interpretation offered was theological, we proceeded to work with it both psychodynamically and theologically, sometimes emphasizing one framework of understanding, sometimes another, depending on the needs of the moment. It shows how an interpretation can take on a life of its own, developing in unforeseen directions, while moving the healing process forward with its own momentum.

One day not long after Eva had brought in the metal chain, I listened as she inflicted several of those messages on herself. The "voices" by which she did so were several in their manifestation, destructive in their consequences, and savage in tone. Drawing upon an image that arose in my mind — the New Testament figure of Legion, the demoniac, wandering among the tombs, filled with self-hatred and contempt — I suggested that these voices were "demonic."[5]

Without quite being aware of the implications, I had, as it were, challenged the authority of Eva's parents head on. The parental sayings had commandeered an unquestioned dominion in Eva's inner world. Dethroning them from "divine" to "demonic" in one fell swoop was startling. Yet, it seemed to fit what I saw. Eva, like the demoniac, lived among the dead. Her mother, nearly twenty years in the grave, was a daily companion, and Eva's fear of the imminent deaths of her father and sister haunted her continually. During her depressive episodes, Eva, like the demoniac, seemed to be wandering among the tombs, cut off from her fellow human beings and from all sense of hope. She, too, inflicted great harm on herself, crying aloud day and night, filled with alien, destructive energies over which she had no control. She, too, needed to be liberated from the abusive forces that inhabited her very being.

Eva began to work creatively with the interpretation. Before our next session she had meditated on the story about the demoniac in the Gospels, drawing explicit parallels between his situation and hers. Although intrigued by the image, she resisted the idea of acknowledging her powerlessness over the voices that inhabited her. The demoniac may have been powerless, she was convinced, but she herself was not. Ironically, the form taken by this belief seemed to arise from a parental message that she "should" indeed be in control. To avoid depressive episodes, she told herself, all she really had to do was to "pull herself together" or "put it all behind her" and get on with her life. She could not accept the interpretation that she, like the demoniac, was fighting against powers much stronger than she and over whom she had little, if any, control. Nevertheless, the interpretation initiated a process in which she began to differentiate their voices from her own. She began to recognize them as something other than and alien to herself. They were *not* in fact her thoughts or feelings but thoughts and feelings that inhabited her against her will. She began to speak out against them, telling them that they were not welcome.

5. The method of interpretation employed at this point might best be seen as Jung's "amplification of the archetype." See C. G. Jung, *The Structure and Dynamics of the Psyche,* Collected Works, vol. 8 (Princeton: Princeton University Press, 1960), pp. 204-6.

One of the tasks that lay before us was to discern the underlying psychodynamic pattern of the "demonic" attacks. In what kind of situation were they called forth? What function did they seem to serve in Eva's personality? How were they related to what Eva was thinking or feeling? When did they most take over, drowning out alternative thoughts and feelings? How might we go about effectively reducing their power over Eva? While all these questions were essentially psychodynamic, they were also entwined at the same time with theological questions that were urgent for Eva. What spiritual or religious attitudes might help her to withstand inner attack? How might she call upon the power of the gospel to cast out these "demons"? What reconceptions, what disciplines, what weapons of the spirit were needed for this kind of struggle?

The psychodynamic questions may be examined first. It seemed important to observe the ebb and flow of the inner voices. For example, did something in particular trigger them? If so, what? We observed how anxiety and fear seemed to be their best weapon. Eva began carefully to note under what kind of circumstances they grew in magnitude. Once, when Eva said something that she feared had displeased me, the following thoughts occurred to her in rapid succession:

1. "I shouldn't have said that."
2. "I hope I haven't damaged that relationship."
3. "Eva, you're insensitive."
4. "You should *never* have said that."
5. "What is the *matter* with you?!"

What started out as anxiety and worry over possibly causing harm to our relationship (#1 and #2) quickly escalated into an attack on her character (#3), to an authoritative and shaming comment that she had acted wrongly (#4), to a final attack that was global in its implications (#5). It should be noted that between the second and third comment, the "speaker" switched from the first to the second person (from "I" to "you"). It was no longer Eva who was thinking and feeling these things but "another" inside her, who addressed her in the second person.

As we continued to work in the ensuing weeks, Eva began to perceive the intimate connection between the "demonic" voices and the inevitable descent into black despairs. She also began to see how her own attitudes, belief structures, and responses kept these "demons" powerful. As we examined the inner psychodynamics of the demonic voices, Eva compiled a list on "How to Feed, Nurture, and Protect Your Demons."[6] It had seven main points.

1. Believe them.
2. Repeat them over and over.
3. Find examples in your behavior that show how they are right. (For instance, look for examples of acting despicably to support the accusation, "You are despicable.")
4. Acknowledge that they are 100 percent correct by believing them *totally* and not questioning any aspect of what they say.
5. Recognize your need for them. They motivate you, keep you on track. They assure your mother's love and approval.
6. Do what they tell you to do. If they tell you to "stuff it," for instance, deaden yourself. Do not allow yourself to think or feel whatever it was that was beginning to emerge into awareness.
7. If you are unsuccessful in obeying them, punish yourself mercilessly.

The list provided a number of clues about how to proceed. No longer wanting to nurture or protect them, Eva drew up a kind of rough counter-list. She became determined to question their authority, not to believe them. She refused to find examples in her behavior that would support their conclusions. Instead, she found counter-examples that directly challenged their conclusions. She questioned whether she needed them. Did they really provide true motivation or did they simply keep the deadly status quo in place? She refused to obey them. If they wanted her to suppress a feeling, for instance, she would express it instead and explore it in detail. Each time she was successful in disobeying them, she regarded it as a kind of victory.

Such a programmatic approach evoked a great deal of anxiety.[7]

---

6. For the use of humor as evidence of the capacity to master anxiety, see Heinz Kohut, *The Restoration of the Self* (Madison: International Universities Press, 1977), p. 110.

7. For a detailed description of a psychoanalytic approach to the confrontation

It was as if we had launched a frontal attack on her entire inner
psychic economy. Eva's inner world was being challenged at its core.
"Absolute truths" were relativized or even shown to be blatantly
false. The world of parental authority, in place for so long, began
to crumble. As it did so, Eva began to find her long-repressed rage.
How could her parents have treated a vulnerable child like that,
filling her with shame and self-hatred? Eva hadn't had a chance to
grow normally; her soul had been twisted by these messages from
her earliest years. Eva was now plunged into a new kind of despair:
a despair that what was crooked might never be made straight.
Would she never recover from the wounds inflicted on her at so
early an age?

In the course of seeking psychological understanding and remedy,
Eva was also acutely aware of a more nearly spiritual dimension of
the conflict. She perused the Scriptures diligently for help and assistance. As she worked with the image of a battle raging within her,
biblical passages that had previously meant little to her, or that she
had found offensive, now acquired new meaning. One passage in
particular, which she read to me, stood out.

> Finally, be strong in the Lord and in the strength of his might. Put
> on the whole armor of God, that you may be able to stand against
> the wiles of the devil. For we are not contending against flesh and
> blood, but against the principalities, against the powers, against the
> rulers of this present darkness, against the spiritual hosts of wicked-
> ness in the heavenly places. Therefore take the whole armor of God,
> that you may be able to withstand in the evil day, and having done
> all, to stand. Stand therefore, having girded your loins with truth,
> and having put on the breastplate of righteousness, and having shod
> your feet with the equipment of the gospel of peace; besides all these,
> taking the shield of faith, with which you can quench all the flaming
> darts of the evil one. And take the helmet of salvation, and the sword
> of the Spirit, which is the word of God. Pray at all times in the Spirit,
> with all prayer and supplication. (Eph. 6:10-18*a*)

---

of such "idols," see Wilfried Daim, *Depth Psychology and Salvation* (New York: Ungar,
1963). For a more recent discussion by a pastoral counselor, see Merle Jordan, *Taking
on the Gods* (Nashville: Abingdon, 1986).

The spiritual weapons that Eva would identify for use against inner attack had emerged: truth, righteousness, peace, faith, salvation, the Word of God, and prayer. Although she did not proceed in a systematic fashion, in various ways she called upon each of these weapons in the ensuing months. Her theological reflections on these matters were not detached, intellectual ruminations but, rather, devout meditations on God's Word as a source of light and salvation. Many times she came to a place where she did not know how to proceed. Yet, as she continued to seek guidance from Scripture, she felt as though she were being led from one insight to the next, step by step.

1. "Girding your loins with truth."

A major part of the ongoing struggle was to separate truth from falsehood. Whom was Eva to believe? She felt that she could not trust her own inner voices, for they only led her astray. She increasingly questioned whether they represented her own thoughts or feelings at all. On what basis could she secure truth about herself and her situation? She noted that Jesus had said, "I am the truth," whereas the demons had told only lies. Jesus had said, "The truth shall set you free," whereas the demonic messages had only kept her in bondage. It seemed that each time Eva acknowledged the abuse she had suffered, she discovered the truth of her situation. Whenever she was tempted to minimize it or deny it or to make excuses for her parents, she was again caught in a web of lies. Her struggle for the truth was ongoing and fundamental. Were the messages from her parents really true? Was it true that her problems stemmed from the fact that she was insensitive, selfish, and lazy, as they had repeatedly told her? Was it true that if she would just try harder, she could finally succeed in avoiding those depressive episodes? Did she really bring them on herself, as her inner attackers insinuated?

Eva felt that she was repeatedly faced with that discriminating sword which Jesus had described — a sword which would set son against father and daughter against mother, the truth which would reveal all lies for what they were. At the most theologically ramified level of expression, Eva felt that she was faced with what the Reformation had identified as the truth of the gospel, namely, that though a sinner, she through faith was nonetheless loved and cherished by God. This evangelical truth stood manifestly opposed to the lie of the "demons" that she was worthless beyond all redemption.

2. "The breastplate of righteousness."

This imagery captured the spiritual issue of whether Eva could secure her own righteousness or whether she could learn, instead, to "put on" "the righteousness of Christ," as one might assume a breastplate over one's heart. Eva felt herself to be trapped in a web of self-righteousness, in an ongoing effort to gain God's love and approval. Over time she came to see that her meticulous confession of every conceivable sin itself seemed to betray an inverted kind of pride, as if she could earn God's forgiveness by being lowly and humble. Such efforts never really transcended the parental situation where Eva had felt that she might earn at least a modicum of approval by debasing herself. Yet, the idea that she was powerless to "do it right" before God brought on the familiar feelings of hopelessness. The breastplate imagery challenged Eva with the notion that she did not have to "do it right" before God. God accepted and loved her as she was. She had only to accept Christ's righteousness instead of striving for her own.

3. "Shod with the gospel of peace."

Eva's constant striving and inner warfare brought about a state of emotional and physical exhaustion. Given her mother's accusation that she was lazy, Eva came to realize that she could not allow herself a moment's peace. She had to be busy all the time. She could not allow herself to become physically ill or even to grieve the death of a friend, for then she was not "doing useful deeds for the Lord." If her essential worth as a person depended upon what she did rather than who she was, then she had to prove that worth. The "gospel of peace" as a spiritual weapon was thus the assurance that she no longer needed to strive so ceaselessly.

4. "The shield of faith."

Eva's meditation on this image led her to the conviction that here lay the only effective defense against the inner attacking voices. To be sinful yet loved as she was was unimaginable to Eva. She could not conceive of it, yet she saw it as the faith that the New Testament asked of her. In her childhood as she remembered it, she had never experienced being forgiven for her wrongdoing. Any misdeed might be thrown back at her at a moment of vulnerability. Her parents seemed to have a secret tally sheet in which her debits kept mounting endlessly, for nothing was ever erased or truly forgiven. Over against such accumulated evidence of her wickedness grew Eva's faith in the gospel of God's unconditional assurance of forgiveness.

5. "To put on the helmet of salvation."

Regarded as a "spiritual weapon," this image came to mean that Eva needed to trust in a salvation that was accomplished apart from her own efforts. Her salvation did not depend on her good works nor her right attitudes. It did not depend on her getting it right nor on her dogged perseverance. It was accomplished apart from what she did or what she failed to do. She could do nothing to earn it. She needed only to receive it as the freely given gift that it was. This "helmet" thus not only offered protection but also signified the promise of a thorough reorientation of Eva's inner world.

6. "The Word of God."

Scripturally described as "the sword of the Spirit" (Heb. 4:12), this image offered the possibility of making crucial distinctions between the way of life and the way of death. Eva felt that the words of Scripture had the capacity to subdue the "demonic" voices in a way that nothing else did. Regularly she would quote a passage that had been especially important to her in her struggle during the previous week. Once, while exhausted from a severe case of bronchitis, the inner voices attacked her with the usual insults to her character: that she was a "useless slob," unable to contribute anything in her weakened state. She suspected that, like her parents, God abhorred her weakness and turned his back on her when she was sick. Then she remembered the scriptural word that God's strength is made perfect in weakness. This meant, as she saw in a new way, that she did not have to trust in her own strength, which was non-existent, but could rely instead on the sufficiency and promise of the gospel.

7. Prayer

Regarded as a weapon of the spirit, prayer became a means by which Eva sought theological insight and spiritual nurturance. In prayer, images of hope would rise up and provide her with a kind of sustaining power to go on. Also as she prayed, she would discover the incongruity between the images of God she had in her mind and those given in the New Testament. In prayer she would ask for clearer knowledge of God's true identity and repent of what she regarded as her "idolatry." Eva experienced a kind of freedom in prayer that she saw as amazing, not only the freedom to express her anger and impatience, like the psalmist, but also to become like a little child, receiving whatever gift God had to give. Once in church, as she gazed at a picture of the risen Christ on a stained glass window, she imagined Jesus lifting his shirt, where underneath were breasts full of the spiritual milk that would nourish her depleted soul. In prayer, she heard him say, "Take what you need, Eva."

Epilogue

It is very difficult to capture the close interweaving of psychodynamic and theological perspectives that occurred in any given session. While each language was distinct, we moved back and forth between them freely, like a conversation between bilingual people. After several months of working with the voices as "demonic," something new emerged to move the process forward in a notable way. The new element was an image from a vivid nightmare.

Eva dreamt that she was possessed by her mother's spirit. She saw her mother inside her own body, with bony, clawlike fingers, clutching her vital internal organs, clinging onto Eva for dear life. She was a dead person trying desperately to live. Eva was a mere vehicle, a means to an end. Her mother had no concern for her as a person. Eva was forced to carry this inner demon that sucked her life from her. She awoke in terror.[8]

The image of her body as a host for demonic forces seemed to strike a deep chord within Eva's unconscious mind, for she felt impelled to develop the image further. Her mother was residing within her, draining her of her life force as she parasitically sucked away life at Eva's expense. In her depressive episodes Eva was actually, as she now saw it, merely a vehicle for her mother's alien voice, beliefs, and attitudes. The effect of the nightmare was dramatic. Eva exclaimed with unexpected intensity: "What the hell *right* does she have to live through me? I'm sick to death of being possessed by my mother! I hate it. I'm sick of trying to figure her out. I'm sick of having compassion on her. I'm sick of swallowing her vomit and pretending I like it." It was as though anger were coursing through Eva's blood vessels like a cleansing fire. She could feel it moving through her, purging her, giving her back her own energy, life, and passion. As we prayed together at the close of the session, an image of Jesus driving the money changers from the temple came to Eva's mind. She, Eva, was God's temple and the Lord was consumed with a zeal for the Lord's house. It was as though Christ himself were angry on her behalf. No longer ashamed or afraid of her anger, she received it as a holy fire, a transforming, purifying conflagration that was clean, desirable, and good. The feeling of an imminent depressive episode, which had been intensifying with the usual manifestations was suddenly ameliorated. Eva did not fall into one of her black despairs but was dramatically delivered from it. A major turning point seemed to have arrived in our work.

---

8. Melanie Klein's understanding of the introjected mother (or parent) is pertinent here. She writes: "Both in children and adults suffering from depression, I have discovered the dread of harboring dying or dead objects (especially the parents) inside one and an identification of the ego with objects in this condition." See Klein, *Love, Guilt and Reparation* (New York: Dell, 1975), p. 266.

Part Two. A Psychological Interpretation: The Dynamics of Shame

How were Eva's depressions to be understood from a psychological perspective? What was the major interpretive thrust of the psychological investigation? While it is very difficult to capture the wide range of exploration in a single conceptual scheme, I found it helpful to think about Eva's suffering in the context of her experience of shame.[9] In my judgment, Eva had what Gershen Kaufman has called a "shame-based identity." In this part, therefore, we will examine the central role of shame in the genesis and perpetuation of Eva's black despairs, drawing primarily upon Kaufman's seminal work, *Shame: The Power of Caring*.[10]

1. The Interpersonal Origins of Shame

Kaufman begins his study by describing the felt experience of shame. He describes the acute sense of exposure, of being seen as basically deficient in some fundamental aspect of being human. Accompanying this sense of deficiency is a feeling of powerlessness; there seems to be nothing one can do to make it right. Shame about the self is not like guilt over specific actions. It is more all-encompassing and total. It seems to pertain not to one's mere deeds but, rather, to one's essential being. One feels worthless or diminished as a human being and unable to make oneself worthy or acceptable. Moreover, there is shame about shame. One cannot speak of one's sense of worthlessness; by acknowledging it, one risks finding oneself further ex-

---

9. Freud, of course, tended to associate depression (or melancholia, as it was called) more with neurotic guilt than with shame. But a number of researchers have linked it more directly with the experience of shame. For a classic description of shame and its place in identity formation, see Helen Merrell Lynd, *On Shame and the Search for Identity* (New York: Harcourt, Brace and World, 1958). Lynd makes careful phenomenological distinctions between what she calls the "guilt-axis" and the "shame-axis" in human experience. See especially her chart comparing them, pp. 208-9.

10. Gershen Kaufman, *Shame: The Power of Caring* (Cambridge, Mass.: Schenkman Books, 1980).

posed. Hence one feels isolated from others, harboring secret shame about the self.[11]

Where does this painful process originate? Kaufman's central metaphor is that of an interpersonal bridge between human beings. From earliest infancy and throughout life, human beings need and utterly depend upon genuine mutuality in their interpersonal relationships. They need to feel loved and respected in their uniqueness and truly important to those around them. As others respond to their basic needs, an emotional bond of trust and interpersonal connectedness arises. Kaufman writes:

> Relationships begin when one person actively reaches out to another and establishes emotional ties. . . . In this way relationships gradually evolve out of reciprocal interest in one another along with shared experiences of trust. Trusting essentially means that we have come both to expect and to rely upon a certain mutuality of response. An emotional bond begins to grow between individuals as they communicate understanding, respect and valuing for one another's personhood, needs and feelings included. . . . The bond which ties two individuals together forms an *interpersonal bridge* between them.[12]

Shame, according to Kaufman, occurs whenever this basic interpersonal bridge is broken. Shame thus signals a breakdown or failure of mutual human responsiveness.

Kaufman traces variations on the shame experience from earliest childhood through adolescence and into adulthood. Harsh, angry words spoken to a pre-verbal child can sever the interpersonal bridge, while physical touch and holding may restore it by communicating affirmation and security. Young children may experience shame whenever emotional or physical abandonment takes place. Whenever a needed parent is emotionally unavailable to a child, the child is vulnerable to a shame response. The child surmises that there must

---

11. For a developmental approach to the place of shame in the life cycle, see Erik Erikson, *Identity: Youth and Crisis* (New York: Norton, 1968). Erikson links shame with doubt and contrasts it with autonomy in the epigenesis of identity. Developmentally, it occurs before the formation of the conscience and the consequent experience of guilt.

12. Kaufman, p. 12.

be something wrong with him or her, with his or her basic feelings and needs, feeling shame about even having them.

In some cases, parents actively try to shame their children as a way to manipulate them into desired behavioral ends, saying, "You should be ashamed of yourself," or, "Shame on you." Other forms of shaming are comparing one child to another, highlighting one child's comparative deficiency, blaming, name-calling, contempt, disgust, ridicule, and humiliation. Excessively high standards of performance, where a child receives the discouraging message that she or he will never be able to measure up, are another source of shame. Finally, Kaufman describes the heightened vulnerability to shame that occurs during adolescence, when one's need for privacy combined with one's sense of exposure about the physical and emotional changes one is undergoing are especially acute. The increase in self-consciousness and the increased importance of one's peers make one particularly vulnerable to episodes of shame at this time.

When we turn to Eva's experience, the interpersonal origins of her sense of shame are perhaps already obvious. The failure of Eva's parents adequately to provide the emotional conditions for basic self-esteem and personality growth is glaringly apparent. Nearly every form of shaming behavior described by Kaufman was a daily feature of Eva's life.[13] The messages on Eva's metal chain, for example, all fall into all of Kaufman's shaming categories. There is not a saying among them that is not shaming in some way: blaming, name-calling, contempt, disgust, ridicule, and humiliation were all there in varying degrees. Eva was also saddled with excessively high performance standards, was repeatedly criticized for not measuring up, and was ridiculed for having simple human needs that could not be met or simple human feelings that could not be tolerated.

2. The Internalization of Shame and the Origin of Identity

Kaufman carefully traces how repeated experiences of shame become internalized in such a way that one's very identity becomes "shame-

13. For a theological perspective on these kinds of patterns of parental abuse, see Dorothy Martyn's remark as quoted above in Chapter Three, p. 101.

based." Once internalized, shame can be perpetuated totally within the self, needing no external person or situation to induce the feeling of shame. As it becomes bound with certain affects, drives, and needs, it may also become unconscious and autonomous, making it difficult to recognize. Unless made conscious, it will remain impervious to change. Kaufman begins by describing the universal human need to identify with others, to belong, to be a part of something or some group larger than oneself. The origins of identity lie in the psychological process of identifying with others, first with those in the family and then significant others who play an important role in the child's life. This process is both conscious and unconscious; it includes conscious modeling as well as unconscious imitation of parental character traits, attitudes, and communication styles. The child's fundamental dependence on the parents provides the basic condition for such identification to take place. Kaufman describes the complex process of psychological introjection in easily understandable terms. He identifies three ways in which the introjection of certain identification patterns of thought, affect, behavior, and relationship become the basis for individual identity. Internalization, says Kaufman,

> involves three distinct aspects: (1) We internalize specific affect-beliefs or attitudes about ourselves which come to lie at the very core of the self and thereby help to mold our emerging sense of identity. (2) We internalize the very ways in which we are treated by significant others and we learn to treat ourselves accordingly. . . . (3) And we internalize identifications in the form of images — we take them inside us and make them our own.[14]

When those around us have attitudes of devaluation or contempt toward us, when they treat us in a blaming fashion, and when we internalize the image and voice of the shaming parent, then we become subject to a shame-based identity. The conditions are then established for shame to be perpetuated intrapsychically.

Kaufman goes on to describe affect-shame binds, drive-shame binds, and need-shame binds, "in which shame can generate and eventually bind whatever has become associated with shame."[15] Drawing on

14. Kaufman, p. 37.
15. Kaufman, p. 39.

Silvan Tomkins's work with primary affects, Kaufman shows how particular affects can be bound with shame when the expression of any affect is followed by a parental shaming response. Thus for example, if a child is consistently ridiculed for being afraid, the child will not only remain fearful but will also feel ashamed about feeling afraid. The two affects — fear and shame — are thus bound together. Any emotion that the parent finds intolerable might be actively ridiculed or shamed. In each case, the child learns to feel ashamed whenever he or she feels the primary affect that was initially shamed by the parent.

The basic instinctual drives, such as sexuality, may also be bound by shame. A drive-shame bind might occur if a child is taught that his or her sexuality is bad or disgusting in some way. As the reactions of significant others are internalized, the boy or girl then feels a sense of shame or inadequacy over an essential part of the self.

Finally, Kaufman shows how children are taught to feel shame over basic human needs. These become what he calls need-shame binds. Kaufman identifies six basic needs:

1. Need for relationship — to be in close interpersonal relationship with others who want to be in relationship with you, the most fundamental emotional need of all;
2. Need for touching and holding — to provide a primary basis for the development of security and trust;
3. Need for identification — to know others "from the inside" and to gain a sense of belonging;
4. Need for differentiation — to experience oneself as a separate being and capable of mastering developmental tasks;
5. Need to nurture — to feel that the love and care one has to give is good and valued by others;
6. Need for affirmation — to feel worthwhile and valued for one's uniqueness.

Any of these basic needs may become bound with shame if a parent disparages the child for having the need, ignores the need, or openly refuses to meet it. The child might even grow to feel ashamed for having needs at all. In acutely painful situations, the child might repress the shameful need altogether, so that there would be no awareness of ever having a particular need.

When shame becomes internalized in this way a significant shift takes place. Instead of experiencing oneself as *feeling* ashamed, one experiences oneself as actually *being* shameful, deficient, or worthless. Kaufman writes: "'I feel shame' becomes transformed, given new meaning: 'I *am* shameful, deficient in some vital way as a human being.' Shame has become internalized. It is no longer one affect among many, but instead comes to lie at the core of the self."[16] Shame can now be activated autonomously, internally to the individual. Something from the environment may or may not trigger it; the external triggering event may look at first glance to be of little importance. But within the individual an "internal shame spiral" has begun in which "shame feelings and thoughts flow in a circle, endlessly triggering each other . . . until finally the self is engulfed. . . . Shame becomes paralyzing."[17]

The concept of the internal shame spiral was helpful to Eva as she learned to notice the onset of paralyzing shame. She was able to trace how the very slightest trigger from the environment could set off an internal avalanche of shame. The shame spiral seemed virtually to have a life of its own, having little relationship to Eva and her objective situation or what her feelings might be in response to a situation. The slightest disapproval of another (actual or only perceived), a feeling of mild anxiety or slight depression, were all capable of triggering a shame spiral. So were a variety of different emotions. As a child, it seemed that Eva had been shamed for feeling angry ("Don't get sullen with me, sister, or I'll. . . ."), for feeling anxiety ("Don't be such a worry-wart!"), for feeling sad ("Just rise above it! Put it behind you!"), for feeling happy ("Get off your high horse young lady!" or, "I'll take you down a peg or two!" or, "You think you are such a much!"). Many of these affects became unconsciously bound with shame in one way or another so that no matter *what* Eva felt, it seemed to her that there was something bad or shameful about it.

When Eva started counseling she was especially ashamed of her black despairs, as she insisted that there was "no good reason for them." Why couldn't she just "put them behind her anyway?" "What in the world was the matter with her anyway?" She had internalized

16. Kaufman, p. 65.
17. Kaufman, pp. 66-67.

her mother's attitudes toward herself to such an extent that she was completely identified with them. She genuinely thought these attacking thoughts and attitudes represented her own thoughts and feelings.

Need-shame binds had taught Eva to repress many of her basic emotional needs. Merely to have certain needs, let alone to acknowledge them or to try to get them met, was at times acutely embarrassing. Eva experienced her neediness as a bottomless pit. She once said that she felt there was no breast in the world that would be large enough to feed her inner emptiness. Another time she said that she feared that if I were to try to meet her emotional needs, I would be sucked dry; my body would become like a husk of grain that would dry up and float away. Such acknowledgments of need were a major step toward healing. She had long struggled to become as self-sufficient as possible, keeping her emotional needs secret and well-hidden from others.

For most of Eva's adult life, she had tried to get her needs for touching and holding met through relationships with men. But the need to be held in a nurturing way was still not fully met. Once, as an adult, Eva was visiting her father and accidentally stepped on a nail. She came into the house, distraught, with the nail still stuck in her foot. When she showed it to her father, he commented wryly, "I've been looking for that nail." To Eva, his words epitomized his attitude toward her need for comfort and attention when she was anxious, distressed, and in pain. It reminded her of occasions as a child when she had felt ridiculed for reaching out in need when she was hurt.

The effect of this pattern was magnified whenever Eva would begin to experience a depressive episode. She would feel distress and then disparage herself for the feeling, saying to herself in an exasperated fashion that there was no good reason for her distress. The distress would then increase to panic proportions. Similarly the inner image of the parent would become intensely shaming whenever Eva felt needy in a panicky way. The central feature that marked a black despair from an ordinary depression in Eva's mind was the inner scathing attack upon the self, combined with extreme feelings of panic and helplessness, which triggered each other endlessly in a downward shame spiral.

3. Defending against Shame and Disowning the Self

Kaufman describes several strategies that people develop to defend against intolerable feelings of shame. How do we protect ourselves from it and how do we deal with it once it is activated? One strategy is to transfer our feelings of shame onto someone else through blaming. Shame is usually transferred from top to bottom, down the dominance hierarchy of the social group. Rage, contempt, blaming, striving for power and perfection, and internal withdrawal are the categories of defense elaborated by Kaufman. Rage, a natural reaction to the sense of exposure that accompanies shame, serves to protect the self from further exposure and to distance the person who activated the shame. Extroverted individuals might express the rage outwardly, while a more introverted person may tend to keep the rage hidden inside or direct it at the self. Contempt is usually learned by the child from parental modeling. Feelings of shame or inferiority are successfully banished as one sets oneself above others, rejecting them as grossly inferior or even as disgusting.[18] Finally, internal withdrawal is the preferred defense of some who withdraw deep within the self, where none can reach or harm the self.

In his discussion of disowning the self, Kaufman talks about the self's relationship to the self, the myriad ways in which we learn to shame and blame ourselves or to hold ourselves in such contempt that we actually split off and disown a part of the self. Thus one part is identified with the contemptuous parent (whose image has been completely internalized) and the other part with the contemptible child. In this way, the adult is able to perpetuate within the self a relationship that is identical to the previously external parent-child relationship. The drives, affects, and needs that were shamed in the past are now partially or completely disowned and effectively split off from the self. The split off or disowned part is then seen as "not-me" and treated with contempt, both internally and in one's relationships with others. Disowning such a vital part of the self by definition weakens the self and increases one's sense of insecurity and vulnera-

18. For an important discussion of how contempt is passed from one generation to the next, see Alice Miller, *The Drama of the Gifted Child* (New York: Basic Books, 1981), especially chap. 3, "The Vicious Circle of Contempt," pp. 64-113.

bility. One is objectively less secure for one is subject to attack from within at any time. Kaufman writes:

> The internal shame process has become painful, punishing and enduring beyond what the simple feeling of shame might produce. The internalization of shame has produced an identity, a way of relating to oneself which absorbs, maintains and spreads shame even further. And the internalized relationship between owned and disowned parts of the self recreates directly within the inner life the very same shame-inducing qualities which were first encountered in interpersonal living.[19]

Kaufman's description of the complex inner processes that come into play when one has a shame-based identity and must continually defend against the crippling effects of shame seems to be a precise and illuminating description of Eva's core issues. Eva used many of the defenses described by Kaufman in her attempts to adapt to her environment and to grow in spite of crippling shame. School seemed to be the only environment that provided any kind of emotional counterweight to her home. Eva excelled in school and was liked by her teachers. Eva remembered that her third-grade teacher was concerned about her consistently high level of anxiety about doing her assignments correctly. She had called her a "worry-wart." Tendencies toward perfectionism thus seemed to be fairly fully developed by the age of eight. Her innate intelligence and ability to work hard, however, made school a sphere where she had some sense of control over her life and a measure of self-esteem.

Even though she was gratified that her teachers liked her, Eva did not gain as much of a sense of self-worth as one might surmise. Instead, she felt that "if they really knew her," they, too, would reject her. After all, her mother "knew her better than she knew herself," and what she knew her to be was spoiled and contemptible. Apart from occasions of internal withdrawal, Eva's main strategy of defense seemed to be "identification with the aggressor."[20] She identified with her mother's estimation of her, modeled her mother's rage and contempt, aiming them at herself.

---

19. Kaufman, p. 104.
20. See Anna Freud, *The Ego and the Mechanisms of Defense* (New York: International Universities Press, 1966), pp. 109-21.

Kaufman makes an explicit connection between the diagnosis of depression and the internal shame spiral when he says,

> When an individual has additionally learned to direct that rage inwardly against the self, this becomes a second means of perpetuating, of literally reproducing, the very shame which then protracts the depressive mood. And a self-sustaining cycle has been created which, if uninterrupted, will continue *ad infinitum.*[21]

The self-sustaining cycle of perpetuating shame, self-contempt, self-blame, and rage against the self, which Kaufman so aptly describes, was the cycle we needed to break. How might such an ingrained pattern be challenged? Was it possible to learn an entirely new way of relating to the self that would interrupt the automatic repetition of destructive patterns learned so deeply and at so early an age? Kaufman suggests a way out of this destructive inner process. He offers a vision for restoring the interpersonal bridge and a strategy for healing shame. We turn to that now.

4. Restoring the Interpersonal Bridge

In his final chapter, on healing shame and restoring the interpersonal bridge, Kaufman identifies four essential processes that need to be integrated in psychotherapeutic work. Although they are interrelated, these processes can be differentiated for the purposes of discussion. All dimensions are needed in the complex task of healing. The four processes that he identifies are:

1. The therapeutic relationship, which involves restoring the interpersonal bridge;
2. The developmental process, which involves returning internalized shame to its interpersonal origins;
3. The internal process of the self, which comprises identity re-growth and healing shame;
4. The interpersonal process, which centers on developing equal power.

21. Kaufman, p. 106.

If shame comes about through a severing of the interpersonal bridge, then the healing of shame must occur in its restoration. If shame is internalized through parental identification, then new ways of relating to oneself might occur through the internalization of a new parental figure, such as a therapist or counselor who has attitudes of acceptance and caring. If shame first occurs in association with specific human feelings, drives, or needs, then the validation of those feelings, drives, and needs as completely normal and human, along with related corrective experiences, will help dissolve the paralyzing effect of those binds. If one can become aware of the sources of shame, one will no longer need to internalize shame and can eventually intervene consciously in the internal shame spiral and stop its destructive effects.

In order for shame to be healed, the counselee's essential interpersonal needs must be met. Otherwise, she will continue to feel ashamed of these needs and will spend her energies denying them. Meeting basic emotional needs must, therefore, be a part of the therapeutic process, according to Kaufman.

The process that Kaufman calls "returning internalized shame to its interpersonal origins" is a complex one. The counselor needs to be able to acknowledge and validate the person's felt experience of shame. If a person is convinced of his or her essential defectiveness or worthlessness, he or she cannot be talked out of it by insisting that he or she is really worthwhile or lovable. Rather, the therapist needs to see and validate precisely those feelings, needs, or personal characteristics about which the person feels most exposed, imperfect, and ashamed. By approaching the shame actively, the counselor offers the person a corrective experience; what was previously a source of shame now no longer need be. Those things previously interpreted by a parent as shameful or disgusting are now reinterpreted as an essential part of one's humanity, indeed, at times even the very source of one's strength as a human being (for example, being able to identify and express one's feelings).

In this process, the therapist offers him- or herself as a new identification model, a caring, non-shaming "parent" whom the person may internalize. Thus, the dissolution of the paralyzing need-shame and affect-shame binds begins to take place at the same time that new attitudes toward the self are being formed, based on the therapist's attitudes toward the individual. As the emotional pain associated with the shame is felt, new beliefs about the self can replace old ones. This is not merely an intellectual process but a process at once both deeply emotional and fully cognitive. As the person becomes aware of the sources of shame in the past, he or she can consciously challenge the beliefs that led to that shame and slowly build a new basis for his or her sense of self-worth. If a shame spiral does begin, the individual learns how consciously to intervene and stop it.

If in actively approaching an individual's shame, the therapist inadvertently induces or triggers more shame, it is important for the therapist to take steps to restore the interpersonal bridge. The most effective way to do this, Kaufman suggests, is to acknowledge his or her part in the shaming process. While emphasizing that it was not his or her intention to shame the person, the counselor can nevertheless empathize with the shame reaction and acknowledge that he or she might have done or said things differently. If the therapist is able to do this in a non-defensive and caring way, the person will not internalize the shame. Indeed, the event has the potential for bringing emotional healing. The bond with the therapist may become even stronger than if the shame had not been induced in the first place. The person will have the experience of another taking responsibility for his or her actions, and not attempting to transfer the blame elsewhere, but openly acknowledging his or her imperfect humanness. These are the precise attitudes and behaviors that the counselee needs to learn. Additionally, by feeling the shame without internalizing it, the person learns consciously to tolerate it. As conscious tolerance increases, there becomes less need to defend against it and more ability to forgive and care for oneself.

The internal process of the self also begins to change as healing occurs. Internally the person is more able to acknowledge and own his or her affects, drives, and needs. No longer needing to disown them, the individual is able to claim and value them and to develop a secure and stable self as a result. As the individual becomes aware of the destructiveness of the internalized parent image, he or she can also begin to choose whether to allow the internal image to guide the self. When one's internalized identification images are destructive or persecutory, the person may be faced with having to let go of the hope that these "parents" will ever be nurturing to the self. Just as letting go externally and separating from the actual parents is a complex and difficult developmental task, so also is the process of letting go of the internalized identification images and replacing them with healthier ones.

Kaufman discusses the psychodynamic bases of personal identity, in both its interpersonal and intrapsychic dimensions in some detail, but he also acknowledges the place of spiritual values in the process of building a solid self-affirming personal identity.

> There is a second, more spiritual base underlying identity as a motivator. Here are subsumed the need for meaning in life, for a sense of purpose to what we do, that quest for belonging to something greater than ourselves, the search for significance which springs from the identification need. And to the degree that shame has been encountered as well as internalized, we have a third motivational base underlying identity, the search for wholeness and worth, for our essential dignity as a human being.[22]

Creating an identity with solid spiritual underpinnings requires us to be meaningfully related to a purpose beyond our own self-fulfillment or personal happiness.[23] Kaufman implies that the experience of shame may be the very motivation by which an individual may seek for deeper sources of human purpose, dignity, and worth. Kaufman again emphasizes the importance of spiritual values when he discusses self-nurturance and its healing potential.

> Learning to accept, no longer fight against, being mortal, human and imperfect is a way of talking to oneself which heals. And learning ultimately to forgive ourselves, no matter how grave the wrong we've done, is another side of true nurturance of self. . . . One begins behaving toward oneself as worthy beyond question.[24]

The source of nurture, affirmation, and forgiveness may originate outside (that is, from the therapist), but the goal is for the person to

---

22. Kaufman, p. 136.
23. For a discussion of the wider identifications, including spiritual purposes, that lie at the heart of a stable and secure identity, see also Lynd, pp. 210-58.
24. Kaufman, p. 140.

internalize these attitudes and values so that he or she will have a secure identity that no longer needs continual reinforcement from the outside. One knows in one's bones of one's essential worth.

Finally, Kaufman writes of current interpersonal relationships and the importance of the individual gaining access to a sense of his or her personal power. The goal is to form an adult-adult relationship with one's parents and others, to be able to choose whether or how to defend oneself consciously, and to learn basic skills in starting and maintaining interpersonal relationships. Expressing feelings and needs, establishing and maintaining clear boundaries, and developing conscious awareness of one's defenses are all skills that are taught to increase the person's sense of interpersonal power.

Kaufman writes, "For the necessary restoring to occur, their relationship [that is, the therapeutic relationship] must be real, honest and mutually wanted."[25] Although they are functioning within an artificial setting, the outcome of the therapeutic process depends a great deal upon the capacity of counselor and counselee to form a significant emotional bond. The counselor needs to be invested in the relationship no less than the counselee.

In my work with Eva, I sought to meet Eva's developmental needs as an essential aspect of the healing process. I let her know in various ways that I was invested in the relationship as a whole person and that she was important to me as a person *(need for relationship)*. Although my focus was appropriately on her, I shared with her from time to time where her issues touched me, particularly in those instances where my own shortcomings may have induced a shame reaction in her. I thus allowed her opportunities to know me from the inside. The fact that we were both Christians and professional women of the same generation and age allowed further opportunities for Eva's *need for identification* to be met.

At the same time it was important to recognize her uniqueness and the many important ways in which we were different from one another. Contrary to her mother's destructive message that she knew her better than Eva knew herself, I made it very clear to Eva that I did not. Eva's inside feelings were known to her alone. Thus her needs for differentiation and separateness were met especially on those oc-

25. Kaufman, p. 120.

casions when I failed to understand her. I was not an all-knowing, all-loving parent but an ordinary, fallible human being struggling to understand who she was *(need for differentiation)*.

In attempting to meet Eva's *need for affirmation,* I tried to describe honestly what I saw, not minimizing her pain, shortcomings, sins, or failures but mirroring back a worthy and lovable human being nevertheless. From time to time, Eva asked me to hold her. On those occasions when she was in the grip of a depressive episode, it seemed that nurturing touch was able to communicate my presence and caring in a way that words could not *(need for touching and holding)*. Finally, there were times when Eva's *need to nurture* was expressed in our relationship as well. She sent me a card, for example, on the anniversary of my father's death and prayed for me during the weeks that I was openly grieving his loss.

The creation of the chain of abusive messages was the beginning of the process of Eva's returning internalized shame to its interpersonal origins. Identifying those messages as essentially shaming and noticing how she perpetuated those shaming patterns in the present were necessary next steps. It was easy for Eva to lose sight of the destructiveness of the messages. She struggled continually with the desire to minimize their negative impact on her. In addition, it was difficult to catch hold of the autonomous process as it was going on in her mind. Even when she was more or less conscious of the way in which she perpetuated the shaming cycle, it was very difficult to intervene powerfully enough to stop the destructive process once it was under way.

While there were a number of occasions in which my words or actions inadvertently induced a shame reaction in Eva, there was one such occasion that might be used to illustrate various dimensions of the healing process that Kaufman identifies: first, to restore the severed interpersonal bridge; second, to identify the sources of the shame reaction; third, to internalize a caring parental figure; and finally, to validate Eva's needs as normal and even as a source of personal strength.

Eva and I had been working for some time, meeting twice a week. In this session she had expressed some hope that she might one day find some respite from her depression and genuine healing. She also told me that she had taken me all the way into her heart, where she had previously let in only the members of her family. She was thus openly acknowledging her growing dependence on me and the importance of our relationship, both to herself and to me. I was touched by what she said and told her so. I then had some scheduling information that I needed to tell her about. I was going to be away for a month at Christmas and wanted to let her know now, since the holidays were generally a difficult time for her.

The juxtaposition of Eva's expressing her need and vulnerability with my informing her of my imminent departure had a powerful shaming effect on Eva. Just when she had told me how much I meant to her, I told her I was leaving her. It felt to her like a repetition of her parents' rejecting message: "Don't need me. Don't depend on me. Don't ask anything of me." It felt as if the moment she had trusted me enough to say that she needed me was precisely the moment that I pushed her away.

Eva's initial reaction had been to withdraw and castigate herself. But she found that she was able to move out of that familiar pattern rather quickly and to risk confronting me with her feelings. In doing so, she had to move beyond her inner paralysis with her internalized mother. First, she questioned authority. (Compare her mother's voice: "I *am* authority." "I am your *mother!*" "Don't you *dare* talk back to me.") Second, she consciously stopped herself from going into the familiar shame spiral of self-blame and self-doubt. For the time being, at least, she was able to break the "identification with the aggressor" and maintain an independent standpoint. Finally, she dared to feel and express her feelings of intense anger toward me. She found that her anger did not destroy me (or herself), as she had unconsciously feared. It did not break the bond between us; instead, it was strengthened. Eva had the experience, perhaps for the first time, of an important other acknowledging her own part in inducing a shame response, thus a step that helped repair the interpersonal bridge.

The incident, with its intensity of feeling, seemed to light up Eva's inner landscape. She had never realized so fully how much she had been a cowering child inside, waiting to be punished or killed by Mommy's wrath. She had also not known how frightened she was of her own anger, how certain she had been that it could and possibly would emotionally destroy another if she were to unleash it. Finally, the experience showed how it was possible to work through extremely

uncomfortable feelings in order to arrive at a new place, both intrapsychically and interpersonally. It demonstrated, in a way that mere intellectual understanding could not, that dramatic change was possible,
for she had in actuality changed her own behavior, with far-reaching
results. Through this work she was also given the opportunity to
internalize a caring, non-punitive parent figure and achieved a new
sense of her own personal power. The incident was to be a watershed
in our therapeutic work.[26]

Part Three. A Theological Interpretation: The Dynamics of Grace

At the same time as Eva and I sought to understand how shame
paralyzed her and contributed to her depression, we were engaged in
another conversation of a different character. In addition to psychological understanding, we also sought theological clarity about the
issues Eva faced. Several themes in Barth's *Church Dogmatics* — specifically, the mercy and righteousness of God, justification by faith, shame
and honor, and demonic possession — seemed pertinent to Eva's core
issues. By examining these themes as they applied to Eva, the theological aspect of our "bilingual" conversation can be shown.

The Mercy of God

The urgent theological question that brought Eva to a pastoral counselor had to do with God's attitude toward her black despairs. Were

---

26. It might be noted, however, that these dynamics needed to be repeated again
and again throughout the course of the therapeutic process. A single such incident,
however dramatic, would not be capable of bringing about permanent intrapsychic
and interpersonal change. The reader should perhaps be apprised of the fact that
Eva's condition worsened as she continued to work through this kind of emotional
material. As the repression lifted she began to recover memories that catapulted her
into a major clinical depression. The healing process itself might be described as a
kind of descent into hell. Such a process of dissolution as a precondition to the
possibility of healing is discussed in the writings of such theorists as C. G. Jung and
R. D. Laing.

her black despairs a sin and, therefore, offensive to God? Eva was convinced that God was deeply disappointed by her inability to avoid this recurrent emotional and spiritual paralysis. In the midst of a depressive episode, Eva could hardly crawl out of bed in the morning. Yet she felt sure God was tired of her self-pity and helplessness and put off by her protests of exhaustion.

At this point it might be helpful to ask the following question. What, as Barth reads Scripture, is God's attitude toward human sin and suffering? In discussing the Gospels' stories of Jesus' healing miracles, Barth takes up the theme of God's mercy. In these stories, Barth notes, God is not seen as standing over against human beings, judging them for their wrongdoing, but as entering fully into their suffering and need, taking on their burdens and pain. In the person of Jesus Christ, God shows compassion to sinners and is ready to heal them of their afflictions. When Jesus confronts the suffering human being, he is not directly concerned with sin as such, nor with identifying the sources of the suffering, but rather with delivering that person from affliction. The evident point of the stories, as Barth reads them, is not human sin but divine healing.

As a striking example, our attention is drawn to the question of the disciples in the story of the blind man's healing: "'Who sinned, this man or his parents, that he was born blind?' Jesus answered, 'It was not that this man sinned, nor his parents, but that the works of God might be made manifest in him'" (John 9:2-3). The story emphasizes God's gracious will to release the man from his blindness, in contradistinction to any human culpability that might lie behind his condition. Barth writes:

> In these stories it does not seem to be of any great account that the people who suffer as creatures are above all sinful human beings, human beings who are at fault in relation to God, their neighbors and themselves, who are therefore guilty and have betrayed themselves into all kinds of trouble. No, the important thing about them in these stories is not that they are sinners but that they are sufferers. Jesus . . . does not ask, therefore, concerning their sin. He does not hold it against them. He does not denounce them because of it. The help and blessing that he brings are quite irrespective of their sin. (IV/2, 223 rev.)

As Barth reads them, the stories take for granted that the human sufferers are also sinners. But they also indicate that God has mercy upon these creatures despite their sin, causing "'the sun to shine on the good and the evil, and his rain to fall on the just and the unjust' (Matt. 5:45)" (IV/2, 223). Who exactly, Barth asks, is the person that Jesus approaches with his compassionate mercy?

> The answer is obvious. It is the person with whom things are going badly; who is needy and frightened and harassed. . . . The picture brought before us is that of suffering. . . . For human life as it emerges in this activity of Jesus is really like a great hospital whose many departments in some way enfold us all. (IV/2, 223 rev.)

Eva's personal sense of God's exasperation and disappointment stands in obvious contrast with the conception that Barth develops on the basis of the Gospels' stories. Eva seems to see God as a punitive parent, reprimanding her for her sloth, while Barth sees God, on the basis of these stories, as essentially concerned with removing whatever might be causing the distress of one such as her. Although God finds people, says Barth, "in the shadow of death, his miraculous action to them is to bring them out of this shadow, to free them from this prison, to remove the need and pain of their cosmic determination" (IV/2, 222 rev.). Here God is seen as standing alongside people as healer and deliverer, not over against them as judge or punitive parent. In another place, Barth expands on this theme of God's merciful action toward the creature in distress.

> The mercy of God lies in his readiness to share in sympathy the distress of another, a readiness which springs from his inmost nature and stamps all his being and doing. It lies, therefore, in his will, springing from the depths of his nature and characterizing it, to take the initiative himself for the removal of this distress. . . . The personal God has a heart. He can feel and be affected. . . . God is moved and stirred, yet not like ourselves in powerlessness, but in his own free power, in his innermost being; moved and touched by himself, i.e. open, ready, inclined . . . to compassion with another's suffering and therefore to assistance. (II/1, 370 rev.)

As here understood, God in mercy is moved to compassion because it is of the essence of the divine identity to be compassionate.

Eva's personal sense of God as a punitive parent also stands in contrast with Barth's depiction of Jesus as the fellow-sufferer who has more compassion on us than we have on ourselves. Understood in such a light, God would be seen as compassionate toward Eva's sense of helplessness, not exasperated by it. God would be seen as working, in her and through others, to release her from her suffering, so that she might be free to live and breathe again. Barth emphasizes that the acts of Jesus self-evidently place him

> at the side of humankind in this respect — that that which causes suffering to human beings as his creatures is also and above all painful and alien and antithetical to himself. As Jesus acts in [God's] commission and power, it is clear that God does not will that which troubles and torments and disturbs and destroys human beings. He does not will . . . entanglement and humiliation and distress and shame. . . . He wills . . . that they should be whole. (IV/2, 225 rev.)

From this perspective, Eva needed to hear that God was on her side and by her side, seeking her deliverance from the painful depressive episodes that so beset her.

Eva's preoccupation with her supposed sin of sloth and God's supposed judgment upon her had, from a Barthian perspective, so distorted the gospel that she was effectively unable to hear it at all. Her view of God's exasperation and impatience seemed to project onto God the unconscious image of her parents, who had continually expected Eva to pull herself up "by her own bootstraps." Perhaps Eva's sin was not her sloth and laziness, as she supposed, but rather her distorted understanding of God, by which she kept her Helper and Savior at arm's length, by seeing God as persecutor and enemy. Insofar as she continued to see God as someone to appease or placate, Eva remained cut off from the knowledge of God's readiness to help and deliver her.

The Righteousness of God

But what about God's judgment and righteousness? Doesn't the Bible, as Eva well knew, refer to God as Judge as well as Savior, to a God holy and righteous as well as merciful? Is it possible that Eva's personal sense of the divine wrath and judgment might be theologically valid after all?

In discussing God's mercy and righteousness, Barth argues that we are mistaken if we imagine them as polar opposites, as if they implied two utterly opposing aspects of God. While God does reveal himself as Judge, it must be remembered, says Barth, that "God's justice is also in fact a determination of his love, and his judgment is an expression of his grace. . . . It is as God forgives sins in his mercy that he judges" (II/1, 382). In other words, God affirms his divine worth and righteousness in the very act of having compassion and mercy on the sinner. The effective exercise of God's righteousness was his decision to enter into covenant with humankind. "For God's righteousness," says Barth, "is that human beings in covenant with him should be righteous; that they should be those who are justified in God's sight because God has addressed them and dealt with them in righteousness, putting them in the right" (II/1, 385 rev.). While Barth discusses this complex topic with great subtlety in detail, his position is essentially that in the cross of Jesus Christ God finds a way to remain true to himself in righteousness while being merciful to the fallen creature in distress, that God's judgment and wrath finally exist in the service of God's mercy, and that God's no is not finally uttered except in the context of God's yes (II/1, 368-406).

If this understanding of God's righteousness were applied to Eva and her situation, it would seem to follow that by God's will Eva, too, whatever her shortcomings and failures, would be received as righteous and acceptable before God. But this would mean that God had canceled out her sin along with that of the world and desired that she, too, should stand before God, with all her shortcomings and failures, justified and forgiven like all the rest. Barth emphasizes that as attested by Scripture and confessed by faith, God's righteousness works on behalf of the poor and helpless, on behalf, therefore, of those like Eva who are overwhelmed by psychic and spiritual forces far more powerful than they.

> To establish justice for the innocent who are threatened and the poor, the widows, the orphans and the strangers who are oppressed . . . God stands at every time unconditionally and passionately on this

and only on this side: always against the exalted and for the lowly, always against those who already have rights and for those from whom they are robbed and taken away. (II/1, 386 rev.)

The truth about God's righteousness that Eva needed to hear is that, as Barth continues, "when we encounter divine righteousness, we are all like the people of Israel, menaced and altogether lost according to its own strength. We are all widows and orphans who cannot procure right for themselves" (II/1, 387). For Eva might be seen as a kind of spiritual and emotional orphan, one utterly without strength to procure right for herself and thus as one whom God passionately and unconditionally affirms.

God's righteousness and God's mercy are here seen as two sides of the same coin. "At this point," Barth writes, "the truth emerges that God's righteousness does not really stand alongside his mercy, but that as revealed in its necessary connection, according to Scripture, with the plight of the poor and wretched, it is itself God's mercy" (II/1, 387). Because it is through the forgiveness of sin, Barth continues, that God's righteousness is most fully and most freely expressed, God's righteousness is itself God's mercy at the same time. From this perspective it would follow that insofar as Eva was a sufferer, God in his mercy was ready to deliver her from her distress. Yet, insofar as her suffering perhaps arose through her complicity in sin, God in his righteousness stood ready rather to forgive than to condemn, or, more precisely, to bear the condemnation in her place and bear it away that one such as her might be forgiven. In neither case could God fairly be seen as an impatient and exasperated divine parent who demanded that Eva wrest herself from helplessness and sin. On the contrary, this God would expect Eva to call upon him for help. Eva's acknowledgment of her true inability and helplessness would be the very condition for her being enabled to reach out to God in her need.

Justification by Faith

An understandable consequence of Eva's upbringing was her profound conviction that her intrinsic worth as a human being depended upon what she did, not upon who she was. This conviction arose quite naturally out of repeated messages from her parents that her worth did in fact depend on what she did. Her conclusion was a carry-over of her childhood situation, where she felt that she could earn her parents' love and approval only if she did as she was told. Her failure to gain their love or approval in any particular instance did not cause her to question her belief that their love was "earnable." Instead, it merely underlined her intrinsic unworthiness and inability to be "good" and therefore lovable. The stage was set for a pervasive and deeply ingrained sense of what could theologically be interpreted as "works-righteousness." When this pattern of thought was transferred into Eva's relationship with God, "God" was forced into the role of the disapproving parent who needed to be appeased and whose love could only be earned by doing the "right" thing. Thus, with "God," too, Eva sought to do it "right."

The theological doctrine of justification by faith reveals the futility of this pattern of thought and behavior. This whole line of thinking, that one can earn love or justify oneself or prove one's worthiness is shown to be empty and false. Love, by its very nature, has what Dorothy Martyn has called a "can't earn" quality.[27] If Eva's parents did not love her, it was not because Eva was unable to earn it. Rather, it was because they somehow lacked the capacity to love. By contrast, if Eva was unable to earn God's love, it was not because God lacked the capacity to love but because God's love was freely given and not dependent upon Eva's having the "right" attitudes or behavior. God's love and Eva's "righteousness" or acceptability before God could only be a pure gift, not something earned or earnable.

While the theological doctrine of justification by faith is analogous to a psychodynamic understanding of shame, the former is more paradoxical in its approach to the subject. As we noted previously, Kaufman acknowledges spiritual dimensions to the psychodynamics of shame. To have an integrated personal identity, he argues, human beings need to find a sense of wholeness and worth. They need to know themselves as "worthy beyond question."[28] They need not only to find their "essential dignity as human beings" but also to forgive themselves when they fall short of their hopes and expectations.

27. Dorothy Martyn, *The Man in the Yellow Hat* (Atlanta: Scholars Press, 1992), p. 151.
28. Kaufman, p. 140.

A sense of worth, as Kaufman shows, grows out of healthy human relationships, where one is treated with respect and care. To know oneself as "worthy beyond question," especially when one's interpersonal relationships have been damaging rather than nurturing, requires a leap of faith. Kaufman seems quite right to emphasize a spiritual dimension at this point, for here we pass out of a psychological frame of reference into one that is somehow theological. Knowledge of oneself as "worthy beyond question" is not, it would seem, immediately or self-evidently ascertainable. On the premise of human sin, human beings are not in fact unquestionably worthy. By virtue of human sin, they do not have the capacity to confer worth on themselves. According to the doctrine of justification by faith, as affirmed by the Reformation and interpreted by Barth, one can know oneself as "worthy beyond question" only as one finds one's worthiness beyond oneself in Christ, that is, only as God makes one worthy. As Barth puts it, a human being "knows and grasps his own righteousness as one which is alien to him, as the righteousness of this other," that is, of Jesus Christ (IV/1, 631). Insofar as a person tries to find her righteousness in herself, or to earn her worthiness by works of merit, such an attempt only mires the person more deeply in sin. Christ's righteousness can be received only as one renounces all attempts at self-justification. With reference to believers Barth writes:

> Even in the action of faith they are sinful persons who as such are not in a position to justify themselves, who with every attempt to justify themselves can only become the more deeply entangled in their sin. . . . Even as believers they can represent themselves to God only as those they are in virtue of their past, only with the request, "God be merciful to me, a sinner." (IV/1, 616 rev.)

The paradox of the knowledge of human sin is that human beings can ultimately know themselves as sinners only in light of forgiveness. Known sin as such, Barth argues, is always finally forgiven sin. We cannot fully perceive ourselves as sinners, he suggests, apart from Jesus Christ. Therefore, knowledge of oneself as a sinner cannot possibly perpetuate debilitating shame (in the sense of low self-worth) but finally only gratitude, for it is precisely as a sinner that one is forgiven and accepted and exalted by God. The sin is not glossed over or hidden but fully evident only as graciously overcome, so that the person's worth before God is nevertheless fully affirmed.

From this perspective it would follow that even as a sinner, the perceived status that in one way or another most immobilized her, Eva was nevertheless "worthy beyond question." Even those things about which she felt most ashamed could not separate her from God's love. As God's adopted daughter, made righteous by Christ, she could just let herself be. She could stop driving herself mercilessly in an attempt to reach a perfection or worthiness that by definition were beyond her.

Of course, knowing that she was "worthy beyond question" was precisely the kind of knowledge that Eva could not readily grasp. Years of parental shaming had had the effect of miring Eva not in real, legitimate guilt that could be confessed and forgiven but in a kind of self-destructive, neurotic guilt that led nowhere and was utterly un-redemptive.[29] The compulsive listing of all kinds of minor "sins" or faults seemed, on a psychological level, to be an attempt to ward off the constant criticism of her internalized parents by identifying with them and making their criticisms her own. Theologically, it seemed to be a strange, inverted kind of attempt at self-justification. Frank Lake, a British psychiatrist who writes astutely about the clinical ap-plication of Christian theological insight, claims that such neurotic guilt is a sure diagnostic indicator of depression. He writes that such self-accusation is "a form of self-righteousness and perfectionism, standing, as it were, on its head, in order to attract attention to the arduous attempts it has made to be good, and to be worthy of approval on grounds of previous meritorious works and reparative toil."[30]

If Eva's litanies of sin were an indicator of neurotic guilt, what was Eva's real guilt?[31] When I asked her, she responded immediately with words to the effect of "Keeping the self-attack going. Going over my sins again and again. Keeping myself steeled for the next blow, staying partly crushed all the time, not letting myself believe God's

---

29. See Ann Belford Ulanov's description of "the false cross" in *The Wisdom of the Psyche* (Cambridge, Mass.: Cowley, 1988), pp. 33-72.

30. Frank Lake, *Clinical Theology* (London: Darton, Longman and Todd, 1966), p. 225.

31. See Ulanov's description of "the true cross" in *Wisdom of the Psyche,* pp. 33-72.

forgiveness, being so self centered." In striking parallel to Eva's words, Frank Lake imagines a kind of internal monologue that goes on as the depressed Christian tries to come to terms with his or her true guilt:

> The depressed *Christian,* and here we must underline the word Christian, for it is of Christians that we are speaking, comes to know what true sin and actual guilt are when he tries to answer the question, "Why, during all these months of misery, would I not respond to Christ's offer of life? . . . Why have I been blind to all He is doing? . . . I have been spending my days poking about in my own ethical navel, circling around my own past in hectic self-appraisal, alternately approving and condemning. I was determined to be my own judge."[32]

The true guilt, then, is seen as failing to grasp the forgiveness and life freely offered, in determining to be one's own judge and executioner rather than allowing the mercy and righteousness of God to have the final word. Lake comments, "That one calling himself a Christian should have so neglected and misrepresented Christ to himself, though explicable in terms of neurotic projection, is a valid ground for a sense of actual guilt."[33]

As Eva herself began to confess the sin of not believing in God's promises of new life and of failing to receive the forgiveness and love that were already hers in Christ, she also began to differentiate the God of the New Testament from the "neurotic projection" of the internalized parents. From a clinical theological standpoint, this was a major step toward healing.

> Neurotic guilt is dissolved so that real guilt may be established, in the specific sense in which the Holy Spirit is concerned to establish it, that is, in relation to Jesus Christ. . . . The aim of the clinical theological approach is to replace neurotic guilt by a true and valid sense of sin.[34]

From this perspective, a valid sense of sin, when confessed, as well as a valid sense of forgiveness, can genuinely be experienced as the

32. Lake, p. 226.
33. Lake, p. 226.
34. Lake, pp. 227 and 229.

individual begins to turn away from the self and toward Christ and his righteousness.

On Shame and Honor

If the dynamics of shame were indeed at the heart of Eva's depression, then only as she found her true worth and honor would she find healing.[35] Threading one's way through the dynamics of shame is a complex process. For while there is the debilitating shame that a person learns in a dysfunctional family, there is also the genuine and, might one say, healthy sense of shame that can accompany the recognition of oneself as a sinner before God. This is a delicate and complex matter.

Even as a pastoral counselor might hope to diminish a sense of inner worthlessness and point to a transcendent and reliable source of worthiness, at the same time, he or she can recognize the validity of a sense of shame about one's status as a sinner before God. Barth is insistent upon our objective situation of shame before God, whether or not we are subjectively aware of that situation.

> But human beings are shamed (whether or not they are correspondingly ashamed) because they find that they are compared with God. With God? Yes, if they are radically and totally shamed it is because they are compared with God, and measured by his holiness they necessarily see their own unholiness revealed. (IV/2, 385 rev.)

This insight is just one aspect of Barth's larger insight that we can finally see and understand our sin only in the light of Jesus Christ. Just as we cannot fully appreciate the magnitude of our sin until it is forgiven sin (that is, sin seen in the light of Jesus Christ), so also we

---

35. Lynd, who also contrasts shame with honor and self-respect, explores some of the paradoxes inherent in the relation between shame and pride. For Lynd, having a secure identity protects one from debilitating shame. She writes: "Trying to understand the relation between pride and humility brings us back to a paradox — the paradox that the more fully one is aware of his own individual identity, the more fully he is also aware of the immensity of the universe and of his place in it" (pp. 254-55). One's self-respect as a human being includes respecting one's human limits.

cannot penetrate the depths of our true and objective shame unless we know it already to have been taken from us. In an eloquent passage Barth drives the point home:

> God has received us so basically and radically that he was ready to make himself our Brother in his own Son, to share our situation, to bear our shame, to be put to shame in our place and on our behalf, thus removing us human beings from the situation which contradicts his election and love and creative will, divesting us of our shame and clothing us with his own glory. (IV/2, 384)

According to Barth, God enters fully into the shamefulness of sin and in Christ takes it upon himself so that human beings might share God's honor and glory. Barth goes so far as to call Jesus "the one great sinner" (IV/1, 239). Not because of any sinfulness of his own, but because of the sin and shame of the entire human race that he bears in his body, Jesus knows human sin in its awful depths and bears the shamefulness of it to an extent greater than human imagining.

Because of sin, all human beings are equally and objectively shamed before God, but only those who know God's true identity (that is, God's holiness) also feel subjectively ashamed in a non-debilitating sense. As Barth points out, both the publican and the Pharisee in the Gospels' story are objectively shamed in light of the divine holiness, but only the publican actually feels ashamed of his sin and cries out for God's mercy. The Pharisee remains in blind ignorance as he congratulates himself on his own goodness and worthiness (IV/2, 385). As depicted in the story, he clearly does not know the One to whom he addresses his prayer. Similarly, it is just when Peter recognizes Jesus' identity as the Holy Lord that he cries out, "Depart from me; for I am a sinful man, O Lord" (Luke 5:8). From Barth's perspective, an encounter with God as the Holy One goes hand in hand with a particular kind of self-knowledge, that is knowledge of oneself as a sinner.

Along with that self-knowledge comes the affect of shame.

> The joy in which we can boast in relation to [Christ] is absolutely bound up with the humility in which we are necessarily ashamed in relation to him. . . . Hence none of us can confess him and therefore be a Christian, unless we confess that we are totally shamed by him. (IV/2, 396 rev.)

If Christ has taken the shame of human sin upon himself and has made it fully his own in order to redeem the sinner, then in the great redemptive pattern of exchange, as embedded in the mystery of the gospel, human beings also may take on and receive the honor before God that belongs to Christ alone. While on the one hand, human beings find themselves "totally shamed" in confronting God's terrible holiness, on the other hand, God yet shares with them freely and graciously a portion of the honor properly belonging to God. Those people humbled by an accurate recognition of their objective unworthiness before God are yet the very ones exalted by God to partake of a measure of God's glory.

Barth's discussion of honor is placed in the larger context of his theological ethics, that is, in the context of "the command of God" and "the freedom of the creature" to respond to that command (III/4). In this material, Barth focuses on human "freedom in limitation." Within the allotted span of any individual's life, God calls one to freedom; God calls one into a covenant partnership. This is the honor that God is seen as conferring on human beings: the call to be in relationship with God. Barth writes:

> What remains is the unsurpassable honor done to us when the commanding God who is our Father calls us as his own child, not just anywhere or to any great or small achievements and activities, but to himself. To be with this Father as the child of this Father is freedom. (III/4, 648 rev.)

God's honoring of the creature in Barth's sense is twofold. First, human beings receive a portion of God's glory by virtue of their creaturehood, and second by virtue of their being called into God's service. God creates human beings and also calls them into partnership as "an expression of his esteem, a distinction. . . . He considers human beings worthy that he should confront them as their Commander and stand on their level as Partner with partner" (III/4, 649).

As suggested by various scriptural texts (for example, "I have called thee by name, thou art mine" [Isa. 43:1]), each person, Barth believes, is called individually by God (III/4, 650).[36] Even though a person may

36. For a possible psychological analogy to Barth's understanding of God's unique call to each particular individual, see Jung's comments on "vocation" in *The Development of the Personality,* Collected Works, vol. 17 (New York: Pantheon, 1954), pp. 175-86.

deny the call, overlook it, or misinterpret it, God continues to bestow the honor by continuing to offer fellowship and to call the person into service. Thus while human beings might sin against their own honor, they cannot objectively lose it. "The honor itself, precisely because it is not theirs, but the reflection of the glory of God falling upon them, cannot be lost" (III/4, 652 rev.). Human beings are thus seen as sharing in God's own glory and as invited to attest that glory through service in the world; this invitation and thus the honor remain in force regardless of the human response.

It seemed to me that Barth's understanding of the objectivity of human honor, apart from human effort or human failing or human shame, might have the potential to stop Eva's endless descent into ever deeper levels of shame. Everyone is deemed worthy of God's honor, even the most wretched.

> What are all human declamations about the intrinsic dignity of human beings compared with the foundation which it is given here according to the witness of the Bible? On the other hand, how can this honor be overlooked, forgotten or denied in the face of this foundation? How can "dignity" be denied to even the most miserable of human beings when the glory of God himself was the honor of that person as nailed in supreme wretchedness to the cross? (III/4, 654 rev.)

The honor and value that God accorded Eva was, from this perspective, clearly something, and perhaps the only thing, that could put an effective stop to the apparently endless spiral of shame.

There were, in fact, occasions in which Eva spoke in terms analogous to Barth's understanding of her honor as a creature and covenant partner of God. Her core belief, that God had delivered her from alcoholism, was one way that she had reflected upon the honor bestowed upon her. If God had rescued her from that cycle of self-destruction, she reasoned, surely it was because God had a purpose for her. If God had begun a work of salvation in her, surely God would complete the task (Phil. 1:6). Eva felt awed, humbled, and honored whenever she reflected on her deliverance from alcoholism. Her very gratitude seemed to motivate her to serve God. She further reflected that this service to which God called her was itself further evidence of God's honoring her. She thus began to be motivated by a perduring desire to bear witness to this God who had shown such mercy to her. Thus a benign spiral upwards became a countervailing force to the shame spiral leading her back into self-hatred and depression. Barth writes:

> God tells each one of us that he needs us in a definite and concrete respect, that he has a use for us. Not one of us is to pass our short span of life in vain. . . . God wills for each one of us that in our limited time and at our limited place we should be his witness. (III/4, 657 rev.)

The worth, distinction, and honor of a human being, then, according to Barth, is something objective but not intrinsic. One cannot find it by looking within or even by looking to one's fellow human beings for affirmation. For human ideas of honor vary from culture to culture and epoch to epoch, but God's honor is unchangeably related to God's call. "Human beings have not called forth their honor, any more than they could call forth themselves out of nothingness, or call, justify, or sanctify themselves. . . . They have it only because God is there for them" (III/4, 664 rev.). Each person is called and commanded in a way unique to his or her own history, for it is a living, active God who calls. Discerning God's concrete calling for this particular person entered, then, into the task of the pastoral counseling.

From a perspective such as this, Eva's honor before God was secure. There was nothing she could do to threaten it. A belief such as this would have the potential to be a strong counterweight to the negative effects of the shame spiral. While she may have cast herself down again and again, she slowly came to believe that God would continually reaffirm her worth and dignity, by expecting something from her, by calling her to be a witness. "We each have our honor before God and from God. No circumstances and no human being can increase or diminish it, can give it to us or take it from us. Even we ourselves cannot do this. God alone is competent to decide our dignity and worth" (III/4, 678).

On Demonic Possession

While Eva felt herself to be the battleground where intense spiritual conflict was being waged, were we justified in imagining her spiritual bondage as a kind of "demonic possession"? On the one hand, it seemed that Eva and I both used the term loosely and metaphorically, where "demonic voices" could just as easily be described as internalized parent representations. The voices that seemed to have "demonic" power were understood in some broad sense as merely the internalization of repetitive destructive messages from Eva's mother and father.

On the other hand, when Eva had the nightmare in which her mother had been pictured as a demon living inside her and at her expense, it almost seemed as if we had crossed an invisible line where "internalized parent representation" could perhaps no longer capture the full reality of the phenomenon. The "internalized parent" from childhood had grown into a grotesque demonic figure who, Eva felt, was sucking her very life from her. The urgency and uncanniness of the nightmare was such that Eva felt it was literally a matter of life and death for her to become free of the insidious influence of her mother's evil hold upon her. The image of the nightmare was not of her mother but of a "demon-mother."[37]

A sense of psychopathological and spiritual complexity is evident in Barth's discussion of "demonic possession." Barth became interested in such phenomena through his study of the exorcism of a young woman in the parish of Pastor Johann C. Blumhardt (1805–1880). After months of meeting for prayer and pastoral conversation, Blumhardt had performed an exorcism in which the woman was finally freed. According to Blumhardt's account, as the demons left her body they were heard to have cried out, "Jesus is Victor!" Barth, clearly impressed by this story, not only entitled one of the sections of the *Church Dogmatics* "Jesus is Victor" but also reflected in a critical way on several possible levels of meaning implied in such an event.

Given what he knew as contemporary tools of discernment and

---

37. For a non-reductive theological discussion of "demon possession," especially as it relates to various psychopathological phenomena, see Marguerite Shuster, *Power, Pathology and Paradox: The Dynamics of Evil and Good* (Grand Rapids: Zondervan, 1987).

frames of reference, Barth distinguished three aspects of the phenom-enon.[38] "Like similar events in the New Testament," Barth writes,

> the occurrence during which Blumhardt heard the cry "Jesus is Victor," has three aspects. On the first, it is realistically explained in the sense of ancient and modern mythology. On the second, it is explained in terms of modern psychopathology or depth psychology. On the third, it is not explained at all but can only be estimated spiritually on the assumption that the two former explanations are also possible and even justifiable in their own way. (IV/3, 170)

Although Barth's own interest is in the spiritual (the third) aspect, he does not thereby dismiss or minimize the importance of the other two.

From such a standpoint each of these three perspectives would be allowed its own validity within the limits of its own explanatory or descriptive framework. The first which Barth distinguishes is that of a "realistic explanation" set forth in the terms of ancient and modern mythology. To speak of "demons" in the contemporary world is to enter into a mythological frame of reference, where personified forces of evil more powerful than the self seem to be intent on destroying all one's efforts. Curiously, Barth refers to such mythological description as a "realistic explanation." How could an admittedly mythological description be regarded as realistic? Clearly Barth is not categorically rejecting the term "mythological" as, for example, Rudolph Bultmann has done.[39] By "realistic" I take Barth to mean that such "mythological" description is, in its own way, as accurate a description of the actual phenomenon in such a case as one can approximate. It is realistic (that is, analogically valid) rather than "literal" or "symbolic."[40] Such "mytho-

---

38. I am indebted to Daniel J. Price for this insight. See his unpublished doctoral dissertation, "Karl Barth's Anthropology in Light of Modern Thought: The Dynamic Concept of the Person in Trinitarian Theology and Object Relations Psychology" (University of Aberdeen, Scotland, 1990), p. 393.

39. Bultmann apparently found these stories about the Blumhardts to be "an abomination" and was dismayed that Barth would dignify them by including them in his *Church Dogmatics*. (See Price, p. 392.)

40. Cf. George Hunsinger, "Beyond Literalism and Expressivism: Karl Barth's Hermeneutical Realism," *Modern Theology* 3 (April 1987): 209-23. It should be noted that this article does not take up the question of the "demonic" nor of Barth's uncharacteristic espousal here of the term "mythological."

logical" description, when trying to describe elusive and transcendent aspects of reality, is considered, in certain cases, to be at least as "realistic" as the scientific language that categorically disallows certain kinds of description at the outset.

From the second perspective, such demon possession is explained in terms of modern psychopathology or depth psychology. Barth allows that such explanations are both "possible" and even "justifiable in their own way." In explicating Barth's position, Daniel Price moves cautiously back and forth between the thought worlds of depth psychology and Barthian theology, concluding that there exists an analogy between "human brokenness as a revealed broken relation to God and others, and on the psychological level as internalized bad object relations."[41] He raises significant questions that point to the mysterious area of overlap between the two frameworks for knowing.

> For Barth, the term, "demonization," is used somewhat metaphorically; yet Barth does not discount the possibility that demons are "real" — even though their reality is ontologically negative. For Fairbairn, the demons are psychological. Yet they might not be exhaustively described in terms of endopsychic human states — for they represent an unhappy interpersonal history; and a history of bad object relations can very readily become repressed and stored in the unconscious with the result that they may become a sinister psychological force in the life of the individual. Who knows if such a sinister psychological force might not begin to assume a life of its own — acting independently of the person whose *soma-psyche* it occupies?[42]

Contemporary object relations interpretations of the psychopathological explanations of demonization would, I think, come to a conclusion similar to Fairbairn's. Indeed, such is the thrust of Rizzuto's more contemporary study, as discussed in Chapter Four. Yet when we examine the same phenomenon from a theological perspective, can the kind of question that Price is asking simply be dismissed out of hand?

However, there is yet a third possible perspective on the phenomenon, this being the one that most clearly interests Barth as dogmatic

41. Price, p. 391.
42. Price, p. 392.

theologian but that is also of interest to the pastoral counselor. In the third or spiritual perspective, these demonic forces cannot be explained at all but must be understood, along with the other two perspectives, in a spiritual or theological frame of reference as well. While freely acknowledging the validity of approaching such phenomena from a psychiatric perspective — for, he says, "in what took place it was really a matter of human and therefore also psychical conditions and processes" (IV/2, 228) — Barth then goes on to say:

> The only thing is that we must not think that what the Gospel passages have in mind in relation to these sufferers, and especially to the action of Jesus, can be exhaustively described, let alone grasped in its decisive spiritual and theological meaning and character, in this explanation. (IV/2, 228)

The third way of looking at demon possession attempts to probe just this meaning and character, as they can come to be understood through a study of Scripture.

At this point it might be helpful to recall the story of the healing of the demoniac (Mark 5:1-20). As Barth reads it, the story is a dramatic rendering of the cosmic confrontation between the power of God and the power of evil and of God's final victory over evil. In the story Jesus is seen as entering into conflict with the powers of evil and death and, by the sovereign power of God, as emerging victorious. The exorcism reveals in an especially dramatic way that all forms of human misery are against God's will.

> That which causes suffering to the human being as his creature is also and above all painful and alien and antithetical to himself. As Jesus acts in his commission and power, it is clear that God does not will that which troubles and disturbs and destroys human beings. (IV/2, 225 rev.)

God wills life and salvation for humans, freedom from every form of tyranny and healing from pain and torment.

Thus, to look at the story of the demoniac's exorcism in its decisive theological and spiritual character and meaning, as Barth interprets it, is to see its integral connection with the central narrative of the Gospels — the life, death, and resurrection of Jesus. For while in this story Jesus manifests the sovereign power of God, in the passion narratives he increasingly identifies himself with the powerlessness of sinful humanity, as suggested by the demoniac's vulnerability. In the course of the synoptic narratives, Jesus becomes progressively powerless until that moment of total brokenness on the cross, where he himself cries out as one utterly forsaken and lost, cast out from the human community and given up to the realm of destruction and death for our sakes. Into this situation of complete desolation, the power of God irrupts in its most radical and absolute form. In the resurrection of Jesus, even death itself is conquered as that which is alien to God. The realm of suffering and death, to which the demoniac himself was subject and from which he was released by the mercy of God in Christ, is ultimately shown to be powerless.

How might these reflections be applied to Eva's case? It would seem that all three perspectives that Barth differentiates were operative in our pastoral therapeutic work. From one perspective, Eva and I were aware that we were speaking metaphorically when we spoke of the "demonic" element with which she struggled. Although metaphorical, it seemed to capture an essential aspect of the phenomenon that could not otherwise be fully articulated.

From the second perspective, however, the demonic element did seem to derive from an internalized "bad object." Object relations psychology with its ability to describe with precision the effects of internalizing such a "bad object" had extraordinary explanatory power. Eva's "demons," no matter what their ultimate character, were bound up with her concrete interpersonal history with her mother and father. Coming to terms with the demons also meant putting her relationship with her parents on a new footing.

From the third or spiritual perspective, which was perhaps most operative in the time of shared prayer with which we concluded each session, the central concern was not the demonic per se but the scripturally attested power of God in Christ. Although literal "exorcism" seemed to be neither palatable nor particularly pertinent, Eva and I did approach the signs of her "possession" from a standpoint of faith. Thus our prayer was informed by the biblical account of Jesus' sovereign power over demons as well as by the Gospels' narratives that portray Jesus' own suffering and final vindication. Eva prayed, at times fervently, for Christ to cast out the demons that so oppressed her.

Eva thus sought to weave her own life story into the larger sacred story of Christ and the church. Her suffering, once placed within this larger spiritual and theological context, could no longer be understood as completely isolated and therefore meaningless. This kind of "narrative inclusion" into the gospel is itself a form of healing. What one theologian has said of the sacraments could also, I believe, be said of prayer:

> By the sacraments, events occur in the life-stories of individuals and groups that make those stories part of a larger story, of Christ and the church. We need not yet even refer to the ultimate hope that obtains if the story is *true;* in our detemporalized and rootless world, the mere narrative inclusion is already a great blessing.[43]

On all three levels — mythological, psychological, and spiritual — therefore, there seemed to be some warrant for seeing Eva's suffering as entailing some kind of spiritual bondage. We were not able to specify, nor did it seem necessary to specify, just how much of her chronic suffering was due to perhaps transcendent rather than intrapsychic powers. The point was, either way, that they were destructive powers that were beyond her control. Eva believed that no matter what their source or true character, she could finally withstand their inner attack only by her faith in Christ.

Conclusion

This chapter has presented a paradigmatic case — one that required the pastoral counselor's bilingual competencies. Because of the interests and issues of the counselee, the interpretive process proceeded along both psychoanalytic and theological lines. Following the guidelines of the Chalcedonian pattern, the two interpretive frameworks were neither separated or divided from each other, nor were they confused with or changed into one another. Psychology thus remained psychology with its appropriate methods and norms, and theology remained theology. The two were kept distinct even though both were

43. Robert W. Jenson, "Story and Promise in Pastoral Care," *Pastoral Psychology* 26 (Winter 1977): 119.

brought to bear on a single unfolding history. Psychology, while making its own contribution, functioned within a larger theological context, a context implicitly reflected by the institutional setting of the counseling as an outreach ministry of the church.

In Part One the case of Eva was presented. Her depressive episodes were shown to have their origins in years of parental abuse. Eva's internalized parent representations were set forth and the question of what bearing these might have had on her unconscious God representation was considered. Various possible functions of the God representation were suggested. Biblical influences on Eva's picture of God were also indicated. A single theme — the internalized parental messages as "demonic" — was then traced as a way to demonstrate the close interweaving and clear differentiation of psychological and theological interpretation. Psychological interpretation was concerned primarily with exploring the possible genesis, development, and function of these "demonic voices" within the personality, while theological interpretation sought to place them into a biblical context and to discern their possible spiritual influence.

In Part Two Eva's case was interpreted psychodynamically by focusing on what was identified as her "shame-based identity." Although successful by the world's standards, Eva was pervaded by feelings of hopelessness and worthlessness. The concept of shame, particularly as developed by Gershen Kaufman, became the overarching interpretive category that provided the kind of theoretical map needed. The interpersonal origins of Eva's sense of shame were traced by reference to parental shaming messages. The process by which these messages were internalized was also sketched, especially with reference to the way affects, drives, and needs had become bound by shame. Various defenses against shame were then discussed and applied to Eva. Finally, a description of the healing process was set forth, including four distinct aspects: restoring the interpersonal bridge in the therapeutic relationship, learning how to return internalized shame to its interpersonal origins, healing shame in the internal processes of the self, and learning to develop a sense of one's personal power in relationships. An incident in which the pastoral counselor inadvertently induced a shame reaction in Eva was recounted as a way of showing how each of these aspects came into play to bring about a healing of shame.

In Part Three various theological themes that seemed pertinent to Eva's case were explored. Eva's initial question of whether her black despairs were a sin and, therefore, offensive to God was addressed by explicating Barth's understanding of the mercy and righteousness of God. Contrary to Eva's image of God as a punitive parent, condemning her for her black despairs, God was seen (as depicted by Barth) as One who, in mercy, desired only the restoration, salvation, and wholeness of Eva. God's righteousness, furthermore, was understood to be demonstrated in assuming human sin through Christ and righteously condemning it there once for all, thus restoring a right relationship with human beings. These reflections were followed by a brief presentation of the doctrine of justification by faith as it might be applied to Eva's situation. Neurotic guilt, which only led to a kind of emotional and spiritual paralysis, was contrasted with Eva's recognition of her true guilt, a recognition that held the possibility of bringing about repentance and a corresponding change in attitude.

The themes of shame and honor, theologically considered, were then taken up. The validity of one's legitimate shame as a sinner before God was contrasted with the debilitating shame that a person internalizes when growing up in an abusive family. To know God's holiness is also to know the shame of sin. Yet, to recognize one's unworthiness before God is not to be debilitated by it, for in faith one knows the shame of sin only on the basis of God's prior gracious forgiveness. (The psychological and theological dimensions of "shame" are thus kept from the danger of being confused with or changed into one another, as might otherwise so easily occur.) The honor conferred by God on human beings was shown to be twofold: first, human beings were created to be in fellowship with God, and, second, they were each called by God to service and witness within the span of time allotted to them. These reflections were considered in light of Eva's felt sense of God's honoring her. Finally, the theme of "demonic possession" was explored by reference to three aspects of the phenomenon as distinguished by Barth: the mythological, the psychopathological, and the spiritual. All three were seen to be present in different ways in the case at hand.

Something might be said in conclusion about just how the sort of psychoanalytic and theological material discussed in Parts Two and Three of this chapter actually entered into the counseling process.

Certainly such material cannot be introduced in the form of a lecture presented from the counselor to the counselee. There are, in fact, no simple formulas, for the presentation of such material in the right way at the right time is part of the art of counseling. Questions of timing, transference and countertransference, specific treatment goals, and so on all need to be taken into account. In any case such theoretical material, whether psychological or theological, would be used primarily as a way of orienting the counselor to the complex clinical phenomena being considered. The interpretive frameworks thus function as a set of maps indicating what sorts of things to look out for at various points. The counselor would rarely spend time talking about the maps but, instead, would use them as needed in order to determine how to proceed as the process unfolded (for example, to figure out what questions to ask next).

Winnicott's statement about the nature of psychotherapy would thus apply also to pastoral counseling:

> Psychotherapy is not making clever and apt interpretations; by and large it is a long-term giving the patient back what the patient brings. It is a complex derivative of the face that reflects what is there to be seen. I like to think of my work this way, and to think that if I do this well enough the patient will find his or her own self, and will be able to exist and feel real.[44]

While this statement captures something of psychoanalytic work, it must also be noted that Winnicott himself, in the course of "giving back what the patient brings," consistently made wonderfully clever and apt interpretations of his patients' material. The interpretive process, it seems, is an integral part of this giving the person back to himself or herself. The therapist doesn't simply mirror but mirrors and interprets at the same time. When all goes well, the process of interpretation deepens and enriches the counselee's self-perception and self-understanding. As Hans Frei has written, "The language we use is what enables us to experience in the first place. There is no such thing as a non-interpreted, nonlinguistic experience."[45]

44. D. W. Winnicott, *Playing and Reality* (New York: Basic Books, 1971), p. 117.

45. Hans W. Frei, *Types of Christian Theology,* ed. George Hunsinger and William C. Placher (New Haven: Yale University Press, 1992), p. 74.

Equipped with "bilingual" competencies, the pastoral counselor brings the richness of two significantly different "languages" to bear on the counselee's life experiences. What the pastoral counselor reflects back, therefore, is a richer, less entangled, and more finely differentiated narrative of the counselee's history than the counselee was initially able to present, one more attuned to the dramatic interaction and distinction of spiritual and psychological realities.

CHAPTER SIX

Conclusion: A New Interdisciplinary Approach for Pastoral Counseling

IN THIS BOOK a method for relating theology and psychology from a Barthian theological perspective has been set forth. At the theoretical level we have shown that these two distinct disciplines are to be related according to the terms of the Chalcedonian pattern: without separation or division, without confusion or change, and with the conceptual precedence assigned to theology (asymmetrical order). At the practical level we have shown that the bilingual competencies of the pastoral counselor, as one who speaks not only the language of depth psychology but also the language of faith, are also to be used according to the stipulations of the Chalcedonian pattern. Thus the pastoral counselor uses two distinctively different frames of reference for interpreting the counselee's material (that is, especially in what we have called the "paradigmatic" case) without confusing them with each other. At the same time the pastoral counselor recognizes the inseparability of theological and psychological materials in the life events of the counselee and in psychological constructs, such as the God representation. Finally, in order to understand the theological significance of the psychological materials, the two are placed in analogical and asymmetrical relationship, with psychological interpretation operating in a larger theological framework of meaning. At both levels, therefore, theoretical and practical, the Chalcedonian pattern has provided methodological clarity for the pastoral counselor in interpreting theological and psychological materials.

Summary of the Argument

The importance of each of the three distinguishing characteristics of the Chalcedonian pattern — inseparability, differentiation, and order — was brought out both theoretically and practically in various ways. Each of the three features was considered in detail, for example, with reference to a particular theoretical proposal that the pattern would rule out (that is, those of Thurneysen, Edinger, and Tillich). The pattern was thus shown to offer tools of discernment for the pastoral counselor seeking to assess various interdisciplinary proposals from a Barthian standpoint. In addition, several works that bring Barth into dialogue with psychology or counseling were surveyed. These also were assessed (although implicitly) by means of the pattern. Thus the theoretical significance of distinguishing clearly between the two worlds of discourse was brought out positively, for example, by reference to the work of Daniel Price, who was able to draw such fruitful analogies between Barth's anthropology and object relations psychology precisely because he kept the disciplines both distinct and asymmetrically ordered. A similar point was made negatively with reference to a work by Thomas Oden in which he exhibited a kind of confusion of categories at the theoretical level. Although he began by clearly distinguishing between the two modes of discourse, he later collapsed them, showing that he did not finally grasp the full significance of the analogical and asymmetrical relationship between the two sets of concepts.

Some of the theoretical and practical implications of the pattern were considered in a discussion of the relationship between "sin" and "victimization," on the one hand, and "healing" and "salvation" on the other. The concepts of sinner and victim were shown to belong to distinctively different linguistic worlds and to function logically within the contextual wholes of which they were each a part. The underlying formal pattern by which they could be related was Chalcedonian. Although clearly distinguished from each other, it was possible to draw certain analogies between them. Thus it was shown that healing could be interpreted theologically as a sign of salvation. As a concept, healing has its own relative autonomy, so that it is possible to speak of healing without referring to salvation. But when healing is placed within a theological framework, the concept of salvation sets the terms for understanding the theological significance of healing. Healing, as the sign of salvation, takes place on one level (penultimate), pointing to salvation (as the thing signified), which is promised on another, more ultimate level. The significance of healing is temporal, while the significance of salvation is eternal. Thus the two concepts were seen to be operating on two distinct levels with theology having a kind of logical priority or precedence, because the significance of the psychological concepts depends upon the theological concepts rather than the reverse.

The practical value of the distinctions between the "sinner" and the "victim" was brought out first in a hypothetical clinical example of a woman recovering from childhood incest and then again in the discussion of the paradigmatic case. If a pastoral counselor is to use these two concepts in meaningful ways, it is important to understand the implications of their use, so that one does not either "blame the victim," on the one hand, nor deny the sinner the opportunity to take responsibility for his or her own life on the other. Particularly when a counselee's theological and psychological issues are entangled with each other, the pastoral counselor needs methodological clarity about the use of one's bilingual competencies.

When we compared the methods that were internal to each discipline, that is, Rizzuto's psychoanalytic method on the one hand, and Barth's theological method on the other, we were in effect drawing out some of the implications of one of the stipulations of the Chalcedonian pattern ("without confusion or change"). By showing how each method was appropriate to the object of investigation in its own discipline, we were also conveying the importance of not confusing the two modes of discourse. In like manner the normative criteria internal to each discipline — theological adequacy and psychological functionality — also needed to be seen as concepts that made sense only within their own respective disciplines.

The table, or four-part grid, that presented the range of logical possibilities for relating these norms can also be interpreted as illustrating how the norms are related according to another of the Chalcedonian pattern's stipulations ("without separation or division"). The four combinations of theological and psychological assessments (adequacy or inadequacy and functionality or dysfunctionality) indicate that the two sorts of norms cannot be separated in pastoral counseling.

Although the norms are distinguished, according to the intrinsic criteria of their respective fields, the complex material they assess, as presented by the counselee, consists in an intermingling of psychological and theological factors. Although conceptually distinguishable, at least in principle, these factors occur in and with one another in experience. The grid, therefore, presupposes that the joint usage of the two sorts of norms will reflect, in whatever combination, the complex intermingling of the two sorts of phenomena in the counselee's experience.

Finally, we showed how the Chalcedonian pattern would govern the bilingual competencies of the pastoral counselor in practice. What we called a "paradigmatic case," that is, one in which the counselee sought psychotherapeutic help in the context of the Christian faith, was presented. Two distinctively different interpretive perspectives were then brought to bear on the case material, a depth psychological perspective focusing on the experience of shame and a theological perspective drawing on a number of Barth's distinctive formulations. Although the two frameworks sometimes interpreted the same phenomenon (for example, the counselee's God representation), they were kept distinct and were not confused with each other. Although theological and psychological phenomena often intermingled in experience, the conceptual frameworks by which those phenomena were interpreted were clearly distinguished. At various points the asymmetrical order between the two disciplines was also brought out. Thus, for example, the psychological concept of shame was shown to be relativized when it was put into a larger theological context of sin and forgiveness in Christ. Indeed, the relationship between counselor and counselee was itself placed into a theological context by the practice of praying together at the end of every session. In this way the therapeutic relationship was put into an explicitly pastoral setting. The chapter not only demonstrated the Chalcedonian pattern at work in a clinical case but also indicated something of how the richness of Barth's insights may be used in bringing a theological perspective to the interpretive task.

The Pattern in Retrospect:
Without Confusion or Change

Certain features of the Chalcedonian pattern, as they apply to theology
and psychology, may at this point be summed up by drawing upon
the concepts of "autonomy" and "reciprocity" as defined by John P.
Clayton. First, Clayton's definition of a discipline's "autonomy" helps
to clarify what it means to speak of theology and psychology as being
related "without confusion or change."

> An academic discipline is *autonomous* when at least some of the main
> propositions which it generates are irreducible to propositions of
> another type. However, there could still be areas of overlap between
> that discipline and other disciplines. Autonomy will be used princi-
> pally in the sense of self-direction: x has autonomy when the basic
> rules governing its behavior are internally generated rather than ex-
> ternally imposed. No x can be said to have autonomy when the rules
> governing its activity are either reducible to or deducible from some
> sphere outside x.[1]

Thus we argued that the main propositions of a psychology like
Rizzuto's are irreducible to propositions of a theology like Barth's,
and vice versa. Even when there are significant areas of overlap in
assessing the intermingling of theological and psychological factors
in experience, as there seemed to be when we considered the God
representation from the perspective of both disciplines, each discipline's normative criteria were internally generated. In other words,
the basic criteria that would be applied to a God representation to
discern whether it was psychologically functional or dysfunctional
would be generated solely within the rules of psychological discourse
and could not be imposed from without. Theology, for example,
would have nothing directly to say about whether psychoanalytic
judgments regarding functionality were valid. Nor could psychoanalysis directly comment on the validity of theological judgments
concerning adequacy or inadequacy. The rules governing the assessments of each field would thus not be reducible to or deducible from

---

1. John P. Clayton, *The Concept of Correlation: Paul Tillich and the Possibility of a
Mediating Theology* (New York: Walter De Gruyter, 1980), p. 43.

the other field or from any other sphere outside its own internally generated criteria.

The Pattern in Retrospect:
Without Separation or Division

Clayton's definition of "reciprocity," furthermore, helps to summarize what is meant by the Chalcedonian feature of "without separation or division" as it has been applied to the relationship between these two disciplines. "Reciprocity" is defined by Clayton as "mutual influence or mutual dependence." He goes on to say:

> x is functionally dependent upon y when x varies systematically in accordance with variations in y. But if y is also shown to vary systematically with changes in x, then the dependence is no longer one-directional and functional, but two-directional and reciprocal.[2]

At this point it is important to make a distinction between two forms of reciprocity, one conceptual and the other experiential.[3] Conceptually, the reciprocity between theology and psychology is indirect. Experientially, the reciprocity is evident but elusive. The indirect conceptual reciprocity will be discussed first, followed by a discussion of experiential reciprocity.

In order to show how each discipline can influence the other at the conceptual level, it will be helpful to recall the table or grid of logical possibilities as presented on page 131 and to consider the two conceivable "mixed cases" with respect to a counselee's God representation. The "mixed cases" were either those that combined theological inadequacy with psychological functionality (Case #2) or those that combined theological adequacy with psychological dysfunctionality (Case #3). Such cases would suggest a certain strategy of inquiry for the pastoral counselor to pursue.

When a person's God representation appears to be theologically adequate but psychologically dysfunctional (Case #3), certain ques-

---

2. Clayton, p. 45.

3. As will become clear in the course of my exposition, at neither level is the reciprocity in question "systematic"; rather, it is always ad hoc.

tions arise. The dysfunction at the psychological level poses a question of whether the image is really as theologically adequate as it first appeared. Although this question cannot be answered by the direct application of psychological criteria, the presence of dysfunction may indirectly indicate that the image or concept needs to be reassessed at the strictly theological level by a better understanding or use of the criteria internal to theology. Pastoral counseling presupposes that in principle there is no conflict between theological and psychological norms (for the material they assess represents two different levels of reality). However, the presence of a psychological disorder in experience may indicate that there is a hidden theological disorder as well. Psychological norms in themselves would not be sufficient or decisive in settling the question, but in such cases they would influence theology indirectly to reexamine the image or concept according to its own criteria.

The other possible mixed situation (Case #2), where the image was assessed as psychologically functional but theologically inadequate, implies a similar strategy of inquiry, only in reverse. Again the possible influence of the one discipline on the other would be indirect rather than direct. Generally speaking, the presence of theological inadequacy would prompt the pastoral counselor to reassess precisely how functional the image really is at the psychological level. The extent and quality of that functionality (again on the basis of criteria internal to the relevant discipline, in this case psychology) would indirectly come into question. In this case, as in the one above, the optimal situation is presumed to be the one in which both theological adequacy and psychological functionality prevail. Case #1 is the kind of situation toward which the pastoral counselor is working. It may not be realizable. There may, in fact, sometimes be instances of irresolvable conflict between psychological and theological factors (as in the kind of case mentioned where a man's atheism protected him from the internalized image of a sadistic father). There will always be real limits within which the pastoral counselor must work (not excluding his or her own limitations in discerning just what exactly "adequacy" and "functionality" actually mean in practice), and sometimes these will be severe. But the presence of theological inadequacy at least raises questions about the putative functionality of any given God representation. The inquiry prompted by these questions comprises the kind of indirect influence of theology on psychology that is possible at the conceptual level.

Experientially, on the other hand, the focus of reciprocity shifts from theoretical norms to contingent phenomena. In a counselee's life experience the mutual influence or dependence of psychological and theological factors in shaping beliefs or perceptions is typically elusive even when manifest. It would be possible, for example, for a person's early childhood experiences to influence his or her conscious theological understanding of God. Conversely, the same person's study of Bible and theology in the context of a Christian community may have a kind of reciprocal influence on his or her unconscious God representation, affecting deep psychological patterns in the way he or she imagines God. Or it is possible that such reciprocal relations may not be manifest in a given instance. The presence, degree, and intensity of the influence in either direction all depend upon the specific situation and can not be predicted in advance. But in principle the lines of influence can be mutual and complex.

If we again recall the table or grid of logical possibilities as presented on page 131, we see that a person's God representation may be assessed as theologically adequate or inadequate and as psychologically functional or dysfunctional. Let us reconsider Eva's God representation in light of her initial concern. Eva began counseling with the concern that her black despairs were a sin and offensive to God. What kind of God was implied by such a view? As we explored this and other questions in the process of counseling, a complex picture of Eva's God emerged. On the one hand, God seemed to be a wrathful, punitive parent, one who was just as contemptuous of Eva and her sniveling self-pity as her parents had been. On the other hand, there was the gracious and merciful God of Scripture who had, she believed, delivered her from the living hell of alcoholism, an event that she knew she could not have brought about by her own power. Was such a God to be considered theologically adequate or inadequate, psychologically functional or dysfunctional? Furthermore, how did Eva's spiritual growth affect her psychological growth and vice versa? How was there reciprocity shown, in other words, between the two kinds of materials?

Real life is, of course, always more complex than a table of "ideal types." Yet, it was helpful to consider in what ways Eva's sense of God was theologically adequate and psychologically functional (or not) and to try to provide the conditions, insofar as it was possible from the human side, for both psychological and spiritual growth to occur. In some ways, Eva's God representation could be seen as a mixed or complex case. On the one hand, it did not seem to be theologically inadequate. For example, her understanding of God's gracious power, as exhibited in her deliverance from alcoholism, seemed to correspond to a biblical understanding of a God for whom all things are possible, even those inconceivable from a human standpoint. Yet, her picture of God as an angry, impatient parent who wanted to "shake some sense" into Eva seemed deeply ingrained. Such a picture would be evident in many of Eva's prayers, where she would beg God's forgiveness for things that were essentially outside her control but that she feared were displeasing to God, such as her depressive episodes. By the criteria we had established (that is, needing to correspond to the picture of God in the New Testament), such a God representation would seem less than theologically "adequate."

At the same time, Eva's God representation, viewed psychologically, also seemed a complex case, at once dysfunctional and yet functional in different ways. Her God representation was "functional" in that it helped secure a kind of precarious psychic equilibrium. If God was on the side of her parents, it would be much too dangerous to risk her parents' anger. "God" seemed to keep the lid on much of Eva's righteous indignation, for Eva had been encouraged by her parents (and bolstered by their "interpretations" of Scripture) to think of herself as a miserable offender against the rightful order that prevailed in her childhood home. On the other hand, this precarious emotional balance exacted a very high cost. During the course of therapy it became clear that Eva could no longer afford to direct her anger and rage inwardly, for it had become extremely damaging to her emotionally, spiritually, and even physically.

The changes that took place over time as the therapeutic process unfolded showed that theological and psychological materials must have affected each other in a kind of reciprocal fashion. Since they were inseparable in experience (though conceptually distinguishable), they had effects on each other in observable ways. Theologically focused work often seemed to have psychological effects, and psychologically oriented interpretations sometimes seemed to affect her theological understanding. One could not predict the consequences or the outcomes of any given (psychological or theological) interpretation. Even in retrospect it was not clear precisely how the two worlds of meaning penetrated and affected each other at the level of lived experience, for what we are seeking to grasp is finally a mystery that can be described only inadequately and that can only be pondered anew with each new situation from the standpoint of both language worlds. Edward Thornton, having in mind a particular young woman's situation as she faced the possibility of marriage, pondered similar questions with an essentially "bilingual" approach when he asked:

> How does spiritual growth occur? What is the process of change, not only at the level of sexual identity and emotional freedom for entering into marriage [that is, psychological perspective] but also at the level of discerning the will of God and making decisions in faith without the presence of any kind of guarantee [that is, theological perspective]? Does spiritual growth require psychological growth and change?[4]

With Eva, spiritual and psychological issues were so entwined that growth on one front often meant growth on another, though such would not necessarily be the case, for these relationships cannot be systematized into formulas. Thus as Eva prayed for a deeper trust in God and to believe in God's providential goodness toward her, she was also able to take risks in her relationship with her father. She was able, for example, to confront him with some of her feelings about the abuse she had suffered as a child. On the other hand, as Eva consciously worked on letting go of her perfectionism and began to allow herself to be as she was, faults and all, she also began to gain a new appreciation for what the doctrine of justification by faith alone might mean. She began to glimpse what it might be like not to have to justify every minute of her life, doing the "right" thing at all costs.

Although some sort of reciprocal influence can be seen, it is impossible to specify causal relationships forth and back between just what occurred at each level, psychologically and spiritually. While the two

4. Edward Thornton, *Theology and Pastoral Counseling* (Englewood Cliffs, N.J.: Prentice-Hall, 1964), pp. 21-22.

worlds did sometimes seem to interpenetrate and influence each other in the perceptions of the counselee, it could not be said that this happened in any kind of systematic or predictable way. Generally speaking, the relationship between the two seems to be essentially contingent and complex, making it virtually impossible to specify how these kinds of influences occur. Among the complexities to be taken into account, there is, of course, from a standpoint of faith, the specifically theological factor of the mystery of God's freedom, whose Spirit blows where it will.

It is also possible to imagine other kinds of cases, ones where this kind of reciprocal influence would be blocked for some reason. Because of the relative autonomy of the two factors, one could imagine a situation where spiritual growth occurred without concomitant psychological growth or vice versa. In such cases, no significant analogies could be drawn between the two modes of discourse. Growth in faith, from this perspective, is not seen to be simply a matter of psychological development with "faith" tacked on as an afterthought. Genuine faith could conceivably be found in psychologically immature or underdeveloped people (as in children or the mentally disabled, for example). Even people who are filled with neurotic fears may faithfully serve God, in spite of their neurosis. Their neurosis may even be the very thing that drives them to risk trusting God in spite of everything.[5]

The Pattern in Retrospect: Asymmetrical Order

Finally, recalling Cases #1 and #4 in the logical grid will help summarize what is meant by the Chalcedonian feature of "asymmetrical order" as it has been applied to the relationship between these two disciplines. Asymmetry means that the norms of theological adequacy and psychological functionality pertain to phenomena representing different levels of reality. For this reason there is no necessary conflict between them. When a person's God representation is both theologi-

5. One thinks of the poignant story of Blanche in Gertrud Von le Fort's novel, *The Song at the Scaffold* (New York: Sheed and Ward, 1933), whose life was filled with extreme neurotic fears, yet who faithfully served God to the point of martyrdom. It would seem to involve a confusion of categories to think that only the mentally healthy or those with "good-enough" mothering may enter the kingdom of God.

cally adequate and psychologically functional (Case #1), an analogy can be drawn between what is the case at each level of reality. We have shown that, for example, an analogy can be drawn between healing (as the sign) and salvation (as the thing signified). Similarly, an analogy of well-being can also be traced between the two aspects of the God representation in Case #1. People who have had nurturing parents who truly cherished their children may internalize a biblically based view of God as one who is unconditionally loving and forgiving, with relative ease, for a parable of such a God was experienced in their childhood homes. Similarly in Case #4, an analogy of need may also be drawn. People who grow up in situations of abuse and fear may develop God representations that are both psychologically dysfunctional and theologically inadequate, for at some of the deepest levels of memory and experience they have been taught not to trust. Analogical relationships may thus be drawn between the negative materials as assessed by the two disciplines as well.

In the paradigmatic case, when psychological healing is sought and found by a Christian who seeks it as one of God's good gifts, then an analogy may be drawn between healing as the sign and salvation as the thing signified. Healing in such an instance can be seen as a parable of grace. Whenever Eva was able to make substantive progress toward psychological health, for example, she rightly offered thanks to God for making such movement possible. Similarly when she felt stuck and unable to move forward, she lamented to God over the extent and length of her suffering. In these ways, her emotional suffering was put into a larger theological context and her psychological goals were altered in light of this larger theological framework. For Eva did not simply desire to have a God representation that would afford her enough emotional equilibrium to avoid depression, she wanted a relationship with God. Emotional equilibrium was an essential good to be sought for its own sake, but for Eva it was sought within the context of a greater good, namely, faith in God.

Non-Paradigmatic Cases

Obviously not all cases a pastoral counselor undertakes are "paradigmatic" in the sense of requiring both explicit theological and psychological interpretation. In some instances, people of other faiths (or no faith) seek help from a Christian pastoral counselor. In other instances, Christian counselees may desire only spiritual or theological guidance without any concomitant psychological reflection or interpretation. How might these kinds of (non-paradigmatic) cases be understood theoretically on the basis of the Chalcedonian pattern? Such cases, it might be suggested, can be thought of as instances of de facto separation or division. When the bilingual pastoral counselor needs to use only one of the two languages of his or her expertise, it may be conceived of as a de facto separation between the two modes of discourse.

Non-paradigmatic cases cannot be considered apart from the therapeutic process as a whole. Generally speaking, the focus of this book has been on the interpretive aspect of this process and, in particular, on how a pastoral counselor thinks about the dual nature of the interpretive task. While from time to time mention has been made of the interpersonal context in which such interpretation arises, the importance of the relationship between counselor and counselee in the healing process has not been underscored. Others whom we have surveyed (particularly Martyn and Price) have made this a central focus of their reflection and study. While it has not been our primary focus, it must be acknowledged that the significance of a genuine, empathetic, and caring relationship between counselor and counselee for emotional healing at the heart's core cannot be overemphasized. That this is true theologically as well as psychologically is indicated by the central role interpersonal relationships play in the formation of human identity. If our being in relationship with one another is a reflection on the human plane of God's own being in relationship, then our capacity for interpersonal communion is a sign of the *imago Dei*. It is also the fundamental prerequisite for psychological health. As Daniel Price has commented:

> The curative power of a good relationship cannot be underestimated. Establishing a relationship with a good object, it would seem, is the *sine qua non* of human wholeness, and the only path to healing the "sinsick soul."[6]

6. Daniel J. Price, "Karl Barth's Anthropology in Light of Modern Thought: The Dynamic Concept of the Person in Trinitarian Theology and Object Relations Psychology" (unpublished dissertation, University of Aberdeen, Scotland, 1990), p. 394.

Good interpretations in themselves are not sufficient to bring about change. The most fluent bilingual pastoral counselor would have little impact on counselees if he or she were not also skilled in establishing and maintaining good interpersonal relationships. John Patton puts it succinctly: "A good interpretation is born out of a good relationship."[7] T. W. Jennings likewise concurs that theological reflection "is not a substitute for, but an instrument of, the attentive and compassionate regard for the other which is at the heart of pastoral care."[8] The most astute interpretation, finely differentiated, well-timed, and symbolically apt, would matter little without this "attentive and compassionate" attunement of the counselor toward the counselee.

Because of the uniqueness of each pastoral therapeutic relationship and because interpretation depends upon the qualities of the relationship at least as much as on the kind of "linguistic" competencies we have outlined, for these reasons the "how" of interpretation cannot be directly taught. Apart from a few rules of thumb, which provide only general guidelines, interpretation depends upon the personal creativity of the pastoral counselor, on his or her ability to listen attentively and compassionately, to take what is symbolically essential in what is communicated, and to give it back to the counselee deepened, richer, more differentiated, in a word, interpreted.[9]

7. John Patton, *Pastoral Counseling: A Ministry of the Church* (Nashville: Abingdon, 1983), p. 219.

8. T. W. Jennings, "Pastoral Theological Methodology" in *Dictionary of Pastoral Care and Counseling,* ed. Rodney Hunter (Nashville: Abingdon, 1990), p. 863.

9. Among such "rules of thumb" might be guidelines that emphasize the importance of (1) focusing on the particular questions of the counselee and learning as much as possible about his or her inner symbolic world; (2) conveying essential respect for the counselee, including his or her spiritual understanding; (3) refraining from moralizing or giving advice; (4) taking responsibility for one's own personal therapeutic issues and making continued disciplined efforts not to contaminate the therapeutic process with them; and (5) developing a sense of timing.

Theological Questions Without Explicit Psychological Questions

The first non-paradigmatic case to be considered is Mary, a middle-aged woman, a conscientious and devout Christian, who sought pastoral counseling because she had been unhappy in her marriage for many years. Initially unsuccessful in persuading her husband to enter marriage counseling, Mary sought individual work. She contacted a pastoral counselor because she felt it was important to see someone with views similar to her own regarding the sanctity of Christian marriage. Her presenting concern had to do with the meaning of her marriage vows. After years of struggle to reach her husband and feeling utterly defeated, she was now considering divorce, despite her church's clear teaching on the subject and her own anguished misgivings.

As I listened to Mary I noticed that nearly her entire focus seemed to be on what she felt God expected of her and on what the Bible taught about marriage and divorce. It was almost as if Mary herself were of no account. While her questions were important and ethically serious, they seemed somehow to sidestep the particularities of Mary's history with her husband. I found myself wondering if Mary had freely chosen this marriage, indeed if she could now freely choose it, or if it were not now little more than a joyless duty to be performed because she had once made promises that she must now keep.

Perhaps more to the point, however, there seemed to be an underlying pattern by which Mary somehow used her faith as a defense against knowing herself, against knowing her particular thoughts and feelings in this painful situation. It seemed, in fact, that her almost exclusive focus on theological questions about God's will, though obviously important, was somehow being used as a defense against the anxiety that would be aroused by a more direct psychological focus. If I was on the right track, it was possible that she may have developed a pattern in her life of somehow using her faith as a way of avoiding confronting herself.

While I formed this hypothesis rather early in the therapeutic process, I did not bring it forth as a tentative interpretation until some weeks later. The relationship, I felt, could not yet contain the anxiety that would be generated by a more direct consideration of psychological themes. In the meantime it was more important to Mary to explore the theological and ethical questions on their own terms. In doing so, I was not using a mere technique or therapeutic ruse of "going with the defense" but, rather, was entering into a series of considerations that were important to address for their own sake. I was convinced, moreover, that in time the core psychological issues would emerge in their own right, because I understood that they could not finally be separated or divided from her theological concerns. With the development of a trusting relationship, one in which Mary felt that her theological questions were taken seriously on their own terms and not dismissed as neurotic or irrelevant, Mary was eventually able to face and manage the anxiety that was aroused when she allowed herself to become more fully aware of her repressed thoughts and feelings about her marriage.

It might be noted that in this case the Chalcedonian pattern served as an implicit guide in at least two ways. First, it helped the pastoral counselor clearly to distinguish between one set of concerns (more strictly theological in focus) and another (more strictly psychological in focus). Second, the clear differentiation between the two foci helped to raise the question of how they might be related in this case and to form the hypothesis that the one set of concerns was perhaps somehow functioning as a defense against the other. The apparent absence of psychological materials in the counselee's self-understanding seemed to indicate a kind of de facto separation or division between the two modes of understanding, which I felt could eventually be overcome. As Mary's therapeutic process unfolded, she was able to find the part of herself that was split off. She was then able to move forward into a new phase, one that included open communication with her husband about their marriage, a conversation that had previously been impossible to undertake not simply because the husband was resistant but because Mary had not had access to large parts of her emotional life. At that point Mary and her husband were eventually able to enter marriage counseling together to address a range of issues before them.

Psychological Questions Without Explicit Theological Questions

An alternative type of "non-paradigmatic" case would be one in which the counselee had only psychological interests and concerns and was apparently uninterested in theological or spiritual matters. In many such cases, the pastoral counselor would interpret the counselee's material almost exclusively from a psychological perspective. Theological interpretations may or may not occur to the counselor as the process unfolds; as they do he or she would make a choice about whether to bring them explicitly into the conversation. At times there may be latent spiritual or religious issues that are unresolved, and the pastoral counselor has been chosen unconsciously, so to speak, so that these issues might eventually come to the surface. The bilingual pastoral counselor would be attuned to spiritual or theological issues that might be embedded in any given psychological issue. She may or may not choose to bring them out in an explicitly theological form.

An example of explicit theological material being introduced into a counseling relationship where the focus had been almost exclusively psychological occurred in my work with a couple, Bob and Joy. This couple sought counseling because their marriage of thirty years was ridden with destructive arguments that left each of them feeling angry, hurt, misunderstood, and alone. Their sense of isolation was compounded by their practice of avoiding each other as much as possible between outbursts. They came to me in what Joy described as a "hopeless Mexican standoff." "Neither of us is going to move," she said. This rather typical power struggle — where each partner was waiting for the other to change and where each saw only his or her own virtue and his or her partner's shortcomings — had a unique history of thirty years behind it, or more if one also considered the childhood roots of the marital impasse.

From the beginning of my work with this couple, my own normative vision of what constituted a good, healthy, fulfilling marriage guided me in my interpretations. This vision was derived not only from psychological sources but also from theological ones. Thus I considered Joy's expressed goal of "detachment" and Bob's conscious ideal of "self-reliance" to be basically defensive postures — a kind of counter-dependence born out of childhood pain. In tracing the early roots of their present impasse it became clear that they had both undergone traumatic experiences in which they had learned not to rely on their primary caregivers to meet their basic emotional needs. For months I raised questions about their apparent conviction that emotional interdependence was a sign of weakness and that emotional vulnerability was to be avoided at all costs. After an extended period of time, they had taken a number of risks and had begun to become more involved with one another on a daily basis. As they turned from merely trying to avoid the worst and began to dream about what they actually wanted in their marriage, I guided them through a process of developing a vision for their marriage.

After they had specified their own goals, I reflected on them from a theological perspective. In particular I decided to discuss with them the theological materials that had guided my thinking from the beginning of my work with them. What was previously implicit now became explicit. I briefly summarized Barth's fourfold determination of human beings as being-in-encounter. According to Barth, human beings were created by God for mutual *openness* (seeing eye to eye), mutual *speech and hearing,* rendering mutual *assistance* to one another, and giving and receiving with mutual *gladness* (III/2, 243-65). After much focused work on their communication patterns, Bob and Joy immediately resonated with the first two items. Achieving the goal of good, open communication where each genuinely felt heard by the other had been hard won. They even acknowledged that there were certain basic things for which they needed the other's assistance. But they both agreed that they didn't like it. They didn't like the fact of their own neediness, nor of their partner's. The element of *gladness* was definitely absent.

The interpretation, explicitly theological in a case that had heretofore focused only on psychological issues, was accepted by both Bob and Joy. The absence of gladness, the sense of the marriage being so much hard work, effort, and drudgery, came to the forefront in a new way. They adopted this fourth point as a focal point in their own goals; they didn't know how to get to the mutual gladness, but they knew that they wanted it. Guthrie's comment, cited previously, is relevant here:

> Christian pastoral counseling motivated by a theology of grace will give up all neutrality about the *goal* of change, growth, or becoming.

It will not encourage people to become whatever they want to be, or hide from them the fact that the counselor has a very definite goal in mind for them. Without manipulating people to attitudes and actions they do not freely choose for themselves, the counselor will openly stand for the Christian understanding of what fulfilled humanity looks like.[10]

It may be important to note that neither of these non-paradigmatic cases dealt specifically with the counselee's relationship to God. Nevertheless, theological norms still functioned in the way the bilingual pastoral counselor conceived of the issues at hand. Because the psychological and spiritual dimensions of life cannot be separated or divided from each other, the pastoral counselor with a dual perspective may perceive psychological issues hidden within putatively theological issues and theological issues within psychological ones. This does not mean that the pastoral counselor tries to "translate" the material from one idiom into another. The issues, whether theological or psychological, still function within their own linguistic frame of reference. When Mary focused exclusively on what she thought were important theological concerns, she did not pause to consider her own wants. Yet the issue of desire is not only a psychological issue but also a theological one. Loving another from the heart's core with gladness is very different from staying in a marriage grimly determined to do one's Christian duty at all costs. When Bob and Joy faced the same essential issue, they came at it from the psychological side. The normative theological frame of reference challenged them directly and deepened their understanding of what was at stake.

A third and final non-paradigmatic case to be considered would be a situation where the counselee is of a different faith or has a different spiritual orientation. Again it must be emphasized that each case is unique and that one cannot develop systematic principles of interpretation. The decision to bring a theological perspective explicitly to bear on a case depends upon a variety of factors, the idiosyncrasies of the particular relationship, the reasons why the pastoral counselor was chosen by the counselee, and what the counselee is

10. Shirley C. Guthrie, Jr., "Pastoral Counseling, Trinitarian Theology, and Christian Anthropology," *Interpretation* 33 (April 1979): 143.

seeking. As each relationship develops, a shared or common language also develops. In this instance a kind of theological interpretation was brought to bear on a case where the counselees were not Christian. Both husband and wife had been devout followers of an Indian spiritual teacher for approximately fifteen years. They spoke of their beliefs in counseling as it seemed appropriate, especially as they made an impact on practices or attitudes within their marriage. Their reason for seeking counseling had to do with a sense of despair and futility that pervaded their marriage. The wife felt that the husband did not really want her for who she was; the husband felt that according to his wife, he couldn't do anything right. (Each of these perceptions, of course, had a pre-history from their respective childhoods.)

On this particular occasion the husband wanted to propose a plan for changing the general atmosphere of mutual criticism that pervaded their relationship. His suggestion was that each day they would tell one another about at least one thing their partner had done that they appreciated. His wife immediately objected to this plan. As she explained further, it became apparent that she had no objection in principle to the idea; it was only that she was certain it would backfire if he expressed appreciation for particular kinds of things. That is to say, if he were to tell her he appreciated that she had made a meal for him or had done his laundry — any such task done for him — it would not make her feel appreciated at all. She felt sure she would only feel contempt for him and for what she considered his sense of "male entitlement." If he was going to appreciate something, it needed to be something *about her,* about who she was in herself and not about what she had done or could do for him.

As I listened to what seemed to be an emotionally significant distinction for her, I recalled a similar distinction I had learned in theology, the familiar one between loving God for God's own sake versus loving God for God's benefits. By way of analogy I suggested that the wife in this case wanted to be loved for who she was and not for any benefits her husband might enjoy by being married to her. "Yes," she replied, "that's it *exactly.*"

Such an interpretation, of course, was not strictly theological at all. The analogy I drew had merely illustrative power. It could just have easily come from myth or literature or another spiritual tradition and still have had the same basic impact. Although for a client of

Christian faith, the analogy would also have been meaningful on another level, in this kind of non-paradigmatic situation that level was not immediately accessible to the counselee.

A similar kind of distinction might be made in a pastoral counselor's use of Scripture. There is a difference between understanding Scripture as the Word of God and understanding it as a psychologically profound book of stories and wisdom that capture some essential aspect of being human. The normative force of hearing Scripture as the Word of God is different from hearing it as possibly illustrating a significant psychological insight. Of course, Scripture may function in both ways and the pastoral counselor may legitimately use it in both ways. The bilingual pastoral counselor who has methodological clarity about the interpretive task will understand the implications of this possible twofold use and would not confuse them with each other.

Even in the paradigmatic case, however, one cannot assume that Scripture or prayer would be used in certain predetermined ways. There are levels of complexity here that are aptly indicated by Kierkegaard's aphorism that "existence is not a system." Neither human existence, nor interpersonal relationships, nor our relationship with God is a system. When it comes to choosing to read Scripture (or not), using Scripture theologically or using it illustratively, choosing to pray (or not), all these decisions depend finally on the pastoral counselor being guided not only by the idiosyncrasies of the particular relationship but also by his or her response to God's leading. Frank Lake, British clinical theologian, captures the living character of these choices.

> Sometimes we are given the freedom here to wield "the sword of the Spirit which is the Word of God." We may, with permission, turn to the Bible. . . . At other times we are obedient to a sense of restraint here. . . . We ought to be ready for either course, but never stereotyped or mechanical in our method.[11]

The pastoral counselor who believes that he or she has been called by God to do this work will also trust in God's continued guidance in each particular case.

11. Frank Lake, *Clinical Theology* (London: Darton, Longman and Todd, 1966), p. 52.

Conclusion

The Chalcedonian pattern, which has received so much of our attention in this work, has been derived from Barth's theological use of it, even though he himself did not apply it to the interdisciplinary questions of pastoral counseling. Nevertheless, it might be noted in conclusion that Barth himself was not unaware that the pattern could be used in any number of different connections. For example, after relating the soul and body of Jesus according to the familiar stipulations of the pattern, Barth reflects on the implications of his procedure.

> It is not impossible, and even in different degrees promising and fruitful, to ask whether the soul and body of Jesus might not be related to one another like heaven and earth in the totality of creation; or justification and sanctification in the atoning work of Christ; or Law and Gospel in the Word of God; or faith and works in the human response to God; or preaching and sacrament in the divine service of the community; or the confessional formula and the corresponding attitude and action in its confession; or church and state in the inner articulation of the kingdom of Christ. The mere enumeration may arouse reflection. (III/2, 343)

The mere enumeration not only arouses reflection but also indicates something of the range of Barth's Chalcedonian imagination.

The analogies Barth is entertaining here are between the use of the Chalcedonian pattern in understanding the central case (the Incarnation) and its use in understanding other cases. While most of the other cases he mentions fall properly within the sphere of dogmatics itself, the last on the list — church and state — begins to move in an interdisciplinary direction. Since Barth himself was apparently uninterested in any kind of extended dialogue with the field of depth psychology, this book has tried to extend the logic of his theology into such a dialogue, especially with respect to the theory and practice of pastoral counseling.[12] Despite his relative lack of attention to such interdisciplinary questions as we have explored, Barth seemed to know something of the territory and its possible hazards, for he left us with

12. For a brief statement by Barth on the "cure of souls" as one of the basic forms of the ministry of the community, see IV/3, 885-87.

a warning pertinent to our own undertaking. After listing possible fruitful areas to explore, he issues the following characteristic proviso:

> We are certainly not required either to systematize this formal connection or to discern it everywhere. There are important points of Christian knowledge where we cannot speak of such analogy and where only a combination of lack of taste and direct error would try to discover it. For example, there is no totality in which the Creator and the creature in general, or in which the freedom and initiative of God and of the human being are so unified as are the soul and body of Jesus. . . . We have good reason, therefore, to refrain from an indiscriminate pursuit of analogies. And even when we may speak of real analogies . . . in each case we must consider whether and how far the points concerned may be brought into mutual relationship, in cross connections. At this point no certain conclusions result from logical possibilities alone. For theological truths and relationships of truth have in their own place and way their own worth and fullness, the light of which can be increased but may also be easily diminished when they are set in relation to others. (III/2, 343 rev.)

In the course of our presentation, we have sought to heed this warning by actually adapting the Chalcedonian pattern to fit the subject matter rather than the reverse, which would have meant squeezing the subject matter into a fixed and predetermined form. As applied to the interdisciplinary questions of pastoral counseling, the pattern undergoes certain modifications that distinguish it from the form it takes in Barth's discussion of the Incarnation as well as from the notably different form it takes when he discusses the relationship in human nature between body and soul. In particular, the closer specification of what it means to speak of two terms being related "without separation or division" differs significantly in each case.

For the Incarnation it means a mysterious relationship of hypostatic union between Jesus' deity and his humanity. For human nature it means a natural or creaturely union between soul and body. For the questions of pastoral counseling, it means a form of inseparability that is at once contingent and ad hoc. To describe this inseparability, it has been necessary to distinguish between the conceptual and experiential levels. At the conceptual level, theological and psychological interpretation exist without separation and division, because the complex phenomena they seek to interpret are often intertwined in experience. Yet, no conceptual synthesis or essential equivalence can be developed between the two disciplines, because the intertwined factors to be interpreted represent fundamentally different levels of reality.

From a Barthian perspective, there is simply "no totality" by which divine being and creaturely being are systematically united and thus none for the complex material dealt with by pastoral counseling. Any actual connections that occur are contingent and ad hoc, being strictly grounded in divine initiative and freedom; yet, on the basis of these contingent connections reciprocity is possible not only indirectly between the two disciplines but also more directly (if elusively) between a person's psychological and spiritual perceptions of theologically oriented material (for example, the God representation). Moreover, the asymmetry governing the relationship between divine and creaturely being implies that although there is no way from psychological to theological interpretation, there is nonetheless a way from theological to psychological interpretation. Psychological healing or well-being can thus be interpreted theologically as pointing by way of analogy to that more ultimate form of well-being attested by faith as salvation. By interrelating theological and psychological materials in this way, without reducing either to the other but allowing each to make its own distinctive contribution to the therapeutic process, a new interdisciplinary approach to pastoral counseling as a ministry of the church has emerged.

Index